PARVEI

A well-known film journalist, Karishma Upadhyay is considered to be a specialist on Bollywood. Working across media, she has led editorial teams at several prominent media houses. She has been the entertainment editor at Times Now, the celebrity editor at *People* magazine, and has contributed articles for a number of publications, including *India Today*, *Times of India*, *Hindustan Times*, *Telegraph*, *The Hindu* and *Forbes* magazine. On Twitter she goes by @karishmau.

Praise for *Parveen Babi*

'Upadhyay is able to create an unforgettable picture of a woman who loved not too wisely but too well.'

– *The Hindu*

'Takes a fresh look at the late star and dives deep into her life's challenges and background.'

– *Hindustan Times*

'Upadhyay strings a lucid account of Babi's public breakdowns and her leaving the industry at the height of her popularity.'

– *New Indian Express*

'Considering the lack of literature on Babi in the fifteen years since her death, *Parveen Babi: A Life* is unique in its level of detail. Upadhyay paints a dark picture of Babi's life – how her circle of friends grew smaller until it ceased to exist, how her condition repelled people who were once allies.'

– *Caravan*

'Here are several such delicious anecdotes in Upadhyay's meticulously researched, smoothly-put-together volume of the life and times of Parveen Babi, who burnt bright for a short while before being consumed by the demons of her mind.'

– *Indian Express*

'Along the way emerges a picture of Bollywood in its flower-power era, and the misconceptions about mental health that prevented a vulnerable woman from receiving the care she needed.'

– *Firstpost*

'The author intelligently puts forth a rather heart-wrenching truth about Parveen's life and death.'

– *Asian Age*

'From her "sex-kitten" stardom to her schizophrenic outbursts, the biography published by Hachette starts off wide-eyed and bloated, and ends with a sledgehammer.'

– *Film Companion*

'The book is an excellent read, it flows like poetry.'
– *Tribune India*

'Upadhyay is as gentle in the book about all parties and sides involved. It's objective, fact-led and information-rich – just the right badges to make a journalist proud.'
– *Free Press Journal*

'Upadhyay, a seasoned film journalist, unpacks the life and legend of the bold and beautiful Babi with meticulous research and care.'
– *Week*

'A meticulously researched, empathetic telling of the tragic life of an actor who forged her own path and redefined the Hindi film heroine. The book also captures a time and place in Bollywood. Fascinating and heartbreaking!'
– Anupama Chopra, 5 Oct 2020, Twitter

'The book paints a picture of Bollywood in its flower-power era and captures the truth about a life lived in the limelight.'
– *Cinestaan*

PARVEEN BABI
A Life

Karishma Upadhyay

First published in hardback in India in 2020 by Hachette India
(Registered name: Hachette Book Publishing India Pvt. Ltd)
An Hachette UK company
www.hachetteindia.com

This edition published in 2021

SRD

Copyright © 2020 Karishma Upadhyay

Karishma Upadhyay asserts the moral right to be identified as
the author of this work.

All rights reserved. No part of the publication may be reproduced, stored in a retrieval system (including but not limited to computers, disks, external drives, electronic or digital devices, e-readers, websites), or transmitted
in any form or by any means (including but not limited to cyclostyling, photocopying, docutech or other reprographic reproductions, mechanical, recording, electronic, digital versions without the prior written permission of the publisher, nor be otherwise circulated in any form of binding or cover other than that in which it is published and without a similar condition being imposed on the subsequent purchaser.

Images on pp. 78, 102, 128, 147, 184 and 274 courtesy Dinodia Photo LLP. Images on pp. 58, 64, 153, 186, 202, 209, 224, 233, 238, 245 and 283 courtesy Magna Publishing Company Limited. Images on pp. 217, 268 and 301 courtesy the personal collection of Xerxes Bhathena. Images on pp. iv, 21, 25, 37 and 44 courtesy the personal collection of Donald Marks.
Image on p. 109 courtesy Karishma Upadhyay.

The views and opinions expressed in this book are the author's own and the facts are as reported by her and have been verified to the extent possible. The publishers are not in any way liable for the same. While every effort has been made to trace copyright holders of quoted material and obtain permission, this has not been possible in all cases. Any omissions brought to our attention will be remedied in future editions.

Hardback edition ISBN 978-93-88322-93-5
Paperback edition ISBN 978-93-5009-578-2
Ebook edition ISBN 978-93-88322-94-2

Hachette Book Publishing India Pvt. Ltd
4th & 5th Floors, Corporate Centre,
Plot No. 94, Sector 44, Gurugram – 122003, India

Typeset in Adobe Text Pro 10.5/14
by Jojy Philip, New Delhi – 15

Printed and bound in India by
Manipal Technologies Limited, Manipal

For my three precious monkeys – Trisha, Tanishka and Anastasia

'I hold a beast, an angel, and a madman in me...'
—Dylan Thomas

Preface

When I moved to Mumbai in the late 1990s, I lived in Juhu. There's a particular, relatively quieter section of the beach that I visited often. As I'd breathe in the salty air and take in the sunset, I often found myself thinking about the lucky few who lived in apartments and bungalows on the beachfront. There was – still is – one particular building complex at the intersection of the beach and the road leading up to it that always caught my attention. There was no discernable reason for my fascination with this nondescript building, but I could never take my mind off it.

In the last three years, I've learnt that the apartment complex – Riviera – was where Parveen Babi lived the last years of her life. She died there, alone. I've learnt about her professional triumphs, her mental lows and her lifelong search for love. Now, when I walk down that same stretch of Juhu beach, I find myself thinking about the importance of family, the lure of fame and the stigma around mental health that persists even today.

Three years ago, when an editor at Hachette India asked me if I'd want to write about Parveen Babi, I knew almost nothing about the glamorous actress besides a handful of hit songs that featured her. There was always an air of mystery about her; it intrigued me. The prospect of digging through hundreds of old magazines, speaking to an entire generation of people in the film industry and tracing sources who would be authentic was daunting and exciting at the same time. As I began my attempt at rescuing Parveen's legacy from the bondage of myth and gossip, I was all too aware of my own limitations. They say every story has two sides, and Parveen wasn't here to tell me hers. So, every scene and every fact recorded in this book has been double- and triple-checked to keep the narrative as true to her story as possible. To tell her story with surety I have had to rely on a decade-plus worth of interviews she had given during her years in the limelight.

Parveen Babi: A Life is the fruit of three years of research, over a hundred interviews, numerous files of photographs, articles and interviews, many sleepless nights and travelling to innumerable locations, from Ahmedabad to Gangtok. As many places as I physically visited, I have to admit that my research took me just as much to unexpected emotional spheres. There were moments of great elation when the extremely private Danny Denzongpa shared his memories of Parveen, or when I held in my hand a note of apology written in her beautiful penmanship for her friend, costume designer Xerxes Bhathena. Yet, for every joyful discovery, there were moments of almost unbearable heartbreak as I navigated the troughs of her life, through to her final days.

My goal with this book was to piece together the known and unknown parts of Parveen's life without judgement. This was only possible because of the generous cooperation I received from everyone I reached out to – her lovers, her co-stars and directors, her closest friends, her employees, and the only surviving family member of her family who was close to Parveen and her mother Jamal. Not only did they share their memories and candid insights, and verify facts and anecdotes, but they also steered me in the right direction when unnecessary nuggets tended to distract me.

In the end, Parveen's story is so much more than a story of fame. It's a story of ambition and expectation, love and betrayal, obsession and mental illness – and its consequences. My only hope is that I have presented it with empathy and insight.

Karishma Upadhyay
Mumbai
January 2020

1

'If you try to stop me, I'll jump out of the car and strip right here!' the manic woman warned the man accompanying her. Having worked with her long enough as her manager, he knew this wasn't an empty threat.

Anyone peeking into the well-maintained blue Toyota idling at the traffic signal at the beginning of the Andheri flyover would have instantly recognized the woman in the back seat as one of Bollywood's most famous actresses. She may have been on the verge of a mental breakdown, but you wouldn't have known it if you saw her that night. To most the exchange would seem like an argument was ensuing between two people. Although it was close to midnight, there was enough traffic on the flyover to ensure that if she did strip, as she was threatening to, the act would make the headlines. For the actress in question was Parveen Babi and her companion her trusted manager, Ved Sharma.

The Toyota's occupants completed the rest of the journey to the city's international airport in an uncomfortable silence. Once at the airport, Parveen, with Ved in tow, made straight for the airline offices. She was looking for Rashna and Bishu Basu, relatives of her costume designer Xerxes Bhathena. The couple worked at Qantas and Swiss Air and Parveen knew they could help her get a last-minute ticket to fly out of Bombay (now Mumbai). Those were the days before cell phones and it took some time for Bishu to be located.

'When I got to my office, I saw Parveen standing there with Vedji,' Bishu recalls. 'She told me that she urgently needed to fly to London because a relative was unwell.'

Almost all Europe-bound flights for the night were in different stages of departure, but Bishu managed to block the last available first class seat on an Air India flight.

'Vedji accompanied me to the cashier, where he took out wads of notes to pay for Parveen's ticket,' Bishu remembers. Once all the formalities were completed, he accompanied Parveen to her flight.

⸙

When Bishu had returned to his office after seeing off the actress, he found a stack of messages from Xerxes. Each one told him to 'call back urgently'. He immediately called his cousin-in-law.

'Don't worry,' he assured an agitated Xerxes. 'I got Parveen a ticket. She's left.'

Xerxes exclaimed, 'But I was calling to tell you *not* to help Parveen!'

It was too late, however. By then, the aircraft had already pushed back, pre-flight checks having been completed and the cabin doors closed. There had been no way to stop Parveen Babi from leaving Bombay that night.

The call from Xerxes left Bishu confused. He couldn't understand why the designer was so distraught.

'I had no idea there was anything wrong,' he now muses.

On the face of it, he feels in hindsight, Parveen had looked like any other movie star waiting to board her flight. While she waited in the first class lounge with Bishu and Ved, she had smiled at eager fans and signed autograph books for them. That she was travelling with just one suitcase was somewhat unusual for her, but Bishu had concluded that this particular trip must have come up unexpectedly. There was no way he could have known of the havoc that had ripped through the Babi home in the days preceding that fateful night.

⸙

Earlier that year, Amitabh Bachchan had headlined a series of stage shows across North America that featured his leading ladies. This was a first of sorts. Until then, Bollywood's stage shows abroad had been the domain of musicians and singers. There was very little dancing and lots of singing. Instead of a star-studded line-up of singers, however, the show which featured Bachchan as the dominant star included performances by actresses like Zeenat Aman, Rati Agnihotri and Parveen Babi. While Amitabh sang hits like 'Rang barse' and 'Khaike paan Banaraswala', the actresses lip-synced, like they did in the movies. After a successful run in the US, the show travelled to London in the summer of 1983 with a new addition to the glittering line-up – Reena Roy.

Parveen had been really enthusiastic about this trip to London. Friends describe her as being almost 'giddy with excitement'. She had packed her best clothes and asked her friends to recommend new restaurants she could try out. London was one of her favourite destinations and being on stage in front of thousands of adoring fans was an electrifying experience. And then there was Amitabh Bachchan. She had been obsessed with him for years and, according to those she had confided in, hoped that being away from the city would mean getting to spend more time with him.

The Parveen who returned from that stage show in London in the middle of July, however, was a very different person. A dark cloud of melancholy seemed to have engulfed her. She had returned to a house full of happy faces, but it seemed as if she herself had forgotten how to smile.

'She had come back with six suitcases full of presents for everyone. She had even bought a gorgeous Royal Doulton dinner set for herself,' says Xerxes.

But she was so depressed that she could barely get herself out of bed.

The fact that she hadn't unpacked right after getting home was the first sign that something was wrong. This was quite unlike the normally fastidious Parveen who liked the house to be spotless, with everything in its place. During the first forty-eight hours of her return, at least, neither her mother Jamal, who was visiting from their ancestral home in Junagadh, nor her staff paid much mind to Parveen's changed mood. It was attributed to jet lag.

Accordingly, Ved cancelled the next two days of shoots so that Parveen could recuperate. Yet, for the third day in a row, she simply refused to get out of bed. After much cajoling by her mother and her maid Maggie, she did, finally, get up, but walked around the house aimlessly, her movements disjointed, her expression blank. Although her eyes were wide open, it seemed as though she were sleepwalking. She remained silent for long periods of time, but when she did speak, Bachchan featured prominently in her conversation. She sounded envious and resentful because of her perception that he had largely ignored her and paid more attention to Reena Roy.

Later that night, she told Xerxes that she wanted to watch a movie. She picked Peter O'Toole and Richard Burton's *Becket*. Everyone around her saw this as a sign that Parveen was beginning to perk up a little. Maggie was in the kitchen preparing to leave, and Jamal, whom everyone called 'Mummy', had sat down to roll the last paan of the day for herself. Xerxes popped the tape into the VHS and the duo settled down in the guest room that also served as a den for watching television. An uneasy but hopeful calm settled over Flat No. 401 in Juhu's Kalumal Estate.

An hour later, Parveen asked Xerxes to stop the film. She was bored, she declared. Even as he was wondering if he should leave, she asked him to throw out the VHS tape. It was a brand-new tape that she had brought back from London and he wanted to know how the film ended. So Xerxes took it out of the machine and kept it in the living room. By the time he returned to the den, Parveen was pointing to a small table clock on top of the television set and muttering, 'There's a bomb in it. They have come to kill me.'

In the three years that he had designed outfits for her, Xerxes had spent almost every single day with her. They were friends who holidayed together, who were in and out of each other's homes; there were no secrets between them. But he had never seen this side of Parveen. Until that night, he believed she was play-acting since her return from London to get out of shooting for K. Prasad's *Kanoon Meri Mutthi Mein* with Marc Zuber, a film that would eventually release in 1984. So he tried to reason with her.

'I picked up the clock and kept saying, "Look, it's only a clock and nothing else," and took it close to her,' Xerxes recalls. 'Parveen screamed like I was attacking her with a knife. I couldn't understand what was going on.'

Parveen's mother, on the other hand, knew this side of her daughter all too well. In Gujarati, she warned Xerxes, 'Don't indulge her paranoia or it will get worse.'

On hearing Jamal's words, Parveen suddenly turned on her, making her the focus of her suspicions. She began accusing her mother of conspiring to get rid of her. Xerxes's relief that the actress hadn't targeted him turned to disbelief and dismay when he saw Parveen attacking her mother. What seemed to be a much-needed distraction for him had taken an ugly turn. To defuse the situation, the designer started taking every object out of the room. Over the next thirty minutes, Parveen made him strip the room down, until two hanging light fixtures were all that was left.

'She told me to take them down too,' he says. 'I tried to explain to her that I didn't know how to.'

That's when she turned on him as well. 'Sit in that corner,' she ordered him. 'You are with *him*.'

He was already so befuddled by the bizarre turn the night had taken that he couldn't understand whom she was referring to.

'Who is "him"?' he asked.

'Amitabh Bachchan!' she hissed, her face betraying intense fear and hatred.

The more he denied any complicity with Bachchan, the more manic she became. Exhausted and confused, Xerxes didn't know how to help Parveen.

'Finally, I went to her and hugged her tight,' he says.

In that almost empty room, they stood there for what felt like hours, but must have been a few minutes. His arms encircling her, he slowly felt all the fight and fear leave her body. And she clung to him.

After a sleepless night, Xerxes knew that the kind of help Parveen needed was beyond him. He reached out to film-makers Aruna Raje and her then husband Vikas Desai. He knew they had lost their young daughter Gaagi to cancer just days earlier, but didn't know who else he could turn to. Fresh off the critical success of their first jointly directed film *Shaque*, starring Vinod Khanna, Shabana Azmi and Utpal Dutt, the couple had first met Parveen in 1976 for a film that never materialized. It took a few years for their friendship to take shape. By 1983, they had become close friends of the actress and, by extension, of Xerxes.

When Gaagi was diagnosed with a rare but aggressive cancer, the actress had become a regular visitor to the film-maker's Peddar Road home.

'She'd come over to cheer [up] Gaagi. My daughter had many Barbie dolls and Parveen would play with her. She even got Xerxes to make new dresses for the dolls. She'd sit on the floor, serve herself food from the kitchen and just spend hours with Gaagi, talking to her and making her laugh,' Raje remembers fondly.

When the couple decided to take Gaagi to the Memorial Sloan Kettering Cancer Center in New York, they didn't have enough time to get their finances in order. Parveen had immediately lent them the money they needed.

It took just one call from Xerxes for the grieving parents to rush to Parveen's aid. Raje found her crouched in a corner of her bedroom. She looked dishevelled and terrified. She told them there were bombs hidden everywhere in the house.

'She said she couldn't move, because "they" had planted bombs in her bedroom, living room and kitchen. She just wouldn't move from that corner,' Raje remembers.

Instead of challenging Parveen's delusions or trying to reason with her, the couple attempted to build a bridge of trust.

Gradually, they discovered that it had been days since she'd had a proper meal, because she was afraid of being poisoned.

'I asked her multiple times if she trusted me and if she'd eat if I cooked. Once she said "yes", I went to the kitchen and made her an omelette. She ate it without any fuss.'

When Raje suggested that she might feel safer living with them, Parveen immediately agreed. A few clothes were hastily packed and she left with the couple. Apart from a brief period in the 1970s when she had consulted a psychiatrist, Parveen stayed away from doctors, because she didn't trust them. So the couple requested their own psychiatrist Dr Ashit Sheth to examine the actress.

'When I saw her, she was floridly psychotic,' the doctor now recalls. 'She was hallucinating, was deluded and [feeling] persecuted. I gave her some medicine. This was the first of the two times that I treated her.'

There was a marked change in Parveen once she started taking the medicines. She ate well and interacted with everyone around her. Until the day a friend of the Desais came by on a condolence visit to see the grieving parents.

Parveen peeped out of her room and, on spotting the visitor, reacted violently. She was convinced he had been sent to kill her.

'She was so afraid that I took her to our room and told her to lock herself inside, so she'd feel safe,' Raje says. 'I had a key to open the bedroom from outside, so I wasn't very concerned.'

Dr Sheth was called once again to give her medication and calm her down.

Parveen stayed with Raje and Desai for three days. On the last evening, she told them, 'I am feeling better now. I think I'll go home.'

'She seemed quite normal, so we let her go,' Raje recalls.

Parveen's driver Hanuman picked her up from Peddar Road and dropped her off at her home in Juhu. The next morning, Xerxes called Raje and Desai to tell them that the actress had left the country. At 2.20 a.m. on 30 July 1983, hours before the fashion designer delivered the news, Parveen Babi had flown out of Bombay, her departure marking the end of her decade-long Bollywood career.

2

The legend of Parveen Babi being of royal lineage and hailing from the erstwhile Gujarati kingdom of Junagadh took root when she started making movies. Sanjay Khan, a friend and co-star of many films, remembers defending his decision to sign her on for *Chandi Sona* by telling his brother Feroz Khan that she was from the Nawab of Junagadh's family. While they were shooting their debut film *Charitra* together, Parveen's first co-star, cricketer Salim Durrani, had heard the rumour that the actress belonged to a royal family, but 'she never made a big deal about it'. 'She had no airs about herself, but she conducted herself with a lot of grace,' Durrani remembers.

It wouldn't be showbiz, after all, if there weren't any rumours trailing Parveen. There was some chatter that before she came down to Bombay, she was so 'down and out' that she'd often drop in at friends' homes at mealtimes so she could eat her fill.

The subject came up during an interview in the September 1974 issue of *Stardust* magazine. In response, Parveen laughed and said, 'Oh hell, this is the most amusing thing I've heard [in] ages! Look, there's no shame in poverty. If I had been down and out, why would I deny it? I still say it, and I mean it, that we are living, and we are living very comfortably. We have a car, a house with quite a few comforts, we have farms... In the hostel in Ahmedabad, yes, we hostelites did drop in at friends' places for meals, but that is only because we longed for home-cooked food, not because I was down and out, damn it!'

Parveen's family belonged to the ever-widening circle of aristocrats who were the lesser remnants of what had once been revered as Indian royalty. They would, typically, be close relations of a king or a nawab, who had been placed in positions of power by the country's British colonial rulers to help with local administration. Following Partition, all these royals had been left with were titles that meant precious little in the new India.

The Babi dynasty of the state of Junagadh in southern Saurashtra had been founded in 1654. At the time of Partition, its ruler was Sir Muhammad Mahabat Khanji III Rasul Khanji, an eccentric nawab, well known throughout British India for his love of dogs. According to local lore, he owned 800 of them, each with its own room, complete with a telephone and an attendant. A white-tiled hospital with a British vet attended to their ailments. In fact, according to a report in the 24 May 2003 issue of *Tribune India*, when one of the nawab's dogs died, state mourning was declared and Chopin's *Funeral March* played.

In keeping with the feudal system that prevailed in those days, the responsibility for administration of the region's villages was handed over to the nawab's extended family. These '*bhayyats*' or brotherhoods, as they were known, served at the nawab's discretion and pleasure. While enjoying local autonomy, they were obliged to pay a regular tribute to the nawab and provide soldiers when the kingdom was at war. Like his father Mojdeen Khanji, Parveen's father Wali Mohammad Khanji was a part of the *bhayyat*. He was the *Girasdar* or yeoman of a number of villages around Bamangam, about 10 kilometres from Junagadh. The nawab also appointed Wali as a *Vahiwatdar* or vice-regent to represent him.

Wali was married to Jamal Bhakte, a distant relative from within the Babi clan. The eldest of four sisters, Jamal had moved from her village Devgam in Amreli district after her wedding to live with her much older husband in Junagadh. In the early years of their marriage, the couple travelled to small villages and towns around the capital, depending on where Wali was posted.

Those were the dying days of the British Raj in India and even as the chants of 'Quit India' reverberated through the region, Jamal and Wali continued to live a seemingly charmed life. What marred this picture of domestic bliss was Jamal's inability to conceive. After an entire decade of marriage, the couple's unfulfilled yearning for a child seemed to follow them like a shadow.

Jamal's younger sister Umrao, who had married a few years later, but borne three children in quick succession, empathized with her sister's desperate desire to experience motherhood. Having shared her pain for almost a decade, Umrao finally sent her eldest daughter Noorjahan to live with Jamal.

But even as the couple took on the role of foster parents, meeting the demands it made on them, fulfilling the responsibilities that came with it and experiencing its joys, they were forced to make what would be another life-altering decision. On 15 August 1947, the Nawab of Junagadh, on the advice of his diwan Sir Shah Nawaz Bhutto (father of Pakistan's future prime minister Zulfikar Ali Bhutto), announced that his kingdom would become a part of the newly created country – Pakistan. This decision sent shockwaves everywhere. Not only was the state predominantly Hindu, Junagadh, situated on the southernmost tip of Saurashtra, was geographically nowhere close to Pakistan. More importantly, in the months preceding this announcement, the nawab had promised the Indian government that his state would integrate with independent India.

While the governments of the two countries grappled with the fallout of his declaration, the nawab, along with a few senior officials of his court, migrated to Karachi. Wali, however, decided, for reasons that remain unexplained, to continue living in India. The couple, like the rest of the state, was mostly spared the horrors of Partition, but they did live through some tense months when the Indian government blockaded and invaded the state. In a plebiscite held on 20 February 1948, 99.95 per cent of Junagadh's population voted to join India.[1]

---

[1] Mohammad Ali Jinnah, ed. Z.H. Zaidi, *Jinnah Papers: Pakistan: Pangs of Birth 15 August–30 September 1947*, Series 1, Vol. V, Quaid-e-Azam Papers Project, Islamabad: Culture Division, Government of Pakistan, 2000.

For Wali Mohammad, the first step towards normalizing their life after the nawab's departure was to find themselves a home in the city. It's unclear how the couple came to live in Danbai Haveli in the heart of Junagadh, but the Babis lived in that two-storeyed mansion at Diwan Chowk for decades after. Like the rest of the nawab's court, Wali lost his land, job and title during the country's partition. Under the Land Acquisition Act that offered compensation to those affected, he received a little over 100 bighas of land in Bamangam. Wheat and groundnut would be cultivated on a large portion of this land and serve as the family's major source of income for a couple of decades.

On a smaller plot, covering about 36 bighas and located across the road from the fields, Jamal started planting saplings to create her dream orchard. Relatives remember it as a place where she was most content and speak of her being happiest when she had soil under her fingernails. In the orchard that was a source of pride for her, Jamal planted varieties of mangoes and chikoos (mud apples) and set aside smaller patches for the cultivation of bananas, papayas, guavas, pomegranates and custard apples. There was even a small vegetable patch in a corner.

While Jamal wasn't particularly well educated, her husband had realized early in their marriage that she was worldly-wise. He had, unlike most men of that era, almost completely handed over the control of the agricultural land in Bamangam to his wife, along with the reins of their household in Junagadh.

By the early 1950s, the couple had almost given up hope of having a biological child. By then, Wali Mohammad was on the wrong side of sixty and Jamal was on the cusp of forty. As a childless married woman, Jamal had had to bear the stigma of barrenness but she had learnt to ignore the cruel whispers about herself.

When she eventually conceived in the summer of 1953, Wali Mohammad greeted the news of the unexpected pregnancy with a mix of joy and relief. On 4 April 1954, she gave birth to Parveen Sultana Wali Mohammad Khanji Babi. The arrival of the baby girl was a minor miracle, not just for her parents, but also for the extended family. If there was any disappointment over the baby's gender, it was well hidden. Noorjahan, who was twelve when Parveen was born, had to come to terms with not being the only child in the family any more, but she doted on her younger 'sister', nonetheless. A few years after Parveen's birth, Noorjahan was married off to Noor Ahmed Sheikh and left the Babi home.

༺༻

Parveen's early childhood was no different from that of the other young girls in the neighbourhood. She grew up in a household that was strict but thanks to her family's wealth, privileged as well. When she was old enough to start her formal education, she was enrolled at the local Gujarati-medium school and spent her holidays either at the family farm or on the rocky beaches of Chorvad.

Parveen wouldn't realize until she was much older that there had, indeed, been a subtle difference between her childhood and that of her peers. Unlike her friends or cousins, who lived within extended families or in homes teeming with children of similar ages, she grew up in a fifty-four-room haveli she called home, where the only other people were her parents, a family friend's young son, who was Wali Mohammad's apprentice, and half-a-dozen staff. Given that Wali and Jamal were at a stage of life where world-weariness outweighs the enthusiasm of new parenthood, Parveen never really enjoyed the warmth of parental affection that most children take for granted. Of course, her needs were taken care of and she was looked after, but there was no real emotional engagement or bonding between Jamal and her daughter. Wali was a kind presence, but Parveen didn't see enough of her father to compensate for the lack of intimacy with her mother.

Parveen was just four when tragedy struck the family. Wali Mohammad was diagnosed with a rare and aggressive form of throat and mouth cancer. The family spent the next two years rallying around him as he was subjected to a battery of tests and underwent multiple surgeries and treatments at the Tata Memorial Centre in Bombay to remove malignant tumours.

When it seemed as if Wali might never recover from the insidious disease that had taken hold of him, there were whispers of 'making his last days comfortable'.

These two years changed the family forever. Wali's apprentice, who had lived with the family for over a decade, but whose name no one seems to remember today, helped Jamal as she took charge of their finances. She sold a portion of the agricultural land they owned to pay for the expensive treatment her husband was undergoing. Parveen was too young to know the odds her father was battling, but seeing him under harsh hospital lights and attached to IV lines, surrounded by a blur of stethoscope-wielding medical staff and the constant, insistent beeps of unfamiliar, intimidating machines, left her with a deep-seated fear of doctors and hospitals that would stay with her forever.

Although she was still very young, Parveen instinctively knew that time with her father was limited. Noorjahan's eldest son Javed, who was born many years later, remembers having heard from family elders that she stayed by her ailing father's side through every blood test, every trial and every heartbreaking moment. She was just six when Wali Mohammad, who was in his seventies then, breathed his last.

Although her world had crumbled, Jamal didn't have the luxury of grieving. She had a young daughter and the family estate to look after. Parveen was immediately sent back to school and her mother busied herself with matters relating to the estate she had inherited. Wali's apprentice continued to live on in the haveli with the mother and daughter. He is said to have been a source of great strength for Jamal.

After the intensity of their initial grief had subsided over a period of time, Jamal asked her niece Noorjahan to send her firstborn Javed to live with her and Parveen in the haveli. Just eight years old at the time, the boy went on to become an integral part of the family and stayed by Jamal's side almost until her death in 2002. A few years after Javed moved in, Wali Mohammad's apprentice finally moved out.

Painfully shy and quiet as a girl, Parveen had two close friends at the local Gujarati-medium school she attended – Meena, who lived in the house opposite the haveli, and Asha, another family friend's daughter. The three girls were inseparable. Parveen wasn't a particularly diligent student. In class, when she wasn't daydreaming, she would doodle endlessly in her notebooks, turning out portraits and designing dresses for her dolls. What did make her stand out in school, however, was her photographic memory and her exceptional performance in exams. She did so well in them, in fact, that she was granted a double promotion and skipped two grades ahead of her classmates. Decades later, her sharp memory would give her an edge over other actresses. Co-stars and directors were always impressed by her ability to remember dialogues.

From her mother, Parveen inherited a love for the written word. Despite Jamal's sketchy formal education, she enjoyed reading. Some of the earliest books Parveen read were, in fact, borrowed from her mother's collection in Gujarati, Urdu and Hindi. She devoured every word of the books that came her way, regardless of the subject they dealt with or her understanding of them. Until the end, Parveen remained a voracious reader. As an actress on set, she always had a book or magazine with her. In the last decade of her life, when she had all but withdrawn from public appearances and activities, she could be spotted at the bookstore at the erstwhile Holiday Inn Hotel (now the Novotel) in Juhu. Journalist and author Dinesh Raheja recalls a time when he had accompanied her to a bookstore.

'I met Parveen many years after she had returned from her self-imposed exile in the US and I was the editor of *Movie* magazine,' he recalls. 'She dropped in at my office in Mahalaxmi for a two-hour interview, after which I accompanied her to Crossword bookstore to buy books. She was a voracious reader.'

The era of 'helicopter parents' was decades away, but even by the utilitarian parenting standards of the 1950s, Jamal wasn't known to be particularly maternal. Being a new mother who was no longer that young might have had something to do with her disinterest in her newborn. Enduring sleepless nights while taking care of a crying baby is physically taxing for all new mothers, but it must have been that much more difficult for Jamal, who was already in her forties. For her, the baby had increasingly become a responsibility, not a source of joy. But it wasn't a responsibility she would ever shirk. She made sure that her daughter suffered no material deprivation. She was clothed and fed appropriately, taken for vacations to the Chorvad Palace and sent to college in Ahmedabad. But there were no warm, fuzzy cuddles or words of affection exchanged between mother and child. This created a certain distance between them, which prevented them from ever bonding. It also led to Parveen feeling isolated and lonely in her own home; and her father's death merely deepened the void within her.

This sense of emotional alienation would influence all of Parveen's important relationships as an adult. She was territorial as a friend and didn't like sharing. She craved constant attention. And when it came to significant others, her life revolved around theirs. She always clung to her partner of the moment, hankering after a sense of security and a way to fill the emptiness within. Her anxiety and deep-rooted feelings of not measuring up only exacerbated her fears of being unloved and abandoned.

Parveen had realized very early in life that nothing she did could earn her mother's love or approval. So at some point, she had stopped trying. A strained silence permeated their haveli and she couldn't wait to escape its confines. Teenage rebellion is an established reality today, but it was virtually unheard of in a royal Gujarati family in the 1960s. Parveen's defiance of norms, however, in whatever situation life handed her, became a defining and permanent character trait. If she and her mother continued to share a home, it was certainly not out of any love they had for each other; after Wali Mohammad's death, each woman was the only close family the other had left.

Jamal represented everything that her daughter deemed conventional and 'convention' became a word Parveen would never again want to be associated with. She went to great lengths to project herself as 'bohemian', building in the years that followed a certain persona and adopting a particular lifestyle for the world to see. The small-town girl would, however, peek through the façade every now and then, making her a bundle of contradictions for some and an enigma to others.

3

On a July morning in 1968, a young girl stepped on to the tree-lined path inside the St Xavier's College campus in Ahmedabad. She was dressed rather plainly in a loose-fitting salwar kameez and her hair was tied back neatly, every strand held in place in a single plait. Other than a smidgeon of kajal outlining her eyes, there was no trace of make-up on her strikingly attractive face. This was the first day of the pre-university course for the batch of 1968 and Parveen was one of the hundreds of students embarking on a new phase of their lives in what was considered one of the best institutes in the region.

Like some of her classmates, she was a bundle of nerves, overwhelmed by a mix of feelings. She was excited about the future, yet gripped by social anxiety at the thought of meeting new people and insecure over the prospect of living away from her family for the first time. Above all, there was a sense of unreality at finding herself in a situation she hadn't dreamed was possible; she still found it hard to believe that Jamal had actually allowed her to move out of her home town for further studies.

Parveen had left home for the first time that summer with good grades from school and her mother's reluctant blessing. Families from a certain stratum of society had begun to educate their daughters then, but to send a young girl to college over 300 km away from home was still unheard of in the late 1960s. After months of her daughter's begging and cajoling for a chance to pursue higher studies, Jamal had finally given in, but not without a caveat of her own: Parveen could go in for further studies if she agreed to get engaged soon and marry in the not-too-distant future. It was surprising, even for Jamal, that the fourteen-year-old had immediately agreed to her terms and conditions. But for Parveen, this must have seemed at the time like a small price to pay for four whole years of freedom from parental supervision and interference.

Mother and daughter had spent most of that summer making sure Parveen had all the basic necessities, new clothes and school supplies she could possibly require. Somewhere in between the hustle and bustle of that summer, it had dawned on Jamal that once Parveen left, she'd be left alone in that huge haveli. The sudden surges of emotion she experienced at the thought of her daughter being away from her could well have served as an opportunity to repair her relationship with Parveen. But they dissolved, instead, into petty squabbles between the two over the most trivial things. And before Jamal knew it, they were standing in a spartan hostel room off a busy street in Ahmedabad, hugging each other in farewell.

Parveen had been assigned the spacious Room No. 5 on the first floor of the St Xavier's Ladies' Hostel that accommodated three single beds and came with an attached balcony that overlooked the road. Her two roommates were Asha Gaur, a senior, and Mala Shah, who was enrolled in the pre-university Arts course like Parveen. The room next door was occupied by three girls from Porbandar, a town close to Junagadh, and they went on to become Parveen's close friends. But on that first night, she kept to herself.

❦

Before Jamal left Ahmedabad, she had introduced her daughter to two families – the Zaveris and the Marks, who went on to become her lifelines during her college years.

Jamal's brother Zorawar Khan Babi chose Pankaj Zaveri, who was a few years older than Parveen, as her local guardian. A well-known cricketer, Pankaj was the captain of Gujarat's Ranji team and was employed by the State Bank of India. The Zaveris lived close to the hostel and the St Xavier's campus. For the next three years, Parveen's conduct and welfare would become Pankaj's responsibility. She couldn't stay out of the hostel overnight without a signed letter of authorization from him to the warden and if the warden or the college authorities had any complaints about her, they were expected to go straight to him.

Considering that she didn't know anyone else in Ahmedabad, her social life was confined to her daily visits to the Zaveri home. Though the family was Jain, which meant that they were strict vegetarians and ate neither onions nor garlic and their food was very different from what she had been used to from childhood, this was where she headed if she craved a home-cooked meal. On some days she'd go there alone and on others she'd take along a friend or two from the hostel.

The second family she was introduced to by Jamal, the Marks, also lived close to Parveen's hostel. Eric Marks, an Anglo-Indian employed as the palace superintendent, had also worked in the Nawab of Junagadh's court. In fact, Wali Mohammad had known Eric for decades as an integral member of the nawab's inner circle. Like Parveen's father, Eric too had chosen to continue living in India, instead of following the nawab to Pakistan. During India's partition in 1947, the nawab had picked Eric to oversee his move to Karachi. Marks had spent three months in that city for the purpose, before returning to his wife and two sons – Patrick and Donald – in Junagadh. In 1950, the family moved out of the city and settled in Ahmedabad.

Parveen was unlike the girls young Donald was friends with in Ahmedabad.

'Parveen was one of those typical shy girls from a small town, who wouldn't even look up when someone talked to her,' he recalls. 'Even when I said "hello" to her, she shyly said a quick "hello" and walked away. Later, when we became friends, she told me that she wasn't even used to talking to boys who weren't related to her.'

It wasn't just boys that Parveen was shy around. Everyone who knew her until she moved to Ahmedabad describes her as being painfully reserved. Living in a new place with girls who weren't friends yet made her withdraw further into her shell. It didn't help that Parveen barely spoke English or that she was almost two years younger than most of her classmates (her birth records, submitted to meet the requirements of the college admission process, are said to have been fudged to make her eligible). In the initial months following her enrolment, it had taken her so long to summon the courage to say more than a mumbled 'hello' to her classmates that they had moved on.

Despite her debilitating shyness, within weeks Parveen found herself being included by the 'cool' set. Before any meaningful friendships could be forged, the prettiest girls in the batch of 1968 had automatically gravitated towards each other. Though she still found it hard to strike up conversations with others, she was beginning to sense that her looks could be her primary social currency.

'We were like the stars of the college,' activist, classical dancer and actress Mallika Sarabhai remembers. 'St Xavier's was where the best-looking women went and we were the stars even among them. We were very bindaas [carefree]. We'd sit in the canteen, which wasn't something that girls did in those days.'

Apart from Parveen and Sarabhai, the 'it' girls included Kavita Bhambani (née Singh), who went on to become a Miss India, and Khurshid Ravji, who now runs the Ahmedabad-based Karma Foundation that is involved in community-based projects.

'Even today, if you ask long-time residents of Ahmedabad, they'll tell you that St Xavier's batch of '68 was the best-looking class. At 10.45 every morning during our recess, the canteen would be full of boys from neighbouring colleges who would come to gape at us,' Ravji remembers with a laugh.

Parveen might not have found lifelong friends within this circle of 'it' girls, but the attention she received, whether because of her association with them or because of her own striking looks, flipped the proverbial switch within her. Having lived on the sidelines and craved attention for as long as she had, Parveen thrived on all the admiration that was coming her way. It was a euphoric boost, unlike anything she had ever experienced before. Who adored her or why was immaterial; that the spotlight was on her was all that mattered. She had travelled the hard road of a childhood marked by an absence of emotional warmth. To her any attention was more than welcome and she lapped it up hungrily. Parveen's delicate, ethereal kind of beauty instantly captivated strangers, perhaps because she seemed so unaware of the effect her looks had on others.

'She was really beautiful, fair, tall and [she] had a great figure,' says her former roommate Mala. 'Girls in the hostel would constantly tell her how envious they were of her figure

During her first year in college

and flat stomach. And Parveen would just shrug. She never really bothered too much about how she looked. She wasn't one of those who'd constantly primp and preen.'

Jyotsna Odedra, a senior who went on to become a roommate of Parveen's and formed an enduring friendship with her, has a vivid memory of the first time she saw her.

'Though I was senior to Parveen, I joined the hostel in the same year as her. I remember standing in a queue outside [the admissions] office to submit the application form with my sister,' Jyotsna recollects. 'Parveen was right in front of us. She was so beautiful that we couldn't take our eyes off her. Her shoulder-length, jet-black hair was parted in the middle and open. She had such an innocent face, with not a trace of make-up.'

In that first year, Jyotsna and her sister Jai Bala were assigned Room No. 4, making them Parveen's neighbours. She immediately gravitated towards the sisters, because their home town was close to hers. Among her initial friends in the hostel was also Pappu Parikh, who lived in the room opposite. A senior, Pappu was everything Parveen wanted to be – confident, well spoken and smart. She was perhaps Parveen's first role model.

For the three years that she lived in the hostel, Parveen's morning routine remained the same. After her roommates had dragged her out of bed, there would invariably be a mad dash to the bathroom down the hall, followed by the wolfing down of breakfast at the hostel mess. Mala and Parveen would walk together to college or if they had money, they'd take a rickshaw, but that was rare.

'Parveen never carried a bag or books to college,' Jyotsna recalls. 'At the most, she'd have one notebook and a pen. At times, she walked empty-handed into college.'

That does not mean, however, that Parveen was a poor student. Although she was yet to attain perfect fluency in spoken English, she took up English and Psychology for her bachelor's degree and finished her MA in English even after she had started accepting acting roles.

'Asha and I were more studious and would keep telling her to study as well, but she wouldn't,' says Mala. 'Then she would study at the last minute and still get a first class.'

In Jyotsna, Parveen found a kindred spirit who wasn't always studying.

'The day before exams, we'd go out to watch movies,' she recalls. 'And then in the evening, we'd keep postponing our study session. There were times when we'd wake up at 5 a.m. on the day of an exam and then read through our books.'

Watching a film after every single exam was another tradition they never let go of. Their love for films served as a bond between them.

'Those were the days when movie tickets cost ₹2. We'd go for the first-day-first-show of most films,' says Jyotsna. 'There were even times when we'd walk out of one show and go to another theatre immediately for another film.'

In Parveen's mind, these four years of college weren't for acing exams and getting a degree. That she did manage to do both, nonetheless, thanks to her photographic memory, was incidental. She looked upon this period in her life as her only years of freedom. Since she had promised her mother an early betrothal, marriage was an eventuality she was prepared for. Even the idea that she could, perhaps, have a career after college was quite unthinkable for her. Having basked in the attention of those around her, all she wanted to do now was continue to court it.

For Parveen, being fluent in English was just the first step of fitting into the social maelstrom of St Xavier's and she taught herself spoken English almost from scratch. One of her most prized possessions was a dictionary. If there were words she came across that she didn't understand, she'd make a mental note to look them up. She'd ask the nuns for the correct pronunciation of words she found tough. She'd read everything from English language magazines to notices on college boards and then try to use the words she'd learnt in conversations.

She began to pick up little things that she had seen the 'cool' girls do, starting with smoking – an addiction that stayed with her until the end of her days. She also tried alcohol for the first time and contrary to the public perception that dogged her later in life, it wasn't a taste that appealed to her. She learnt basic table etiquette and how to sit in a ladylike manner while wearing a dress. Parveen also began to take an interest in pop culture, so she could tell the Beatles apart from Bob Dylan, talk about Neil Armstrong's walk on the moon or comment on Julie Andrews's performance in *Mary Poppins*.

'She was like a sponge who learnt from the people around her,' Jyotsna recalls. 'For instance, if she was with people talking about a particular musician or book, she'd quietly listen to them and that bit of information was filed away in her brain.'

It was in those initial months in Ahmedabad that Parveen transformed herself into the person the world would get to meet a few years later. An unassuming girl from a conservative small town would morph into a young woman who wanted more out of life. But even as this transformation was taking place, she never let go of the simple, tradition-bound part of her personality.

It was around this time that Parveen first revealed signs of being a social chameleon: she could adapt herself to different personalities and settings around her. As her motivation to 'fit in' grew, this ability became her strength. In different social situations, she'd quietly observe the behaviour of others and later replicate it. She was just as comfortable rolling khakhras (a popular Gujarati snack) and chatting with a friend's grandmother, as she was lighting a cigarette in public and carrying on a conversation on Richard Bach's fable in novella form, *Jonathan Livingston Seagull*.

During the first six months of college, Parveen visited her local guardian's home every single evening. She'd drop in to meet the Zaveris after college and on Sundays. Very often, she'd spend time with the women of the house in the kitchen and learn to make *khakhras*. Parveen would sit on the floor and help the ladies knead the dough, roll out the khakhras and then slow roast them on an open fire. From the Zaveri home, she'd walk to the closest postbox to mail a postcard to her mother and make it back to the hostel for the 8 p.m. roll call.

To those with whom she lived in close quarters, Parveen was initially pleasantly ordinary, except for the fact that her corner of the room was a cluttered and messy pit; her unmade bed always had piles of washed and unwashed clothes. Stacks of newspapers, textbooks and loose sheets of paper lay on the floor. Her closet was a mess of bags, shoes, linen and clothes. Most girls would do their laundry daily but Parveen would wait until her bucket overflowed. The rare occasions on which she did get down to

With a hostel friend, the late Manju Roy

sorting out the clutter she had created, her zeal bordered on the obsessive.

'Suddenly one morning, she'd spend hours cleaning everything she could get her hands on,' Mala remembers. 'Once she'd finish with her clothes, she'd start cleaning the room. She'd obsess with cleaning every corner and hunt for cobwebs, even though the hostel staff would clean our rooms every day.'

It was a trait that would resurface later in her life.

By the time they were in their third year in college, none of the other girls wanted to share a room with Parveen. That's when Jyotsna stepped in.

'Like all rooms, ours also had three beds, but no one wanted to stay with Parveen. So it was just the two of us,' she recalls.

Though they ended up remaining friends for decades afterwards, Jyotsna describes Parveen as 'not an ideal roommate'. 'She hated washing clothes,' she explains. 'Weeks would go by before she got around to doing laundry. This meant that either she'd be wearing dirty clothes or someone else's clothes. Very often, I'd realize that she'd borrowed my clothes only when I'd see her wearing them. Forget about washing your clothes before returning them, Parveen would just forget to return them. At the end of the day, I'd find my nice clothes in a heap, along with her shoes and dirty underwear.'

In the new room she was sharing with Jyotsna, Parveen found another dumping ground for her belongings – the third, unused bed. Tired of living in messy surroundings, Jyotsna would offer to clean the entire room on a Sunday, but Parveen never took her up on it.

'One day, I got really fed up and soaked all her clothes in water and detergent. I thought she'd have no choice but to wash them.'

But Jyotsna hadn't quite understood just how much Parveen abhorred the chore of washing and cleaning.

'Three days later, that bucket was where I had left it,' she remembers with a laugh. 'The water had evaporated and the clothes had started to stink and still Parveen didn't wash them.'

Eventually, Jyotsna gave up.

Clothes weren't the only things Parveen borrowed from the girls in the hostel. The monthly allowance Jamal sent her was so meagre, she was trapped in a perpetual cycle of debt.

'Parveen was constantly borrowing money. She'd pay people off at the beginning of a month and by the middle, she'd be broke again. Girls slowly started avoiding her, because lending her money meant that they'd not have enough for themselves and no one could say no to her.'

Living in a bigger city, away from her mother's intense scrutiny, gave Parveen the kind of freedom and anonymity that she had never enjoyed before. She began to realize that she was free to spend her days as she pleased as long as she attended her classes and returned to the hostel before the evening deadline. She could wear what she wanted to and talk to whoever caught her fancy.

Even as the boys in her college vied for her attention, there was one familiar face that piqued her curiosity. After she had met him through her mother, Parveen had pretty much forgotten about the Marks's son Donald. Six years older than her, he had friends in her college and hostel. In those first few months of college, it seemed like the strapping twenty-something Donald was everywhere she went. He seemed to stand apart from the others; tall, handsome, with nice eyes and a warm smile. There was something that clicked instantly and Parveen and Donald went on to become friends for life.

'We were best friends. We would meet every single day and talk about everything under the sun. After a while, she even started staying the night at our home or would spend the weekend with us. My mummy used to get worried because we'd sleep on the terrace in the summers, but there were never any romantic vibes between Parveen and me. We were just inseparable buddies,' is how Donald – or Donny, as Parveen called him – describes their relationship.

Jyotsna, who was married to Donald for a few decades, confirms, 'If you didn't know them well enough, you'd think they were a couple, but until the end he just remained one of Parveen's closest friends.'

Bankura, a hole-in-the-wall eatery, was where Donald and his friends hung out. It automatically became one of Parveen's regular haunts. The owner, Ramesh Mehta, was so used to the group being here that he would even step out to run errands, leaving them in charge of the place. In between endless cups of coffee or cola, Donald would take Parveen's friends for joyrides on his bike. Every Sunday morning, she would patiently watch Donald spend hours washing and servicing his Jawa motorcycle. It was the same bike Parveen learnt to ride later.

If they weren't hanging around Bankura, Donald and Parveen would drive out to his brother Patrick's home.

'I used to be broke all the time,' Donald remembers. 'There were days when I'd have 2 rupees to spend in an entire evening. Coke would cost 80 paise and we'd buy samosas with the rest of the money. I would have enough petrol in my Jawa to go for a drive. My brother would be busy with his music stuff, so Parveen and I could sit in his *otla* [an enclosed courtyard at the entrance of a house] and eat our dinner – two samosas each – and share a Coke.'

If they were really broke, they'd gatecrash weddings.

'I'd tell Parveen, "Dress well today. Don't wear your shorts or minis; we have to go to eat today." She'd get the hint,' he adds. This kind of mischief presented a new kind of adrenaline rush for Parveen and helped her break out of her shell.

꧁꧂

As the days and weeks flew past, Parveen grew more confident in her new surroundings and those around her began to notice little changes in her. The first obvious indicator of her metamorphosis was the transformation in her choice of clothes. When she left home and travelled to Ahmedabad, her trunk had been full of simple cotton salwar kameezes. But the girls she came across in college were all wearing bell-bottom jeans and dresses.

Considering the measly pocket money she received from her mother that barely covered her monthly expenses, a complete wardrobe makeover was out of the question. So Parveen did what most kids in hostels resort to: she raided the closets of her roommates and neighbours. She'd borrow a T-shirt from someone and pair it with someone else's bell bottoms.

'She wouldn't even bother asking. If she liked something she saw, she'd walk off with it,' remembers Pearl Goswami, one of the only three schoolgirls who stayed in the hostel.

Very soon, most of Parveen's salwars were relegated to the dark corners of her very messy cupboard. These would only come out when either Jamal was visiting or Parveen had to meet Pankaj Zaveri.

However, within a year of moving to Ahmedabad, Parveen's visits to the Zaveri home too reduced considerably. Pankaj Zaveri was firm in his conviction that Donald was a bad influence on his ward and the reason for her behaviour, and he cut off all ties with Donald.

'Pankaj and I used to be friends,' Donald reminisces. 'We played cricket together. But our friendship ended, because he thought I was responsible for how much Parveen [had] changed.' Now Parveen would only visit the Zaveris if she simply couldn't avoid it and that was mostly when her local guardian insisted that she show up. She would grudgingly change into the conservative clothes she had brought from home and join the ladies of the Zaveri household in rolling out khakhras in their kitchen. What used to be, just a year ago, the high point of her day had started to feel like an onerous chore. For a few hours, the new, gregarious and fun-loving Parveen would reluctantly step back and allow the shy and docile one to take over.

While she was preoccupied with testing the boundaries of her newfound freedom, being on her own also meant that Parveen was exposed to a larger world against which she had no safeguards. When she returned to Ahmedabad after her first summer vacation in July 1969, there were developments outside her little cocoon that would have a strong impact on her psyche. This first tryst with the terrifying unknown left her deeply shaken.

Between 1961 and 1971, sixteen districts in Gujarat were rocked by communal violence. During that ten-year period, 1969 was the year that the situation came to a head and Ahmedabad was the worst affected city. This was the first time that communal violence in the state would peak to barbaric levels, leading to wide-scale massacres, multiple acts of arson and rampant looting.

On 19 September, Ahmedabad erupted in violence yet again. In the week that followed, over five hundred people were killed and thousands of homes and properties damaged across the city. All schools and colleges were closed and Parveen, like all the other girls in the hostel, stayed indoors. Intimidated by the turn the riots had taken, the warden of the hostel feared for Parveen's safety and decided that she would be more secure in her local guardian Pankaj Zaveri's home. Under cover of darkness, the young girl was, therefore, hidden under a mattress and a massive pile of blankets in the back of a truck and transported to the Zaveris' home.

Living through the riots would have been a traumatic experience for a young Parveen, but the resilience of youth, the excitement of starting a new life and having her friends around her helped Parveen bounce back quickly.

Decades later, however, the incident would come back to haunt her during one of her lows. Mahesh Bhatt would mention this incident in multiple interviews.

'She told me once, "You don't know what it is [like] to lie hidden under several blankets, dreading the moment when the furious rioters would pull off the mattresses and rape me." The fear, still lurking in her voice, explained a lot as to why her psyche had remained scarred till date,' he was quoted as saying in the January 2007 issue of *Society* magazine.

That first year and a half of living on her own in a big city would fundamentally change the young woman, shaping her personality and habits. She would not only try her first cigarette, but learn a new language that helped ease her into social circles where she might have initially felt awkward. She also came to know what it felt like to be always short of money and experience the kind of fear she had never known before, but all of this was offset by the friends she made for life.

This was also when Parveen fell in love for the very first time.

4

As soon as her daughter had left home to attend college in the summer of 1968, Jamal had marshalled all her relatives and urged them to help her in her endeavour to find a suitable son-in-law.

Keeping in mind the condition Jamal had made her daughter agree to for allowing her to move to another city for higher education, Parveen had accepted that marriage was definitely on the cards. It was no different for every young Indian girl at the time. Almost eighteen months later, even after she had tasted freedom and discovered a world beyond Junagadh and its strictures, the idea of marrying a man her mother had chosen for her didn't seem alien or preposterous.

Jamal had meanwhile managed to identify a suitable groom from within her extended family, but there was just one problem – he lived in Pakistan. During Partition, a significant number of her relatives had migrated across the border. Among them was a distant cousin who had settled in Karachi and had a son of marriageable age – Jamil Khan. Jamil was in his twenties and employed as a pilot with Pakistan International Airlines.

Jamil and Parveen were engaged in Karachi during her college break in the winter of 1969–70. The lavish ceremony, described by many as a 'mini wedding', was attended by dozens of their relatives who had travelled to Karachi from all over Pakistan and Gujarat to bless the couple. Jamal oversaw every little detail, sparing no expense to make it an event to remember.

As was common at the time, Parveen didn't get to see her fiancé at all until she came face to face with him during the engagement celebrations. Sitting on stiff, uncomfortable ceremonial chairs, surrounded by hundreds of guests, she finally set eyes on the man she was supposed to spend the rest of her life with. She liked what she saw. Tall, fair and strong-jawed, he looked as if he had walked out of one of the many romance novels she was in the habit of reading.

When she returned to college after the vacation, Parveen carried with her a photo album brimming with cherished memories of her engagement. She'd bring out the thick, bound album every time she was asked how she had spent her vacation or when someone refused to believe that she was actually engaged to be married. There was one photograph, in particular, of the couple standing shoulder to shoulder – she, shy and totally smitten, and he, handsome and confident – that eventually found its way under Parveen's pillow. Over time, this picture had 'P + J' scribbled on it inside hearts of all sizes.

Her doodling wasn't restricted to pillowcases or notebooks, however. One night in the hostel, Parveen was sitting with a few friends, catching up on gossip and cracking jokes. Sitting on one corner of her unmade bed as she chatted, she twirled a safety pin between her fingers. Even as she laughed at the jokes and complained about the hostel warden, she pressed the pin hard enough on to her wrist to break skin. It was a tiny prick. It barely hurt. Mesmerized by the sight of a single drop of blood, she punctured her skin once more – then yet again. And with every pinprick, she came closer to marking out Jamil's initial on her wrist in blood.

One wonders if what might have been passed off as the ultra-romantic gesture of a girl pining for her first love was, perhaps, the earliest marker of an obsessive mind. Later, the same disturbing behaviour would manifest itself in Parveen's obsession with her co-star of many films – Amitabh Bachchan.

Sustaining a long-distance relationship, that too one across international borders, was particularly hard in those days.

Parveen's daily mailing list of postcards immediately increased from one to two as she began writing to Jamil. She'd spend hours thinking of what to write in the limited space a postcard offered. In her loopy handwriting, she'd give Jamil an account of her days in college, share news of her friends and, most of all, confess to him how much she liked him. Love was a word she was still too shy to use. Then she'd eagerly wait for him to reply from whichever part of the world he had flown to.

Jamil visited Parveen in Ahmedabad about a year after their engagement. This was only the second time they were meeting. That they were away from the watchful eyes of their relatives was an added bonus. Parveen's local guardian Pankaj was on double duty – as a chaperone and as Jamil's host. Though she stayed at the hostel throughout the duration of his visit, Parveen spent every possible moment by his side.

Unable to resist showing off her handsome husband-to-be, she took him to Bankura to meet her friends. Jamil charmed everyone that evening. Some remember that he spoke to them in Sindhi, while others recall a conversation he had with them about his travels and his motorbikes. Parveen's friends were suitably impressed. Jamil was polite, attentive and seemed to be perfect husband material. Fate, though, had other plans for the young couple.

In early 1971, rumblings of trouble started in the Indian subcontinent with East Pakistan demanding independence from West Pakistan. With India geographically caught in the middle, it was inevitable that the country would be drawn into the conflict. As winter gave way to spring, the Pakistan army, deployed to carry out a brutal campaign to suppress the revolt in its eastern province, sprang into action. The atrocities reportedly perpetrated by its soldiers on the local population and the resultant mass exodus of refugees from East Pakistan to India became the grounds for India's armed intervention in the situation by the end of 1971.

In a war that lasted all of thirteen days, the armed forces of India and Pakistan clashed simultaneously on the eastern and western fronts. On 16 December 1971, the fall of Dhaka signalled the end of the war and the birth of a new independent nation – Bangladesh.

Hundreds of kilometres away in Ahmedabad, 1971 had begun like any other year for Parveen. College, her ever-expanding social circle and writing to Jamil kept her busy. Her mother, though, brooded over the increasingly strained diplomatic relations between India and Pakistan. Memories of the bloody partition of India in 1947 and the war with its neighbour in 1965 were still fresh and vivid in her mind. Family members believe that it was Jamal's fear of the hostilities between the two countries affecting Parveen's marriage that prompted her to call off the engagement.

Thus, a little less than two years after Parveen had fallen in love for the first time, she experienced her first heartbreak.

The news of her broken engagement came via a postcard from her mother. As she read the postcard, Parveen felt like her entire being had died — if hearts could shatter into a million pieces, hers had certainly done that. Jamil had disappeared from her life just as suddenly as he had entered it. Parveen spent nights crying into the pillow that had his name scribbled on it. The first night that her roommates heard her sobbing, they were worried and wondered if there was something they could do to help, but as the nights turned into weeks and Parveen's misery continued unabated they gave her the space to heal on her own.

There were good days and bad. There were moments when she seemed completely normal, followed by sudden waves of debilitating grief that led to uncontrollable sobbing when she was in the college chapel. Focussing on simple tasks like eating or sleeping felt like insurmountable challenges. She felt numb.

Slowly, Parveen began to cope by harnessing her sadness to serve as a creative force. She began to write. Putting pen to paper helped her make sense of her emotions. She had done this when her father passed away and continued to enjoy using this creative outlet all through her life. In these years, as she grew more comfortable with English, it would become her language of choice but at the time she wrote Urdu couplets about love and heartbreak. Eventually, with time, she got over her first break-up and Jamil was pushed into a dark recess of her memory that she rarely probed.

5

After her father's death, this was the second time that grief had gripped Parveen's heart and numbed her fragile mind. But slowly she began putting herself back together in her characteristic way – she rebelled, and revelled in her rebellion. Suddenly, just being a pretty face among many wasn't enough for her. She wanted to be noticed and remembered. In a crowd that included the brightest young minds from the region and scions from millionaire families, she wanted to stand out. The new Parveen was defiant, self-assured, ever so provocative and an attention seeker. She opened herself to exploring new experiences and went out of her way to meet new people. She flirted with boys she found attractive, was the life of parties and smoked like the proverbial chimney.

The easiest way for a young girl to attract attention in the Ahmedabad of the 1970s was to light a cigarette in public. It's not that girls Parveen's age didn't smoke; they just took care to do it on the sly. Not Parveen, though. She flaunted her habit.

'Even if no one else around her was smoking, she'd light up, because she knew a cigarette in her hand will make people do a double take,' her friend and roommate Jyotsna remembers.

By the time Parveen stepped into the third year of her course, all the girls in the hostel knew she was a smoker. Her room reeked of cigarette smoke. The warden, who was in the habit of conducting spot checks, constantly warned her to not smoke inside the hostel, but Parveen paid little attention. It is believed that this was one of the reasons why she was asked to vacate the hostel at the end of three years.

Goofing off on Donald's terrace

As Parveen grew more confident, she began to thrive on her ability to scandalize people around her. For a Talent Evening in college, one year, Parveen decided she wanted to wear a gold dress. She had a very specific design in mind and roped in Jyotsna, who knew how to use the sewing machine in the hostel, to make this outfit for her.

'She wanted to wear something no one had seen before – a micro mini dress with a zip fastening at the back,' she remembers. Jyotsna, whose sewing skills extended to nothing beyond simple kurtas and tops, suggested they look for a professional tailor to make this special outfit. The girls bought two metres of slinky, sparkly material and handed it over to a tailor with very precise instructions. The dress turned out to Parveen's satisfaction; it hugged her slim figure in all the right places and showed off her long, shapely legs. She didn't perform at that Talent Evening, but in her eye-catching dress, she made sure that everyone was talking about her.

Yet, Parveen's gracious manners and lack of guile made up for all her lapses. Her charm was potent enough to floor college boys and endear her to cranky grandmothers. It got her out of scrapes and won her unexpected rewards. She may have been aware of the impact she had, but her behaviour never came across as forced or fake.

Mala remembers inviting Parveen and Donald to her sister's home for kite-flying during the Uttarayan festival. Every winter, the pale sky over Ahmedabad is punctuated with a rainbow of simple diamond-shaped paper kites bobbing over the city's higgledy-piggledy skyline. Mala, her guests and members of her sister's extended family spent the morning on their terrace, where raucous kite wars played out in between snack breaks. The family, who were initially taken aback to find themselves hosting a Muslim girl and a Christian boy in their home, were soon charmed by both. That morning, the victorious shouts of '*Kai po che* (I have cut)!' rang out over the warren of brick terraces as clearly as Parveen's lilting laugh.

When she wasn't on the terrace, she spent time with the matriarch of the house.

'Parveen was very warm and polite. Everyone always gravitated towards her. That was just the kind of person she was,' says Mala.

༄༅

Even before he became the frontman and bassist of the band Purple Flower, Neville Damania was a hit with the ladies. Son of a theatre owner, the twenty-four-year-old was classically handsome: tall and fair, with broad shoulders, warm brown eyes and a quick smile. Unruly waves of ebony-coloured hair framed the contours of his face, set off by an angular jaw; his eyes sparkled when he smiled; and when he sang, his deep, velvety voice made the girls swoon. As one of Donald's closest friends, Neville had met and known Parveen for some time, but that was the extent of their friendship.

Months after all memory of Jamil had become a blur in her mind, Parveen attended a party at Mallika Sarabhai's home with a few friends. It was here that Neville finally gathered the nerve to ask her out. She told him to 'take permission from Donny; if he's okay with it, then we can see each other'.

'The poor chap got on his Jawa immediately and came to my house to ask me,' Donald remembers with a laugh.

From that day on, until she left Ahmedabad in 1972, Parveen and Neville were inseparable. She used to be a fixture at every band practice, sitting in the corner as they performed their set drawn from country, folk and rock. Whether they were playing at college shows, weddings or private parties, Parveen was in the audience, cheering and whooping for them.

Jamil might have been the first man she fell in love with, but it was with Neville that Parveen had her first adult relationship. For better or for worse, this relationship established the framework that defined how she would approach love and the kind of partner she eventually became. These patterns formed the foundation of all her future romances. Neville was the centre of Parveen's universe and her life revolved around him. When they were together, she didn't want to share him with anyone else.

This kind of obsession also awakened in Parveen a generosity that had probably been inherent in her, but hadn't surfaced until then, possibly because she hadn't had much to give earlier. When she earned significant money for the first time, it fuelled an unbridled desire in her to give all she had to the object of her affection. Few of her friends believed she had accepted a role in her first film to earn extra money so that she could buy Neville a guitar. The irony that it would be the stepping stone to a career that eventually took her away from him forever was never lost on those who knew her well.

Parveen's relationship with Neville took her deeper into a world she had only just started to explore. Being completely focused on her boyfriend to the exclusion of all else meant that she was listening to the kind of music he loved listening to, reading what he recommended and watching movies that appealed to him. Given that Neville was the frontman of a rock band, Parveen suddenly found herself facing a tsunami of Western influences and she absorbed it all like a sponge. It was during this period that the bohemian girl who would drop into Bollywood a few years later and become a sensation was born. A significant contributing factor to those learning years was Parveen's own resolve to open herself up to new experiences and it was the same determination that led to her first exposure to acting.

DRAMSOC, the dramatic society of IIM Ahmedabad, was informally started in 1970. That year, the plays were primarily performed for the students on campus. The following year, three students and theatre enthusiasts – Anshul Balbir, Achyut Vaze and Siddharth Bhattacharjee – formally registered the society and that's when they started staging public performances.

Balbir, who was originally from Delhi, met both Parveen and Mallika Sarabhai at a common friend's party. They instantly connected.

'We started hanging out occasionally – we'd do drinks, go for plays and dance recitals in Ahmedabad,' Balbir recalls.

He suggested to the girls that they act in a play for DRAMSOC and they agreed. Apart from Parveen and Mallika, the only other female member of the cast was Balbir's classmate Parvin Makhija.

In September 1971, DRAMSOC presented two iconic plays – *Night of January 16th* by Ayn Rand in English and Badal Sarkar's *Evam Indrajit* (*And Indrajit*) in Hindi. On two consecutive days, there were two shows of each play. Tagore Hall, where the plays were staged, was Ahmedabad's largest indoor venue and it was packed to capacity on both days. Both productions called for substantial audience participation and the crowds didn't disappoint.

In *Night of January 16th*, Mallika Sarabhai played the lead role of Karen Andre, the stenographer accused of killing her boss and lover Bjorn Faulkner, while Parveen played his prim and proper wife Nancy Lee Faulkner. Sarkar's abstract, absurdist play which explores the writing process and the search for inspiration had Parveen playing Manasi, one of the only two characters.

'She did a phenomenal job playing Manasi,' Balbir remembers. 'Like Indrajit's three split personalities, Parveen's character also changes. In one scene, she could be a modern, confident girl wearing a tank top, and in the next be demure and submissive, clad in a saree. Parveen's performance in *Evam Indrajit* really got noticed.'

After every performance, there were hordes waiting to meet her backstage. She had never experienced adulation like this before. She was used to a boy or two mooning over her in the college canteen or on a friend's terrace. To be surrounded by crowds asking for autographs and complimenting her was even more exhilarating than the rush of performing to an auditorium full of people.

Sarkar's angst-ridden play made such a profound impression on Parveen that she'd talk about it even years later. Long before being cast opposite her in Hrishikesh Mukherjee's *Rang Birangi*, actor-director Amol Palekar remembers meeting Parveen on a movie set in Film City.

'Our meeting left an unforgettable impression on me,' Palekar recalls. 'Badal Sarkar, the legendary theatre personality from Bengal, was visiting me in Mumbai. On a Sunday, Badal da said he wished to see a film shoot.'

Palekar drove the playwright to Film City, confident that there would be some crew filming there. He wasn't wrong.

After introducing Sarkar to Amitabh Bachchan and Mithun Chakraborty on their respective sets, he drove to the sets of *The Burning Train*.

'Before I could even introduce her, Parveen came rushing [down] to speak to us,' says Palekar. 'She touched Badal da's feet and said, "It's such an honour to meet you, sir." She went on to tell him how his play *Evam Indrajit* had completely changed her life. She shyly mentioned that she had begun her career by playing Manasi, the central character in *Evam Indrajit*.'

Parveen spent the next two hours chatting with Badal Sarkar and Palekar about literature and theatre.

'Far away from her Bollywood image of a sexy seductress, this was a completely different and fascinating Parveen. It's sad that her fans were never exposed to this learned side of her,' Palekar says ruefully.

Having tried her hand at acting, Parveen stepped out of her comfort zone yet again when she was offered an opportunity to be a ramp model.

Before designer Ritu Kumar set up Ritu's Boutique in Delhi in late 1969 and the words 'prêt' and 'couture' became a part of our vocabulary, the Indian fashion scene revolved around textile companies exhibiting new blends and prints. There was only one name these companies relied on to show off their products – Jeannie Nowroji. The Bombay-based catwalk tsarina organized fashion shows for them in the hubs of the textile business – Ahmedabad, Coimbatore, Ludhiana and, of course, Bombay itself.

Nowroji, along with her partner Hilla Divecha, established the country's first modelling agency and event management company rolled into one. Their troupe, which included models from Bombay, would travel to a city for a week or ten days, where they'd showcase a textile mill's latest prints and patterns on the catwalk. Credited with the 'discovery' of women like Rosita Mendonca, Mamta Sahu (later known by her married name Landerman) and Esther Daswani – who were subsequently recognized as India's first supermodels – Nowroji would design the outfits and choreograph the show, while Divecha looked after the logistics of the business. During their stay in a city, they would organize daily fashion shows inside a tent that was open to the public. It wasn't uncommon for the troupe to be on tour for two or three months at a stretch, with models travelling from city to city by train.

In 1971, Nowroji and her troupe landed in Ahmedabad for a week-long fashion show for Calico Mills. The venue for the show was the famous Calico Dome that housed the company's administrative offices and showroom. Inspired by master architect Buckminster Fuller's geodesic domes, this Gautam Sarabhai-designed building was one of the city's modern landmarks. As they did in other cities, Nowroji hired a few locals to model in the show, in addition to those who had travelled down with her.

Among the new recruits was Parveen Babi. And she was everything Nowroji was looking for – naturally slim and willowy, with straight, shiny hair, glowing skin and loads of energy.

'She was beautiful, but without make-up, she looked like a really young girl-next-door. I liked Parveen when she came to meet me,' the nonagenarian remembers.

※

Even as Parveen became increasingly aware of her own potential and her belief in her abilities grew, other, not-so-attractive traits in her personality were beginning to emerge. Insecurity-induced feelings of jealousy and sudden, inexplicable bouts of anger began to rear their ugly heads.

One of the first manifestations of these behavioural aberrations was the increasingly antagonistic relationship she shared with Mallika Sarabhai. They did theatre and partied together, but there was no ignoring the fact that the two didn't really get along. Parveen and Sarabhai were very different personalities.

The former was polite and reserved, while the other was more outgoing. Sarabhai made heads turn every time she entered the campus on her motorcycle. Parveen would eat in the campus canteen and participate in lively group discussions in the dorms. Individually, they owned every single room they walked into. Inevitably, when they were in the same space, it seemed to onlookers that they were competing with each other for attention. Those from St Xavier's and IIM Ahmedabad, who interacted with both the girls, recall sensing a simmering undercurrent of mutual envy and competitiveness. There are some who attribute this to nothing more than teenage cattiness. Air kisses and forced smiles barely veiled the hostility they obviously shared. Eventually, they stopped putting up a show of everything being fine between them.

During the week Parveen spent with Nowroji and her models, she charmed them all. 'Free soul', 'disarming' and 'vivacious' is how they remember her, but there was also a certain evening

With Donald, who remained one of Parveen's closest friends until the end

spent at Bankura that exposed a side of Parveen that shocked her fellow models and made them wary of her. She had invited a couple of them to her favourite haunt for dinner and dancing. Neville was in charge of the music, while Donald sat with Parveen and her new model friends. In between sipping on cola and eating sandwiches, everyone took turns to get up and dance.

'Parveen had this habit, where she'd introduce me to everyone as her boyfriend, even when her actual boyfriend was around,' Donald recalls. 'This continued for years after she had joined films. One of the models asked Parveen if she could dance with me, because she thought I was her boyfriend. Parveen immediately snapped back, "Of course not!" That poor girl, she was taken aback! I tried to reason with Parveen, but she just held my hand, so I couldn't get up. It was odd and unnecessary.'

As the evening was winding down, the models decided they wanted to continue the party elsewhere.

'All of us were planning to go out. She and her boyfriend Neville were also supposed to come. Suddenly, she decided that she didn't want to go,' recalls Mamta. 'The way she told Neville that he wasn't going either threw us off. She almost barked at him, like it was an order. I had never seen someone talk like that. It was off-key, because she was otherwise so well behaved, whether it was during the shows, or later when she lived in our house in Bombay.'

⁂

Modelling for Calico was the first time Parveen earned money she could call her own. Nowroji's regular models made about ₹1,200 each, every week, and got to keep the outfits they modelled. Part-timers like Parveen made a little less, but it was still a princely sum in those days. After years of surviving on the meagre pocket money Jamal sent her, Parveen finally had a tidy sum that was all hers; she could spend it as she pleased without being answerable to her mother. The knowledge that there were a few hundred-rupee notes, some crisp with promise, others worn with experience, in her cloth wallet gave her a heady rush of independence that she hadn't experienced before.

Growing up in Junagadh, Parveen's goal had always been to escape to a bigger city. When she moved to Ahmedabad, she realized that she wanted more, but didn't know how to go about it. Everyone who knew her described her as being not particularly ambitious. She was just coasting through college, until something better came her way. When she got engaged to Jamil Khan, there was at the back of Parveen's mind the thought that marriage would be her route out of Ahmedabad to a destination that was far away from Jamal's influence and control. That hope of escape dimmed with her broken engagement.

The next couple of years etched into her mind a very clear picture of the life she didn't want to lead. The attention she attracted while modelling with Nowroji's troupe, along with the adulation she received after performing in two plays at IIM Ahmedabad, opened her eyes to a world that was alluring – that of show business. She realized that her looks could be her ticket to money, fame and freedom. Only, she couldn't decide what her next step should be to get there.

6

Parveen's eventual introduction to Bollywood was facilitated by a series of happy coincidences.

In the late 1930s, Kishore Sahu had got his first break as an actor in Bombay Talkies's *Jeevan Prabhat* (1937), headlined by the legendary Devika Rani. It was as a director, though, that Sahu achieved greater success, starting with the 1942 comedy *Kunwara Baap*, where he was cast opposite Protima Dasgupta. The box-office triumph of films like *Raja* (1943), starring the same pair again, *Veer Kunal* (1945), where leading man Sahu's co-stars were Durga Khote and Shobhna Samarth, *Nadiya Ke Paar* (1948), a Dilip Kumar–Kamini Kaushal starrer, and *Dil Apna aur Preet Parai* (1960), featuring Raaj Kumar and Meena Kumari, established Sahu as one of the most important film-makers of his time. Having launched his elder daughter Naina in *Pushpanjali* opposite Sanjay Khan in 1970, the film-maker was on the lookout for a fresh new face for his next venture.

At the time, his younger daughter, Mamta, was working as a full-time model with Jeannie Nowroji. Parveen had caught her eye almost instantly when she was hired to walk for the Calico fashion show.

'Parveen had the "new look" – tall, with straight, long hair and a soft face. She had her quaintness; her tooth was a little off,' Mamta remembers. 'She had an animated face, so I thought she might be able to act.'

Having seen potential in the new girl, the model had immediately called her father in Bombay.

'He was always on the lookout for new talent,' she explains and everything he heard about Parveen from his daughter piqued Sahu's interest.

'He wanted Parveen to come to Bombay and do a photo shoot.' Parveen immediately agreed to the proposal. During the photo shoot, Kishore Sahu wasn't just interested in how this young girl from Ahmedabad looked on camera. The director was more concerned about how comfortable Parveen would be in front of the camera and how she responded to instructions.

Sahu liked her so much, however, that he signed her on immediately.

While an elated Parveen returned to Ahmedabad, Sahu began preparing to shoot the 1974 film *Dhuen Ki Lakeer*, where she would be cast opposite Ramesh Arora. As was customary at the time, the director announced the film with an advertisement in the local newspapers and film magazines. The names of his three new 'finds' (as debutants were referred to then) – Parveen Babi, Ramesh Arora and Ashish Bohra – were prominently displayed in the ad.

Days later, film-maker B.R. Ishara claimed in an interview to a newspaper that Parveen was his 'discovery' and that he would launch her first. And just like that, even before she had stepped on to a movie set, Parveen was embroiled in her first controversy. 'This was a bit awkward for Dad, because during all his conversations with Parveen, she never mentioned that she had been in talks with Ishara Saab,' Mamta recalls.

Sahu was curious to know how and when Ishara had signed on this new girl and why Parveen had failed to mention it. On being asked about it, she explained that she had signed a contract with Ishara, but had not heard from him since. Instead of allowing the controversy to rage on in the media, with the latter adding fuel to the fire, Sahu and Ishara met to decide who would launch Parveen Babi.

It so happened that back in 1972, Ishara was shooting his film *Ek Nao Do Kinare* in a bungalow in central Ahmedabad. Among the crowd of onlookers gathered at the spot was a striking-looking young girl who instantly caught his eye.

'She looked very modern, in her T-shirt, jeans, sling-bag, shoulder-length hair and smoking a cigarette. Hippy-like, fresh, careless and striking,' is how Ishara described Parveen in an interview conducted by *Star & Style* and published in their 10–23 December 1982 issue.

Ishara was spellbound by Parveen. Even as the shoot continued with the film's leads – Rakesh Pandey, Mrinal Mukherjee and Manher Desai – the director couldn't stop thinking about her. He asked the film's still photographer to click a few photos of her from all angles.

'The next day, when I saw the results, I liked them,' he said. Parveen was in the crowd on that day as well.

'It turned out that she was close to the family in whose bungalow we were shooting,' Ishara remembered. 'I called her over to see me. When she came, I told her [of] my intention of making a film with her.'

To his surprise, Parveen didn't seem overwhelmed by the offer. She apparently told Ishara, 'I will do your role only if I like the role.' This impressed him even more.

'I liked her approach. Here was a girl to whom the role mattered more than getting a break in films.'

The director had been toying with a mother – daughter story for a few years and that's what he narrated to her.

'Would you believe it, Parveen jumped at the offer of playing the mother of a fourteen [or] fifteen-year-old girl. Her confidence in her own ability to play the role of a woman in her late thirties or early forties impressed me.'

Before he left Ahmedabad, Ishara had a contract drawn up for Parveen as the female lead of his next film.

'I signed her up on a stamped paper of ₹3.50 and I inserted a clause that she wouldn't work for any other film-maker till my film was released.'

Once Ishara returned to Bombay, he became so involved in completing and releasing *Ek Nao Do Kinare* that he completely forgot about Parveen, along with the contract he had signed with her, and soon moved on to working on his next film *Prem Shastra*, with Dev Anand, Zeenat Aman and Bindu.

Parveen might have played down her excitement when Ishara offered her a role in his film, but there was no doubt that she was more than enthused at the prospect of becoming a movie star. She immediately went to the Marks's home to share her news.

'I told her to give it a shot,' Donald remembers. 'She had done two plays in college, but I never thought she could become a film star. I thought she'd do a film or two, experience that world and come back to Ahmedabad. My brother was listening to our conversation. He was very concerned about how her mother and relatives would react to the news.'

Patrick Marks's concern was justified. Given Jamal's deep disapproval of her daughter's fledgling modelling career, movies were completely out of the question.

'In those days, it wasn't considered very respectable for girls from good families to do these things. And Parveen was from a royal family. They were even more conservative, compared to other families,' explains her nephew Javed.

For months, mother and daughter argued and fought over Parveen's decision. Eventually, Jamal gave in.

The other family that Parveen was looking for approval and permission from was her boyfriend Neville's. The Damanias had grown very fond of their son's girlfriend. After she signed the contract with Ishara, she told Neville's father that she'd want to give films a chance.

'Just this one film,' she told him.

Having been a successful theatre owner for decades, Neville's father knew a thing or two about the lure of showbiz.

He told her, 'If you decide to do this, you are definitely not coming back. That's just the nature of the glamour world. It engulfs everyone.'

Parveen's elation, though, was short-lived. After Ishara wrapped up his shoot in Ahmedabad and returned to Bombay, he failed to get in touch with her. She had no idea how to contact him either. Just as it seemed that her dream of escape might fizzle out, the offer from Kishore Sahu came her way. Naturally, Parveen jumped at the opportunity.

In the initial months after receiving Ishara's offer of a role in his film, Parveen had dreamt of starting a brand-new life in Bombay with Neville. In her mind, there was no reason why he should have any objections to moving to another city to be with her. Moreover, he was an incredibly talented musician and very good-looking too, and moving to Bombay, she thought, would make his career. Once Parveen had signed the film with Sahu, she brought up the topic of moving with Neville. Only, he had other priorities and so they decided to part ways.

'He was the only child and his parents were getting old. There was no way that Neville would have left his parents alone. He was very close to his mother and there was nothing that could separate him from her,' explained Parizad Damania, who married Neville years after his relationship with Parveen had ended.

Before Parveen left Ahmedabad, Neville's mother performed the very auspicious *'sagan'* ceremony to wish her luck for her new journey. She drew an intricate chalk pattern on the floor and made Parveen sit on a low seat placed on the design. After putting a tikka on her forehead and garlanding her, she gave Parveen a mithai to eat and an envelope with some money. This was the kind of maternal love and attention that Parveen had grown up craving, but her mind was made up – new adventures beckoned and she felt impelled to pursue them.

Unlike her move to Ahmedabad, a transition in her life that Jamal was involved in every step of the way to ease the process, the Bombay-bound Parveen was left to her own devices. She wrapped up her affairs and bought herself a one-way train ticket from Ahmedabad to Bombay. The promise of an adventure, coupled with youthful innocence, fearlessness and her deep-seated desire for a better life, propelled her to a city and a life she knew little about. She made a decision few girls of her age and time would have dared to, that too without the approval and support of their families.

When they met to decide who would launch Parveen, Ishara gave Sahu written permission to go ahead with his film *Dhuen Ki Lakeer* and present it as her debut vehicle. Considering the fact that he had quite forgotten about having signed her on for his own film and that Sahu had a story and a cast in place, this was the honourable thing to do. Crisis was averted and *Dhuen Ki Lakeer* was on track to become Parveen's launch film.

Knowing that she had no place to stay when she moved to Bombay, Sahu suggested she live with his family in their bungalow in Chembur in the eastern part of the city. Parveen was glad to accept the offer. Since the film-maker's younger son Vikram was studying at the prestigious Film and Television Institute of India (FTII) in Poona (now Pune), the new guest was given his room. 'I would stay in my sister's room whenever I came home for the weekend,' Vikram Sahu remembers.

Parveen fit right in with the Sahus. 'She was very respectful at home and was easy to be around,' the film-maker's younger daughter recalls.

Parveen had never faced a film camera or studied acting. So the first thing Sahu did was hire Roshan Taneja, the acting coach who had set up the Acting Department at FTII in 1963. There, he had subsequently taught and mentored students like Jaya Bhaduri [now Bachchan], Naseeruddin Shah, Shabana Azmi and Mithun Chakraborty, who would all go on to become famous names in Bollywood. Every morning, Taneja visited the Sahu home to train Parveen and her co-stars Ramesh Arora and Ashish Bohra. Over a few weeks, he gave them a crash course in acting that included an understanding of the technical aspects of facing the camera, dance improvisation and voice modulation. Sahu's children, most of whom were inclined towards a career in films, would very often join the classes.

Everyone who interacted with Parveen during this time walked away impressed with her diligence and work ethic. Mamta, who had contributed a few dialogues to the film, remembers one where Parveen had to pronounce the word '*dhuen*'.

'She couldn't say the word. She joked about how I made her life miserable,' the model recalled.

Not one to give up in the face of a challenge, Parveen practised delivering the dialogue containing that particular word in front of a mirror, until she had got the pronunciation just right. She may not have been the best performer on a set, but she was certainly the one who put in the most effort.

'She wasn't difficult to work with and there were no tantrums,' Vikram Sahu says. 'She gave everything... she did her best. My dad was very impressed with her.'

It was on the sets of *Dhuen Ki Lakeer* that Parveen met a man who would stand by her side for the next decade. Lovers, friends and colleagues would come and go, but Ved Sharma, whom she eventually appointed as her secretary, was the only man Parveen counted on in the following years to support her and champion her cause.

Ved, a former dancer, had joined Sahu as an assistant in the late 1960s.

'I handled production and did bit roles. When four of [Sahu's] films flopped, I left him,' Ved would acknowledge to *Star & Style* in its 16–29 October 1981 issue at the fag end of Parveen's career. 'Later, when he decided to start a new film with a new star cast, I was summoned again. At the time, Parveen had just come to Bombay from Ahmedabad. I used to often help her on the sets. "If I continue in films, I'll take you as my secretary," she kept saying.'

Once she had finished shooting *Dhuen Ki Lakeer*, Parveen met Ishara once again. She was still keen on finding out why he hadn't made a film with her after pursuing her in Ahmedabad to sign a contract with him and he sheepishly told her the truth. But having met Parveen again, Ishara's interest in working with her was rekindled. Deciding almost immediately that he should be the one to 'introduce' her to cinegoers, Ishara put his current film with Suchitra Sen in the lead on hold and, within twenty days, finalized another script that he felt would be the appropriate launching pad for his new heroine. He had also found his leading man in former cricketer Salim Durrani and rounded up a crew. The film, *Charitra*, was ready to go on the floor.

On 6 May 1973, Ishara organized a small mahurat ceremony in Bombay to announce the film. Then, following custom, the director moved to Poona for the film's start-to-finish schedule that would stretch over approximately thirty-five days. Parveen was given the role of Shikha, a young middle-class girl who feels obligated to give in to the advances of her much-married boss Anand (a character played by Gautam Sarin). The tall, light-eyed Salim Durrani was cast in the role of Ashok, a rich playboy who has a different woman in his bed every night.

After a decade of playing for the Indian cricket team, Durrani, the all-rounder, still loved the sport, but it wasn't paying the bills. 'I have to earn money and I am looking for a job even now,' he admitted to *Filmfare* on the sets of *Charitra* in Poona. One of the most popular sportsmen of his time, Durrani would be the first Indian cricketer to play a major role in a Hindi film. *Charitra*, though, wasn't the first film offered to him. Kamal Amrohi, of *Pakeezah* and *Mahal* fame, had wanted to make a film with the Pathan, who was born in Kabul and raised in Jamnagar, but the project hadn't taken off. Ishara, in his usual candid manner, acknowledged in the 15 June 1973 issue of *Filmfare* that he had cast Durrani only because 'he is already a public figure and that helps'.

At the end of the shoot, Ishara, like Sahu before him, raved about the new actress.

'I found Parveen to be a reasonably good actress,' he told *Star & Style* in their 10–23 December 1982 issue, when the actress's career was drawing to a close. 'A good role and a good director are necessary for her. For you have to make her do what you want. The director has to extract what is needed from her. However, I knew that she would make a top star one day. She had what it takes to make it to the top.'

As on all Ishara sets, the actors and crew had to follow a 'no smoking or tea drinking inside' diktat, which only the star director, who was known to walk around his set barefoot, had the privilege of violating. The fact that the director described

Charitra as one of his quickest and most economical shoots meant that his crew was working long hours in Poona's oppressive May heat. The frequent power cuts didn't help either. Every person involved with the film handled the issues differently. Even as Ishara's favourites, like actors Manmohan Krishna (who played Parveen's father), Asit Sen and his son Abhijeet milled around in between shots, Durrani struggled with the effort of delivering his dialogues and emoting in front of the camera during practice sessions. Parveen was friendly, but mostly kept to herself.

Of course, there was a lot of curiosity among the cast and crew about the new girl Ishara was launching. Rumours about her had started swirling even before the film's mahurat in Bombay. She was drop-dead gorgeous, but looked nothing like the other heroines of the time, except, of course, for Zeenat Aman. She didn't behave like most leading ladies. She would smoke without inhibition and, unlike many heroines of the time, didn't have a chaperone on the set. That she was warm and friendly with everyone on the set, from the director to the light men, endeared her to them.

There was, however, one incident that fleetingly revealed to them a side to Parveen they hadn't seen before nor would ever witness again. Ishara's cost-cutting measures had obliged actors to share living quarters. Accordingly, Parveen shared a room with Kanchan Matto, whose character in the film was a friend of the protagonist played by Parveen. Kanchan had torn some pages out of a women's magazine on beauty and health care that belonged to her roommate without the latter's consent.

'When Parveen realized what had happened, she barged on to the sets and fired the girl in front of everyone for having stolen those pages. She didn't think twice about making a public scene,' Ishara recalled in an interview published by *Star & Style* in their 10–23 December 1982 issue.

It appears that had Kanchan asked Parveen for those specific pages, she might have handed her the magazine itself, but the fact that her co-star had defaced one by tearing out pages from it irked her. All through her life, Parveen would be generous with money and most of her possessions, but books and magazines remained sacred to her.

⸙

In Bombay, though she was far away from her friends and the kind of life she was used to, Parveen couldn't have been happier. On set, she was the centre of everyone's attention. Beyond it, there was no one interfering in her decisions, telling her what she could or could not do. Moreover, she had her own money to spend as she pleased. Just as she had expected, in the first few months after she moved out of Ahmedabad, her life was pretty close to being perfect. Interestingly, this was also the time she met the three men who would subsequently become an integral part of her life – Ved Sharma, Mahesh Bhatt and Danny Denzongpa.

It was his love for cricket and his interest in Ishara and his work that would induce Mahesh to visit the sets of *Charitra* when the film's director moved the shoot back to Bombay.

'Babu Ram Ishara was a fascinating man who made it from a spot boy to a director of great repute. What was unique about *Charitra* was that they had this great cricketer called Salim Durrani, whom one had seen and one was mesmerized by – a tall, handsome man who used to hit huge, lofty sixes,' Mahesh reflects.

He remembers a girl in high heels walking past him with a cigarette in her hand.

'She walked past us, not even aware that she was being looked at; and what struck me then was that her eyes were not there in that space. In her demeanour, there was no consciousness that she was a lady who's smoking a cigarette on a film set. In those days, and even now, women continue to withdraw into small pockets to get their nicotine fix.'

When Ishara introduced him to Parveen, Mahesh thought to himself that 'the name sounded strange'.

'Little did I know that that word "Babi" would be an albatross, and also a springboard that would take me where I find myself today.'

While Mahesh Bhatt's meeting with Parveen was a fleeting one, the first time Danny Denzongpa met her, the two were immediately drawn to each other. The shooting of *Charitra* was midway through when Danny, whom Ishara had launched the previous year in a film called *Zaroorat*, came down to Poona. He was there to film *Abhi To Jee Lein* with his FTII classmate Jaya Bhaduri.

'We had a month-long schedule. I heard Mr. Ishara was shooting, so I went to meet him. He introduced me to his film's heroine – Parveen Babi. We got talking that day and there was something that clicked. We exchanged phone numbers.'

After that first meeting, Danny lost no time in reaching out to Parveen and their phone conversations immediately led to dinner dates. 'I took her out for a few dinners. She was intelligent and we really enjoyed talking to each other.'

Movies were a subject that came up often in their conversations. 'That's how I got to know that she didn't know much about world cinema. While studying at FTII, I had watched a lot of [them] and I understood the importance of knowing the works of cinema greats like [Federico] Fellini, [Akira] Kurosawa and [François] Truffaut. In those days, it was almost impossible to watch world cinema in regular theatres.'

From his days at the institute, Danny remembered that the Film Archives of India had an extensive collection of classics. Their dinner dates soon turned into educational movie-and-dinner dates.

'The first film we watched was Kurosawa's *Rashomon*. Another film we saw was [Jean-Luc] Godard's *Breathless*. She was very taken by these films and we watched quite a few in those ten-fifteen days. We'd have long conversations about them afterwards.'

They quickly settled into a rhythm of sorts. During the day, the two actors would shoot their respective movies, and if they wrapped up early enough, they'd spend time with each other. While there was an obvious attraction that had drawn them together, they were still just friends and getting to know each other. Neither was inclined to rush into a relationship.

7

One of the first friendships Parveen forged in Bollywood was with actor Sanjay Khan and his model wife Zarine. It started when the latter saw an interesting face on the cover of a magazine.

'My husband was making a movie called *Chandi Sona* and he was looking for a young girl to pair opposite himself,' Zarine Khan explains. 'I was reading Eve's Weekly and I thought the girl on the cover was pretty. I always believed a good heroine should have good eyes, mouth and teeth.'

Her husband asked his office to track down the girl from the magazine and call her for a meeting.

'A few days later, Parveen walked into the office. She was dressed like a hippie – in jeans and a very odd and probably old blouse. She was carrying a bag with a long fringe, wearing chappals and her hair was untied,' he remembers.

While all his staff saw was a shabbily dressed young girl, Khan recognized her potential.

'I completely discounted how she looked at that moment and imagined what she'd look like in costume, with make-up and through the lens of a camera.'

He immediately signed on Parveen for his directorial debut *Chandi Sona*.

Later that evening, Khan met his brother and actor Feroz. 'He must have heard from someone on the staff about Parveen's visit and that I had signed her for *Chandi Sona*.'

Knowing how important the film was for his younger brother, Feroz Khan asked him, 'Who's this bhabhi [sister-in-law in Hindi]? You have all the heroines at your disposal. Hemaji, Mumtaz – you can pick anyone. Why have you signed this bhabhi?'

'I know Feroz was joking, but I immediately felt very defensive on her behalf. I told him she is not "bhabhi", but B-A-B-I,' the younger Khan remembers.

Within days, the industry was talking about this new girl that Sanjay Khan had signed for his big film. Other producers started calling him, so they could cast her as well.

'Balraj Sahni's secretary [Rajendra Bhatia] came to me and said, "Sir, I'm producing and directing a film. Can you help me sign her?"' Khan recalls. 'I sent Parveen a message and she signed up. And then my guru Satyen Bose, for whom I have great regard and respect, said he was making a movie and wondered if she'd work with him. And so I asked her.'

With Sanjay Khan in a scene from Satyen Bose's Mastan Dada

Apart from *Chandi Sona*, Parveen was also signed on for *Trimurti* and *Mastan Dada* opposite Khan.

When the actor told her that it was his wife who had spotted her on the *Eve's Weekly* cover, Parveen wanted to meet her and thank her.

'We immediately connected and soon she started coming over every other day,' Zarine Khan recalls.

At the time Parveen met the Khans, she had already moved out of Kishore Sahu's Chembur bungalow and was living as a paying guest in Dadar's Shivaji Park. In the 1970s, Juhu was considered the hub of Bollywood and Khan felt his leading lady should stay in that area.

'I told her that she should try looking for a paying-guest kind of accommodation. The bungalow next to us had an elderly Anglo-Indian or Parsi lady [as owner], who was very fond of me.'

Khan asked his neighbour if she'd consider keeping a paying guest and 'she jumped at the idea'.

Parveen subsequently moved into the bungalow and, with just a boundary wall separating her new home from the Khan residence, she had soon become a regular at their place.

'My kids were very young and Parveen used to be here from morning to evening,' Zarine Khan remembers. 'She became like a part of our family. She was very warm and nice. I took to her [as if she were] my younger sister.'

Sanjay Khan fondly remembers Parveen's quirky habits, like sitting on the floor.

'It was very odd. We'd all be sitting on sofas or chairs and she'd sit on the floor. Eventually, we just ignored all her quirks, because she was a very warm and intelligent girl. I remember she was reading Jean-Paul Sartre and would discuss existentialism with me. And I was quite impressed with her.'

The press already saw Parveen as being bohemian, while Khan was nicknamed 'Killer Khan', thanks to his reputation as a ladies' man. As expected, their friendship set tongues wagging. Parveen insisted, while speaking to a journalist for the September 1974 issue of *Stardust*, that she hadn't had an affair with the actor and 'considered it an unthinkable future prospect'.

Khan himself was obliged to address the rumour that he and his leading lady of several films had shared a hotel room in Delhi during a visit to the capital. He told the magazine that Parveen was not his type, and that he'd never looked at her from a romantic point of view. 'She's like a sister to me. And I am happy she calls me Abbas [Khan's real name] Bhai. We didn't check into a double room at the Delhi hotel. Both of us were there for a function and we were given two single rooms, side by side,' he clarified in that interview.

෩෪෫

Released within six months of each other, both *Charitra* and *Dhuen Ki Lakeer* sank without a trace. The critics weren't kind to either film. *Dhuen Ki Lakeer*, the love triangle with a murder angle, was described as 'uniformly bad from the word "go"'. In the *Free Press Journal* of 19 May 1974, there was also a mention of Parveen 'in the most atrocious of outfits and hairstyles'. In Ishara's film with a social message, however, the reviewers were kinder to the actress. 'Parveen Babi's debut is promising,' said the *Free Press Journal* in its 11 November 1973 issue. 'The girl has the makings of a good actress if she can keep her head and not be misled down superstarry alleys.'

Quick learner that she was, Parveen had already picked up the ways of showbiz. She knew that she must 'always deflect failure' by adopting the lofty stance that 'art trumps commerce', when called upon to explain her association with a flop film and justify her poor performance in it.

'*Charitra* was not a commercial film – I knew that from the outset – but I took the role because it had good characterization and people have liked my performance,' she told *Stardust* during an interview that was published in the magazine's September 1974 issue. '*Dhuen Ki Lakeer* was my first signed film. I had a stubborn director who gave me no scope for expression. I had no make-up man. I was forced to wear clothes that didn't suit me one bit – it was inevitable that the film flopped.'

Parveen and her newly hired secretary Ved Sharma weren't too worried about the poor performances, because even while she was shooting with Ishara in Poona, Bollywood was buzzing about her in Bombay. At the screening of *Charitra* for its potential distributors, the film met with little enthusiasm, but the select audience was bowled over by Ishara's 'discovery'. The buzz was that Parveen, not the film, was 'selling'.

What helped in her campaign for winning over the not-so-easily-pleased Bollywoodwallas was the media, which had already fallen in love with her. Hard-nosed, cynical journalists, who were used to flitting from star homes to movie sets, couldn't decide what to make of this actress who openly chain-smoked during interviews and didn't bother to hide her glass of wine at parties. What was most refreshing, however, was the fact that they didn't have to wade through a sea of obstructive secretaries or bossy, protective star-mothers to interview her. And then there was her fledgling romance with Danny Denzongpa that she was completely unabashed about.

Filmfare put Parveen on the cover of its 11 January 1974 issue with Rishi Kapoor, another newcomer who had made waves the previous year with *Bobby*, his first film as a leading man. The half-page profile began in the following manner: 'Parveen Babi returned from the shooting at Manali, went to Danny Denzongpa's flat in Juhu and to bed – with a cold. Danny is very sick with jaundice, by the way. She met us unflinchingly at the flat – all credit to her – and said the recent reports about her marrying Danny weren't true.' The magazine did clarify, however, that 'Parveen doesn't quite live at Danny's. She has a place of her own in a cottage where she is a paying guest.'

The media couldn't get enough of her. They wanted to know everything they could about the long-haired beauty with royal antecedents. Interviewed by *Stardust* for its February 1974 issue, Parveen was happy to scotch rumours about being a divorcée ('I've not been married, so how can I be a divorcée?') and talk about everything from drug use ('Yes, I've tried dope') to pre-marital sex ('All that talk about virgin brides is bull') and her smoking habit. It took journalists quite a few years to stop harping on her nicotine addiction. There were even rumours that this was a 'compulsive attention-getting tactic', to which her exasperated response in the September 1974 issue of *Stardust* was as follows: 'I am not an attention-getter. Nothing I say or do is to attract or distract people. I smoke because it's a habit with me. I need it badly, something like paan-eaters. For me, smoking is like drinking a glass of water. I can't be like the others and run to the john every time I want a fag, because then I'd be running there every half-hour.'

Parveen always spoke the truth, even while talking about the profession that would bring her fame and fortune, and her candour succeeded in disarming the most jaded film journalists of the time. In an interview with Bikram Vohra, a much respected journalist from *Filmfare*, 'she confesses through a Dunhill smokescreen that nine out of ten Indian films require no talent, no anything, just a pretty face, some deadpan dialogues and a few slippery movements'. Published in the 27 December 1974 issue of the magazine, the interview also carried her startlingly candid observations on her own place in Bollywood's scheme of things: 'I've earned a lot of money for doing practically nothing... There is hardly any work; it's very elementary. But the money is terrific; so let's leave this art for art's sake business out of it. I am happy as things are.'

While this was an accurate summary of what Bollywood had been demanding of its leading ladies for decades, no one had ever come out with it quite so nonchalantly in public. Parveen's views on singing and dancing on screen were no less controversial. While shooting for her first few films, she was terribly embarrassed at the idea of singing and dancing around trees. It was only after she saw Zeenat Aman doing the same that she felt less discomfited. Quoted in the September 1976 issue of *Stardust*, she apparently told herself, 'If Zeenat can do it, so can I.'

It was the media that would nickname Parveen 'Zeenat Aman II', even referring to her as 'the poor man's Zeenat Aman' when it was inclined to be particularly vicious. This irked both the actresses no end.

'We are two separate individuals, two separate people. There is no similarity between us, no likeness at all. Not even physically. If I push all my hair back, our features are totally different – our eyes, our noses, lips – no resemblance at all,' Parveen was quoted as saying in the 1974 *Stardust Annual*.

Two years before the actress made her debut, it was Zeenat Aman, languidly swaying to the tune of R.D. Burman's 'Dum maro dum', who had captured the heart of the country. As Jasbir/Janice, the troubled chillum-smoking younger sister to Dev Anand's character in *Hare Rama Hare Krishna*, the actress became the face of 1970s hippie culture and a cinematic signpost. Born to a Hindu mother and a Muslim father, Zeenat had done her schooling in Panchgani, before moving to Los Angeles to study at the University of Southern California. After she returned to Bombay, she started working at *Femina* magazine and dabbled in modelling on the side. A second runner-up in the Miss India contest, Zeenat went on to be crowned Miss Asia Pacific in 1970.

Her first two films – *Hulchul* and *Hungama*, where she was paired with Kabir Bedi and Vinod Khanna respectively – crashed at the box office. It was *Hare Rama Hare Krishna* (to which she was a last-minute addition) that would put her on the Bollywood map. Along with her global sensibilities, what made Zeenat stand out from the rest of the crowd were her international looks. A statuesque frame, chiselled cheekbones and luxuriant tresses that cascaded over her delicate shoulders set her apart from Bollywood's curvaceous heroines.

For the Indian audience and even the industry, Parveen and Zeenat came to epitomize the 1970s bohemian mindset. Together, the two actresses would also change the very notion of how a Hindi film heroine should dress. Clingy gowns and flowing maxis, long skirts with thigh-high slits and knotted blouses, halter necks and bikinis – Parveen and Zeenat wore everything with their trademark carefree confidence. Probably for the first time, Bollywood had leading ladies, not vamps, who were unapologetically sexy.

But for the rest of their careers, no matter how much they protested against the odious comparison and stereotyping, Parveen and Zeenat would always be measured up and pitted against each other.

※

While the press had already decided that 'Babi baby' was a star, it was up to Ved Sharma to make sure that the right opportunities came Parveen's way. While the actress was still shooting in Poona, her manager had done the rounds of all the film directors and producers. One of her earliest meetings, after wrapping up *Charitra*, was with B.R. Chopra for *36 Ghante*, loosely based on the 1955 Humphrey Bogart and Fredric March starrer *The Desperate Hours*, made in the *film noir* genre. Sunil Dutt, Ranjeet and Danny Denzongpa played three escaped convicts who hold a

On the sets of Majboor *with director Ravi Tandon*

newspaper editor (a role enacted by Raaj Kumar) and his family hostage. Parveen was cast as Kumar's sister Naina.

Though her role demanded precious little of her, the fact that she was shooting a film under the B.R. Chopra banner made other film-makers want to sign her. Within the first year of Parveen's debut, not only did she have multiple releases but she also signed on eight other films, including Ravi Tandon's *Majboor* opposite Amitabh Bachchan, who had finally attained success in 1973, after having delivered twelve flops.

Written by Salim Khan and Javed Akhtar, the slick and pacy thriller was heavily inspired by Hollywood releases from 1970 – Charles Bronson's *Cold Sweat* and George Kennedy's *Zigzag*. *Majboor* is the story of a travelling sales executive Ravi (played by Bachchan) who discovers that he has a brain tumour. If that were not enough to turn his middle-class world upside down, Ravi is also embroiled in a kidnap-and-murder investigation. Parveen played his rich, attractive girlfriend Neela, who drives around in a fancy red Opel.

Majboor turned out to be Amitabh Bachchan's biggest solo success of the year and Parveen's first box-office hit. Both Farida Jalal, who played Ravi's wheelchair-bound sister Renu, and Pran, who excelled in his role as the kind-hearted thief, walked away with Filmfare Award nominations in the Best Supporting Actress and Best Supporting Actor categories respectively. Parveen, however, continued to lose out, with critics using harsh words to describe her performance. 'If anyone had any doubt still lurking in mind that Parveen Babi can do better than [to be] a painted doll with colourful costumes, *Majboor* has enough to disabuse it,' wrote the film critic for the *Free Press Journal* in its 8 December 1974 issue.

Both Parveen Babi and Amitabh Bachchan had been signed on for the film before Tandon was brought on board as director. For producer Premji, *Majboor* was meant to be a low-budget 'quickie' with actors who weren't in a position to command hefty fees and a director who was still looking for his first big film. In his leads, Tandon found two malleable and disciplined actors.

'If we had a 7 a.m. shoot, our three cars would all reach at the same time,' Tandon recalled. 'They [Amitabh Bachchan and Parveen Babi] were both very hard-working and really understood what the director wanted of them. There were never arguments about why they had to do something. They believed in the vision of the director.' Years later, the trio would go on to deliver yet another hit with the 1982 release *Khud-Daar*.

Even as *Majboor* brought her laurels, the first big project Parveen had signed was destined to remain on the floors for another three years. *Chandi Sona*, the film that brought Parveen and Sanjay Khan together was launched with much fanfare in 1973, but only hit theatres in March 1977. Apart from the leading pair, the film also starred Kamini Kaushal, Pran, Premnath, Ranjeet and Danny Denzongpa, with Raj Kapoor in a special cameo.

In his biography *The Best Mistakes of My Life*, Sanjay Khan writes, 'I was pleased to introduce some leading ladies to the film industry. One of these was Parveen Babi who starred in my film *Chandi Sona*, after which she made a very big name for herself in other films.' The truth, though, is that by the time *Chandi Sona* hit theatres, Parveen had already tasted stardom.

8

Hollywood's 'Rat Pack' was the name by which a group comprising Frank Sinatra, Dean Martin, Peter Lawford, Sammy Davis, Jr and Joey Bishop was known. Its members were hard-drinking, high-rolling celebrities who partied and worked together in the 1960s. The original Rat Pack, however, grew out of Humphrey Bogart and Lauren Bacall's home in the tony Holmby Hills area of Los Angeles in the mid-1950s. This bunch of 'rebel-rousers' included members of the Hollywood élite, like Katharine Hepburn, Spencer Tracy and Cary Grant. After Bogart's death in 1957, Sinatra would take over his legacy, with the non-stop partygoers going on to make Las Vegas their regular haunt.

In the 1970s, Bollywood had its own version of the Rat Pack – the Juhu Gang. Unlike the beginnings of its Hollywood counterpart, the origins of the Juhu Gang aren't really known. In the previous decade, most of the city's nightlife had centred around south Bombay, while Bollywood was beginning to settle in and around Juhu. There were two distinct social groups – one led by Vinod Khanna and the other by actor-director I.S. Johar's son Anil. Most of Bollywood's young brigade belonged to one or the other. Restaurants like Bistro, Volga and Napoli were regular hangouts for them. Johar's group also spent a lot of time at Venice at the Astoria, where singer Biddu was a regular performer.

The groups began disintegrating, however, when Khanna became increasingly busy with his films. Biddu moved to London to pursue his career in music and Johar prepared to debut as an actor in his father's film *5 Rifles*. Later, Johar's younger sister Neelam, who was also known by her screen name Ambika, would take over the mantle. In its new avatar, the group shed its rough-and-tumble image, acquired some glamour and adopted the new moniker, the Juhu Gang.

'It made sense. We were all from the neighbourhood and worked in the same fraternity,' explains actress Anju Mahendru. Journalist and author Dinesh Raheja recalls an interview with Kabir Bedi, where the actor spoke about this loosely knit group and what had brought them together.

'I belonged to a generation of youngsters who pioneered bell bottoms,' Kabir told him. 'The spirit of the moment in those days was to loosen things up a bit, to break free from 1960s orthodoxy. People all over the world were demonstrating for peace. Hippie culture and flower power were "in". The Juhu Gang, comprising Shekhar Kapur, Mahesh Bhatt, Protima [Kabir's wife], Shabana [Azmi], Parveen Babi, Neelam Johar, Jalal Agha, celebrated the spirit. We would gang up every Sunday at my Beach House residence and have a blast.'

Other regulars included Anju Mahendru, Balraj Sahni's son Parikshit, Danny Denzongpa, legendary film-maker Chetan Anand's son Ketan and the Khan brothers Akbar and Shah Rukh, whose siblings Feroz and Sanjay were more recognizable Bollywood names.

For this group of fun-loving night owls, the evening would start with a swim at the Sun-n-Sand Hotel.

'Around 8 p.m., we'd leave and either go to Parikshit's house or mine for dinner,' Mahendru remembers. 'We just did mad things, like hang around the Mount Mary grotto for hours, late in the night. Or we'd take bus rides from Juhu to Bandra and back at midnight. These were just things that most of us couldn't do otherwise.'

When Danny Denzongpa wasn't filming, he'd make it a point to be at the Sun-n-Sand seaside pool by 5 p.m. During an interview for *Filmfare*, published in its 3–16 September 1976 issue, he joked that to establish his credentials as a water baby, he would have, if left to him, 'come wearing bathing trunks to the studios'. A swim, followed by a yoga session, was his idea of a perfect evening.

Most actors had every second Sunday in the month off. 'This meant that we'd party hard on Saturday night and then get into the pool around noon on Sunday. We'd swim, have a leisurely lunch and watch the sun set before heading home,' Danny reminisces.

It was during one of these sessions that he brought Parveen along on a date.

Those were the relatively carefree days of roistering youth, where everyone knew what was happening in everyone else's life.

'At the end of a night, people would crash at each other's homes. Sometimes, I'd leave my clothes at someone's house and go back the next morning to pick them up. Some mornings, you wondered how you got to where you woke up,' Ketan Anand remembers with a laugh.

Parties often ended with impromptu singalongs on Juhu beach.

'Especially on full-moon nights, we'd end up going for a midnight swim. We'd light a bonfire on the beach and someone would bring a guitar and a set of bongos,' Anand remembers.

Around the world, the 'hippie scene' was synonymous with free love, drugs and philosophical musings. The Juhu Gang didn't buck the trend.

'We were the "flower children" of India; we were monkeying [sic] what was happening there in the Mecca of the entertainment world, Los Angeles,' recalls Mahesh Bhatt, who was introduced to the group by Kabir Bedi, the leading man of his directorial debut *Manzilein aur Bhi Hain* (1974). 'Those were the days of *Jonathan Livingston Seagull* and dropping LSD, meditating.'

Many turned to spiritual gurus in search of enlightenment. Some travelled to Rajneesh's ashram in Poona to experience his brand of psycho-physical therapy, while others congregated for lectures by Jiddu Krishnamurti on 'turning inwards' or became followers of Uppaluri Gopala Krishnamurti in the quest for the truth of life.

Mind-altering drugs were an integral part of the quest for spiritual enlightenment. Various members of the Juhu Gang, at different points in their lives, have been quite open about their experimentations with hallucinatory drugs. They smoked Mary Janes, dropped acid and went on psychedelic 'shroom trips together. There was no one standing in judgement on those who fuelled their creative energies with drugs. Nor was there peer pressure on those who abstained.

Later in her life, when Parveen suffered two very public mental breakdowns, large sections of the media insinuated that it was the outcome of substance abuse. However, one of the things friends from different periods of her life agree on is that she didn't take drugs – of any kind.

'The truth is, she never touched drugs,' Mahesh Bhatt observes. 'In fact, she was averse [to] and scared of drugs. She only drank wine, that too, occasionally.'

Parveen's only addiction was smoking.

'She smoked a lot of Dunhill,' Mahesh adds.

༺꧂

After both of them had returned to Bombay from their respective shoots in Poona, Danny and Parveen were back in touch with each other.

'We'd call each other regularly,' Danny remembers.

They might have been in a different city, but all they had to do was pick up the threads of the fast and easy friendship that had developed in Poona over films and food.

Danny fondly remembers one of their earliest non-dates. 'One day, she called to ask me out for dinner. It turned out that there was a producer who was trying to get friendly with her. He was a famous producer with whom I had worked earlier. He kept inviting her out for dinners and she was very uncomfortable going alone with him. I was shooting close by in Juhu. So I told her that I'll finish and join her.'

The unnamed producer was obviously taken aback to see Parveen's companion.

'He couldn't say much, though. Obviously, he didn't want to create a scene. Parveen and I really enjoyed that meal. We ordered the most expensive items on the menu – lobster and champagne – and left the producer with the bill.'

When he first met Parveen in 1972, Danny Denzongpa was an actor on the cusp of stardom. Big hits like *Chor Machaye Shor*, *Kaala Sona* and *Kalicharan* were still a few years away, but his performance as the trigger-happy, jealous, wheelchair-bound husband of a traumatized Rani Ranjit Singh, played by Zeenat Aman, in B.R. Chopra's 1973 release *Dhund* would hit all the right notes and pave the path to greater success.

Born Tshering Phintso Denzongpa, the actor had changed his name within the first month of joining the Film Institute in Poona. He admits that he had simply got fed up of being addressed as 'Hey boy!' or nothing at all. It was Jaya Bhaduri who would rechristen him Danny, which was short for Denzongpa. 'The funny thing is that even my family calls me Danny now,' he told *Filmfare* in an interview for its 3–16 September 1976 issue.

Growing up in the hills outside Gangtok, Danny had dreamt of joining the Indian Army. It was somewhere during his school years in Nainital and college in Darjeeling that his love for films took over. His first brush with acting came early, in school. When students were being assigned jobs for the annual play, he was initially put in charge of set decoration. That quickly changed when the director heard him singing. Danny was plucked from backstage and given centre stage as Naarad Muni.

While graduating from FTII, he lost the gold medal to Jaya Bhaduri. 'I beat her in the earlier exams,' he would tell *Filmfare* during an interview published in their 21 March 1975 issue. His first year in Bollywood was hard; producers kept turning him down because of his Sikkimese features. But that quickly changed after Ishara signed him on for his songless film *Zaroorat*, which launched two other actors as well – Vijay Arora and Reena

Roy. Though the racy film didn't do very well at the box office, it made sure that the industry sat up and took notice of the strapping youngster from Sikkim.

'I still look Sikkimese. The only difference is that everyone has got accustomed to me,' Danny quipped during an interview for the 3–16 September 1976 issue of *Filmfare*.

'Natural' is how he describes the process by which his friendship with Parveen evolved into a relationship. Soon, the two were inseparable. It also helped that they were cast in the same films. One of the earliest 'outdoor' shoots the couple was a part of was for Sanjay Khan's *Chandi Sona*. Khan's wife Zarine describes the long schedule in Mauritius as a 'picnic'.

'It was one of our best shoots. We were treated like royalty, because we knew the prime minister of Mauritius and their foreign minister. These politicians would join us for barbecues in the evenings.'

The film's cast and, of course, the Khans stayed in cottages close to the ocean in Trou-aux-Biches, an area located on the island's northern coast. For both Parveen and Danny, this long schedule in Mauritius, being surrounded by a turquoise ocean and brilliant white sand, was sheer bliss. The beach lovers believed that sand in the shoes and salt in the hair were marks of a day well spent. When they weren't shooting or spending time with the rest of the cast, the couple would swim for hours in the crystalline waters or watch the waves crash on the sand. It was a most picturesque setting and the two lovebirds lapped it up.

Back in Bombay, Parveen and Danny were open about their relationship. They weren't the first couple in Bollywood to have an affair, but they were among the few to defy convention by refusing to keep it under wraps in a milieu where it was expected that any relationship, unless sanctified by religion or law, would be conducted away from the spotlight.

The couple's refusal to keep their relationship a secret triggered the initial rumours that Parveen was using Danny for publicity. When they reached the actress, she promptly squelched them. 'I don't do anything for publicity,' she clarified to *Stardust* in its September 1974 issue. 'My relationship with Danny is something very personal and dear to me. I wouldn't like anything or anyone to spoil it.'

'Intense' is how their friends describe Parveen and her relationship with Danny. Her life revolved around him and their home. This was exactly how she had been around Neville in Ahmedabad. During her time with Danny, she made an effort to understand the Hindustani classical music that he was partial to. He played the flute; so she began carrying one in her handbag. She tried learning to play the instrument herself, but couldn't really carry a tune.

Apart from the flute, Ketan Anand remembers a notebook she always carried in her oversized fringed hobo.

'The book had stories Parveen had written when she was younger. Some of the stories were lovely, but there was something odd about them. Each story was written under a different name and had a very distinct approach to life. If you didn't know that one person had written them, you'd think they were works by different writers. She was aware that this was strange, but she'd laugh it off and say to me "See, I am a nut, Konks."'

At the same time, he also remembers her being playful and really warm.

'These were the days before she became a star. So, like us all, she was quite broke. Some evenings, she'd come over to my house and ask if I wanted to drink good whisky. She'd take me to Feroz Khan's home and charm him into serving his best Scotch to me,' Anand fondly remembers. 'Or I'd hear a voice from the beach shouting, "Hi Konks, what are you doing?" across my boundary wall. She'd be standing there in a brief little bathing suit and drag me [out] for a long walk on the beach.'

It was around this period that Suchitra Sen was shooting with Sanjeev Kumar for Gulzar's political drama *Aandhi*. During the schedule in Bombay, Sen and her daughter Moon Moon were put up at the Sun-n-Sand Hotel. During the day, when her mother was shooting, the star daughter would swim and then study for her exams.

'One night, this very beautiful girl came up to me in the pool and asked me my name,' Moon Moon Sen remembers. 'I didn't know her, because I wasn't really into films, and she told me she was an actress and introduced herself. She told me she'd be hosting a lunch in the hotel the following day and that her friends like Danny, Protima Bedi and Akbar Khan would be with her. She then invited me to join them.'

Soon, the young girl from Calcutta (as Kolkata was known in those days) had become a part of the swim group at the hotel.

'They looked after me and invited me for lunches and things,' she recalls. 'We used to swim together, go for a run on the beach and come back and swim again. Shashi Kapoor would join us sometimes. It was a very nice and fun group of young people.'

When Danny, who used to live in Shivaji Park, moved to a small apartment in Kalumal Estate, a heartbeat away from Parveen's paying-guest accommodation, the rumours of them 'living in sin' started. 'I'm not living with Danny,' Parveen clarified in an interview for the February 1974 issue of *Stardust*. 'But sure, I drop in at his place most times late at night, because both of us are on double shifts. The only time we get to see each other is after midnight. And well... I visit him openly. I don't sneak in and out of his place. If I wanted to live with a guy, I would.'

Eventually, when the couple realized that Parveen was spending more time at Danny's first-floor pad, she just moved in, bag and baggage.

'We like each other, so we live together. What's wrong with that? It's a beautiful arrangement,' she was quoted as saying quite categorically in the 27 December 1974 issue of *Filmfare*.

Like Parveen, Danny had no patience for social pretences. 'We didn't bother about how the industry would react if we lived together,' he says. 'We were two independent individuals, who had roots far away from Bombay. No one criticized us openly, so we never bothered about what they might have been thinking. People just saw us as outsiders who were bohemian, so no one bothered about us.'

Parveen ended up buying an apartment of her own on the fourth floor of the same building where Danny lived. This was around the time that they celebrated their first anniversary as a couple. Excited about owning her very first home, she asked Zarine Khan to help her decorate the space. The living room featured low seating, lots of vibrant colours and mirrors on the walls. Parveen's bedroom had lush floral motifs and Victorian drapes, while the extra room doubled up as a television room and guest room for her mother Jamal when she was visiting from Junagadh. The second bedroom was nicknamed the 'red room', thanks to its monochromatic colour scheme. Parveen's home reflected her personality; it was simple and modern, without being afraid to make a statement.

Even after she had bought the new home, however, the actress continued to spend most of her time at Danny's place. 'She was very particular about cleanliness. She was very particular about things being kept in their right place. If she kept a vase at a particular place, you couldn't move it even a centimetre. She was constantly straightening [up] the house. I loved it, because I also like a neat house. To me, she was perfect as someone to share a house with,' Danny recalls, adding, 'it was only much later that I realized this was a part of her illness.'

As with all long-term couples, Parveen and Danny's life quickly fell into a pattern. Like most actors of that generation, both were working at least two eight-hour shifts a day. When they weren't working, they would take off on long drives.

'We'd go to Lonavla, Mahabaleshwar or even Goa. Whenever we had longer breaks, we'd go abroad — we went to Hong Kong and once even to London,' says Danny. 'Apart from films, we had other interests in common. We enjoyed listening to music and reading; and, if nothing else, there were also lots of parties to attend.'

9

By mid-1974, Parveen's career was on the upswing and her two-year-long relationship with Danny seemed rock solid. But by the end of that year, something had changed. It was obvious that the relationship had run its course and the cracks had begun to show. For a feature titled 'What I Hate about My Mate' in the January 1975 issue of *Stardust*, Parveen said, 'His habit of keeping mum when he is furious with me drives me up the wall. Also, when he gets up at 6 o'clock in the morning and starts playing his harmonium.'

Danny, for his part, admitted to being riled 'when instead of wishing me "Good morning," she starts the day with "Take that harmonium and get out!"'

These observations might have been made half in jest, but there was some truth to them. Little things about each other had started annoying them.

The couple decided that Parveen should move out of Danny's apartment. The actor, however, insisted during his interview to *Stardust* for its July 1975 issue that 'her moving out has not affected our relationship at all. In fact, it'll be good for us, I think. When living together, there are a lot of little things that irritate a person and get on one's nerves. This you avoid when you live in your own flats.'

He was equally at pains to make it clear that they hadn't had any major fight. 'Parveen can't stay angry for long. I can, for two or three days. But not she. At night, before going to sleep, she has to make up and say sorry.'

Danny went on to explain that his actress girlfriend had moved out only because his apartment was too small for the two of them. 'We were getting in each other's way,' he admitted during the same interview. 'In the mornings, when I got up and wanted something, I had to dig through piles of her stuff before I found my things. Her things were lying around everywhere – in my cupboard, in the room. So, when her flat was ready, I quietly started moving her things out. First I sent her clothes, then her other knick-knacks and finally, I shifted her up.'

Though they had decided to not live together, Danny insisted that 'Parveen is a fantastic girlfriend'. 'I've never met anyone like her before,' he claimed. 'One thing I really like about her is her sincerity.'

No matter how much he liked her, though, marriage was out of the question, as he candidly clarified. 'We won't make suitable marriage partners. As a girlfriend – Parveen is fantastic. But as a wife – she won't suit me,' he told *Stardust*.

※

While her personal life was going through a period of upheaval, Parveen's career had finally taken off. Within months of having tasted success with her first hit *Majboor*, Yash Chopra's *Deewaar* released. This was her second film opposite Amitabh Bachchan and it was unstoppable at the box office.

During a conversation with actor Shah Rukh Khan at a public event held not long before Chopra's death in 2012, the director described the film as 'the most perfect Salim–Javed script ever'. Strongly influenced by *Ganga Jamuna* and *Mother India*, the story revolved around two brothers – Vijay (with Amitabh Bachchan in the role) and Ravi (played by Shashi Kapoor). The siblings find themselves pitted against each other when Vijay grows up to become a gang leader and Ravi a policeman. At the centre of this rift is a damp-eyed Nirupa Roy playing their long-suffering mother Sumitra Devi in a more substantial role than those of the film's leading ladies Parveen Babi and Neetu Singh.

With Amitabh Bachchan and Yash Chopra on the sets of Deewaar

While Neetu played the quintessential effervescent and supportive girlfriend Veera, Parveen's character Anita was an unconventional part for a mainstream heroine. The first time we see Anita, R.D. Burman's 'I'm Falling in Love with a Stranger' is playing in the background. Dressed in a scarlet gown with slits that go all the way up her thighs, she slides into the seat next to Vijay in a bar and lights his cigarillo. She has a lit cigarette in one hand and a glass of alcohol in the other.

It's very clear that this character didn't quite fit the 'nice girl' mould most leading ladies preferred to play. Anita owns her sexuality, isn't coy about sleeping with a man without marrying him and even has the confidence to raise their child as a single mother. There is also a stark difference between how the two couples romance each other. Veera and Ravi sing the peppy 'Keh doon tumhein' in a lush garden, while Anita and Vijay share a post-coital cigarette in a dimly lit room. The film doesn't mention what Anita does for a living, but film magazines at the time referred to Parveen's character as a 'call girl' and described the role as being 'small, sleazy'.

Deewaar is credited with being the film that cemented Bachchan's 'angry young man' image. What is completely overlooked, however, is the fact that in Anita the writers had created a new prototype for female protagonists of Hindi films by giving Parveen's Anita economic, social and sexual autonomy unlike anything heroines had experienced in the past. Female protagonists back then were expected to be pious and pretty. If the character wasn't the quintessential golden-hearted *tawaif* or prostitute, she would be steeped in deep sorrow and regret. *Deewaar*'s unabashed Anita was a refreshing departure from the norm and the film passed no moral judgement on her choices.

By mid-1975, Parveen had become one of the most sought-after actresses in the industry and was juggling more than half a dozen films. The new films she had signed included *Mama Bhanja*, opposite real-life uncle and nephew Shammi and Randhir Kapoor; *Amar Akbar Anthony*, again with Amitabh Bachchan as her leading man; *Chamatkaar* with Rajesh Khanna; and *Bullet*, where her co-star was Dev Anand. There was also a film with Dilip Kumar that never took off.

Among the actresses, Hema Malini was considered the most popular with both film-makers and the audience. The names that followed hers on the casting wish-list were those of Zeenat Aman, Rekha, Neetu Singh and Parveen Babi.

What she lacked as an actor Parveen more than made up for with a great work ethic. No matter how many shifts she was doing in a day, she was almost always on time. In an industry where actors were invariably late in reporting on set and ended up adding to delay-related project costs, Parveen's habit of punctuality immediately made her a favourite among producers. On the sets of director Bhappi Sonie's *Bhanwar*, a journalist from *Stardust* found Parveen ready to shoot at 8 a.m. Apart from the actress, Aruna Irani and Ashok Kumar were also present on set to shoot an elaborate party sequence. There was no sign of the leading man Randhir Kapoor, though.

'He'll come in the afternoon and we can't wait. Parveen and Aruna will be going away in the afternoon. They've got to go to other shootings,' Sonie was quoted as saying in the June 1975 issue of *Stardust*.

The director was so impressed with Parveen's sense of discipline that he signed her on for an action thriller titled *Chalta Purza* opposite Rajesh Khanna that released in 1977.

What also set Parveen apart from her contemporaries was her photographic memory, which had served her well through school and college. As an actor, she was expected to endlessly memorize dialogues which, more often than not, were handed to her at the penultimate hour on the set itself. She might not have been the most emotive actress in the business, but she rarely forgot her lines while shooting. Film was expensive and fewer fumbles on camera meant money saved. Shooting songs with intricate dance movements was, however, her kryptonite, and she'd spend hours practising the moves at home. Once she was on set, she was warm and friendly with everyone, from the lighting assistants to the directors. In between shots, she'd sit right there on the set, ready for her call.

At that point, her life was everything she dreamt of as a young girl. She had a career that was on an upswing. She was famous and she had found love. Dreams, though, very rarely stay simple.

10

Long before Parveen came into their lives, Protima and Kabir Bedi were the talk of Bombay society for the unconventional relationship they shared. The two first met in the offices of S.H. Benson, an advertising agency (bought over later by Ogilvy & Mather) that she modelled for and where he was employed. Within months, Protima had run away from her parents' home to live with Kabir. About a year later, on 14 October 1969, when Protima was already two months pregnant with their first child and morning sickness had taken over her life, they were married in an intimate Buddhist ceremony. Within a year of their marriage, Kabir had got a break in Bollywood and Protima, as recorded in her memoir, *Timepass*, couldn't help noticing almost right away how 'the starlets look at him, some with longing and admiration, others with badly disguised lust'.

There was nothing unusual about the situation. What was worth noting, however, was Protima's nonchalance, at least, in public.

'It was clear that I couldn't stop affairs happening, so I took the attitude of "I don't care, because I understand",' she says in her memoir. 'When the starlets asked me how come I didn't mind my husband flirting or having affairs, I would laugh and say, "Well! He'd be stupid to refuse something that came so easily and cheaply," hoping that would put the women off.'

Within another few years, both Protima and Kabir were 'looking for sex and companionship outside marriage', as disclosed by Protima in the memoir. And, yet again, they took no pains to be discreet about the status of their relationship.

By the early 1970s, the hippie ideals of peace, love and happiness had reached Indian shores. An ever-growing group of rebellious dreamers in Bombay eagerly responded to the clarion call of this counterculture that rejected conventional societal norms and urged its followers to look inward for peace and wisdom. Protima and Kabir soon came to be regarded as the proponents and personification of the hippie lifestyle. Kabir spouted new-age philosophies of free love and the role of the individual in spiritual exploration during interviews. This was further compounded by his wife's penchant for making headlines for all the wrong reasons. The story goes that for the launch of *Cine Blitz*, its owner Russi Karanjia advised Rita Mehta, his daughter and the editor of this new film magazine, to 'catch an actress streaking and put her in *Cine Blitz*'. Rita suggested Protima's name and, when approached, she agreed to the proposal. Taiyeb Badshah was the photographer chosen to shoot the scene that featured a naked Protima running through the streets near Flora Fountain in Bombay early one morning. Unhappy with the way the pictures had turned out, Protima repeated the photo shoot on Juhu beach a few days later. In her memoir, however, Protima says that the photo was clicked at a nudist camp in Goa and superimposed on the streets of Bombay.

In an interview to *Stardust* in March 1974, Kabir claimed, 'People are forever mixing up love with possessiveness. Love is a positive feeling. Possessiveness is negative. Most of the misery people go through is because they mix up these two emotions. Love shouldn't create dependence. Being in love should help you to be independent. And independence helps you to become sensitive to each other's feelings.' The industry and the press didn't quite know what to make of his observation.

It was this scenario that Parveen Babi stepped into when she first became acquainted with the Bedis in the early 1970s as members of the Juhu Gang. Already a mother of two by then, Protima was a few years older than most of the women in the group. She was the kind of woman whom women wanted to be and that men simply wanted. It was much the same for the twenty-year-old Parveen. Protima embodied the passionate, independent and intelligent woman. Parveen saw her as someone who had figured out her life, who didn't need a man to complete her and who refused to buckle under any kind of external pressure or care what people were saying about her.

'Parveen wanted to be like Protima. She'd hang on to every word Protima would say,' Anju Mahendru remembers.

For Protima, Parveen was initially just another pretty little thing who had become a part of the Juhu Gang because she was someone's girlfriend. But, gradually, they got to know each other. Seeing how lonely Parveen would get in Danny's absence, Protima encouraged Kabir to invite the younger actress for a swim.

'Parveen was grateful to me for being kind to her,' Protima writes in her memoir. 'Eventually, we became close and she would even ask me for advice. She would come over after her shooting, with her make-up still on, and yell out for me and we'd talk a lot.'

Describing the relationship between Parveen and his wife as 'fairly good', Kabir adds, 'We'd meet at various places, including our homes, and I think they both liked each other.'

It was during one of those visits to the Bedi home in 1974 that film-maker Vinod Pande remembers meeting Parveen for the first time.

'She had come there with Danny and I had gone to sign Kabir for a film that never got made,' he recalls. 'Protima came down to drop me to a taxi, while Kabir stayed in the house. I asked Protima who the girl was and she said, "She's an up-and-coming actress. She will be a star one day."'

The foundation of this friendship wasn't very strong to begin with, and cracks began to appear when Protima realized that Parveen was becoming overly possessive about her.

'We were on the beach once and she started complaining that I was more friendly with Neelam [Johar] than with her, and I never told her any of my secrets,' Protima writes in her memoir. She decided to deal with such inane allegations firmly by telling the actress to stop behaving like a schoolgirl. Expectedly, this conversation didn't go down too well with Parveen.

Being a part of the same circle meant that the two women met frequently, and the cold vibes they now shared were obvious to anyone in the group who cared to notice what was going on. A happy soul, Protima found it difficult to continue living with this festering and unnecessary animosity. After a particularly unpleasant evening with Parveen at Neelam Johar's house, she decided to visit the actress at home the following morning and sort things out. 'When I went over to Parveen's the next day,' she writes in her memoir, 'I found her in tears and the whole house in a mess. She had been trying to find a shirt of mine, which I'd left behind, just so she could throw it out. She disliked me so much that she could not bear to have anything of mine in her house.'

This was the first time since Parveen had arrived in Bombay that this kind of unhealthy possessiveness, acute jealousy and irrational anger had surfaced in her, but these feelings were not new. Yet, just as her classmates and friends from her years in college had dismissed her quirks as 'Parveen being Parveen', so too did members of the social circle she had now become a part of. It didn't occur to any of them that her eccentricities could be a sign of a serious mental health issue.

After years of working as an actor, Subhash Ghai had finally got a chance to direct his first film, an action drama titled *Kalicharan*. For the lead roles he had roped in Shatrughan Sinha and Reena Roy, who were yet to make their mark in Bollywood. The debutant film-maker wanted fellow FTII alumnus Danny Denzongpa to play an important cameo in the film. The actor who was already working fifteen to sixteen hours a day couldn't take on another film, especially one where he only had a special appearance. But with Ghai insisting that no one else could play the character, Danny finally gave in.

He played Shakaa, a one-legged, trident-wielding devotee of the goddess Kali, who shuns his evil ways after a gruelling hand-to-hand fight with Sinha's character. Those were the days before special effects and playing an amputee meant that one of Danny's legs had to be tied up at the beginning of the shoot. He'd spend the rest of the shift hobbling around on the other leg with the help of a crutch. Between having to use a crutch and having a leg folded at the knee for hours, Danny was already in a world of pain; he had blisters all over the foot he had been hopping on. It didn't help that he had to shoot a fight sequence in that condition and that Fight Master Shetty had decided that the scene would look more dramatic if both men were in a mud pit.

By the end of most shifts, all he looked forward to was a long, warm shower and sleep.

One night, when he returned home after a gruelling day at work, he found Parveen getting dressed to go out.

'You forgot that we have to go to Parmeshwar's today,' she said, referring to the late Parmeshwar Godrej who had, by the mid-1970s, established her credentials as the proverbial hostess with the mostest. In fact, parties at the Godrej home were the stuff of legend and not simply because she served the best wines and immaculately turned out servers walked around with platters of lobster and caviar. Her soirées brought together the best of Bollywood, leading industrialists and sports stars under one roof.

'Everyone is coming for the party. Zarine [Khan] just called to say that they are leaving. Get ready quickly,' Parveen called out to Danny, as she applied finishing touches to her make-up.

Danny tried explaining to her that the very thought of spending the rest of the night socializing was exhausting, but she was insistent. She didn't want to go to the party without him. Nor did she want to miss it. After a bitter argument, Danny finally gave in. There was a tense silence in the car as they drove to the Godrej home in posh Malabar Hill, the invisible wall of resentment between them impregnable.

The apartment was huge, and the party was not being hosted in the main sitting room. Next to it was the bar, which is where everyone had gathered. To Danny, walking into that space felt like he was back on set. It was teeming with people; there was a lot of noise and smoke. After a quick round of hellos and picking up a drink for himself, he walked back through the main sitting room and out onto a balcony overlooking the sea. He drew the glass door shut behind him and settled into a chair. The quiet sanctuary he had found transported him miles away from the din that was just behind him. There was a lovely breeze blowing in from the sea and watching the twinkling lights spilling out of the homes below lulled him into a doze.

The next thing he knew, Parveen was waking him up. Disoriented, it took Danny a moment to remember where he was. It turned out that Parmeshwar had seen him dozing on the balcony and gone inside and told Parveen that her boyfriend was asleep. Deeply embarrassed and angry that unlike everyone else at the party Danny wasn't socializing, Parveen shook him hard to wake him up. And just like that they were arguing again. Danny tried explaining to Parveen that he didn't enjoy large parties. His idea of a perfect evening with friends was to have five to seven people over, with whom he could engage in proper conversations without having to shout over the music to be heard. She thought he had forgotten how to have fun and that he wasn't social enough any more. Versions of this spat had played out at different levels of intensity in the months preceding this acrimonious instance. If they had been honest with each other, both would have acknowledged what they already knew – that it was time to pull the plug on their relationship. But they didn't. At least, not yet.

Danny left the party and sent the car back for Parveen who had wanted to stay on. She calmly walked back in and made the appropriate excuses for his sudden departure. The next morning, it was business as usual. Meals were planned and schedules were discussed, but neither could shake off the feeling that time was up for their relationship.

Just a few days after their bitter fight at the Godrej party, Danny left for a long outdoor shoot schedule in Rajasthan. He was away for almost forty days. During this period, he and Parveen kept in touch like they had every time they were apart.

Expensive long-distance calls were booked and letters written, but it all felt a little mechanical, as if they were going through the motions, because that's what was expected of them.

With each call, the rift between them widened. They didn't have anything to say to each other any more. It was obvious that Parveen was pulling away from the relationship and Danny didn't know what to do about it.

When he returned from the shoot, she told him, 'Kabir and I are attracted to each other.'

Danny couldn't believe his ears, not just because Parveen and he were technically still in a relationship, but also because Protima and Kabir were friends of theirs.

He recalls the words he exchanged with her on the subject. 'I asked her, "Don't you feel guilty about this relationship? Protima is your friend."'

According to Parveen, Protima was 'cool' with her friendship with Kabir, because their marriage had been over for almost two years.

'Apparently, they were living together for the sake of their children,' Danny says, adding, 'I found that whole equation very odd.'

The end of his relationship with Parveen was free of drama, almost mirroring how it had started. There were no big fireworks or sob fests.

'I told Parveen that if she was with Kabir, it obviously meant that our relationship was over. We hadn't been getting along for some months, so I thought it was better for both of us.'

And, just like that, an important chapter in both their lives ended.

⁐⁐⁐

By the time Parveen became acquainted with the Bedis, both Kabir and Protima were openly involved in extramarital relationships. Protima thought the film industry was wrecking Kabir, while Kabir considered his wife too volatile and unconventional. By

1974, Protima had begun to feel increasingly disenchanted with her life. 'I had reached a stage where everything seemed devoid of colour and meaning and I took refuge in spiritualism and drugs,' she writes in her memoir. 'I needed the stimulus and I got it. I experimented with acid, and studied Buddhism – spending three months at the Rumtek monastery [in Sikkim] with Kabir's mother. [Kabir Bedi's mother Freda Bedi is said to have been the first Western woman to be ordained as a Buddhist nun.] It was one of the most intense and enriching periods of my life. But the restlessness remained.'

Parveen and Kabir started seeing each other in the summer of 1975.

'There were a lot of problems in my ongoing relationship with Protima and it was pretty much on its last legs for various reasons,' Kabir recalls.

What drew him to Parveen was the fact that she was observant and quick-witted. 'She was an extraordinarily sensitive human being, very perceptive. She had a very alert mind and would come up with all sorts of interesting observations. We were both in the same industry and shared a lot of friends, and we had a wonderful chemistry between us,' he adds.

According to her memoir, Protima encouraged 'Kabir and Parveen to have an affair'. 'I was then busy trying to untangle complications in my own life and I wanted Kabir off my back. In fact, it was at a party in our house that I had first seen the two of them giving each other those special vibes and then I went out of my way to encourage them,' she writes in her memoir.

When they gave in to the attraction they felt for each other, both immediately told Protima. 'Parveen came to me and told me all about it,' Protima elaborates. 'Kabir had never really kept it a secret. In fact, almost every night, he would kiss me and the children goodnight and say, "I'll be back in the morning, darling," and we'd go to bed and he'd go off to Parveen's.'

Though there was a seven-year age difference between them, Protima believed Parveen and Kabir were perfect for each other. A month after the relationship began, Protima stumbled upon something that would go on to become the big passion of her life – Odissi. In August 1975, she chanced upon a live Odissi dance recital in Bombay that left her enthralled. In that dark auditorium on a rainy night, she finally found her calling. She immediately decided to move to Cuttack, Orissa (now Odisha), to learn the dance form from Odissi maestro Kelucharan Mohapatra. Before she left Bombay, Protima asked Parveen to look after her kids – Pooja and Siddharth – while she was away. 'I must say she looked after them very well and they loved her,' she writes.

When Protima returned to Bombay following a three-month intensive dance course, Kabir was at the airport to pick her up. After dinner that night, as she was getting ready for bed, he told her he was going over to spend the night at Parveen's. 'My heart thumped. I refused to believe I had heard right. I knew he was having an affair with Parveen even before I'd left for Orissa, but his wanting to go to her on the very night I had returned shattered me,' she records. Instinctively, she knew that this relationship of Kabir's was different from the many she had had to witness and live through in the past.

'"Do you love her?"

'He nodded yes, and I asked, "Does she love you too?"

'"Yes."'

This is how Protima records the exchange of words she had with her husband. There was nothing more to say and Kabir left for Parveen's that night.

The next day, when he returned home, Protima gave him an ultimatum. 'I've been thinking about the situation all day and I don't think that it's fair on me, or on you, or on her. You both love each other, you should be together. As long as it was only an affair it was all right, but since you yourself say that you're in love, then something must be done. Either I'll leave or you leave,' Protima apparently told Kabir.

She adds in her memoir that even as she was asking him to choose between her and Parveen, she didn't really mean him to go ahead and do it. She was only hoping that this would make Kabir feel guilty and choose her over the other woman.

When her husband returned home after two days, Protima was ready to retract her ultimatum, but his mind was made up.

Kabir remembers the moment. 'She said, "It's fine. Go see her. Just don't leave [our home]." But Parveen and I had fallen in love completely by that time, so I moved out [of the house] and in with her.'

Within a few weeks, he had permanently moved out of the Beach House apartment he shared with Protima and their children to go and live in with Parveen in her Kalumal Estate home a few lanes away.

No matter how unconventional their relationship had been, its end was devastating for Protima. While Kabir moved on and got involved in another relationship, she was left with two young children and a broken heart.

11

Protima may have encouraged the affair between Kabir and Parveen, but once her marriage actually imploded, she found it hard to come to terms with her situation. In her memoir she writes how she wept on Juhu Beach that New Year's Eve, anguished by the thought that Kabir was just a few bungalows away at Parmeshwar Godrej's party, probably dancing with Parveen. The bitter truth had finally dawned on Protima that her marriage was over and there was no going back; that the man she loved had lost interest in her and their common friends had picked Kabir and Parveen to socialize with, forgetting that Protima had ever been a part of their circle.

One day, she dropped in, uninvited, at Parveen's Kalumal Estate home. It's not clear what she hoped to accomplish by doing so. In her book, she writes, 'If Kabir's happiness lay with Parveen, I thought, I'd try and reassure her and make her feel secure about my man.' Since the couple was still asleep, Protima knocked on their bedroom door and sat down in the living room with a cup of tea. When Parveen and Kabir came out of their bedroom to meet her, their attitude was tentative, as if they were uncertain about what to expect from Protima. 'I thought my casual attitude would relieve any tension, but Kabir came out looking nervous and panicky. Parveen came scuttling out behind him and the two of them huddled together.' It was apparent that they were prepared for a showdown of some kind.

According to her memoir, Protima looked Parveen in the eye, instead, and said, 'Kabir is yours, yours completely. I don't want him back ever, you are absolutely made for each other. In four months you've managed to give him what I couldn't in seven years.'

So what was different about Kabir's relationship with Parveen? Protima believed that she herself 'was too much for Kabir'. In an interview to *Stardust* for its February 1976 issue, she had said with her trademark bluster, 'I am the exact opposite of Kabir. But Parveen is made like him. There are so many things that Kabir wanted in his woman that he found in Parveen. Basically, Parveen is a one-man woman. Kabir needed such a woman – someone secure, someone he could depend on.' It is ironic that Protima should have thought this way, because as time would reveal, Parveen's insecurity and overpossessiveness when it came to her boyfriends could easily be mistaken for loyalty.

❦

One of Parveen and Kabir's earliest outings as a couple included attending a glittering industry event, helmed by Dilip Kumar, Raj Kapoor, Dev Anand and G.P. Sippy, organized to raise money for the Prime Minister's Famine and Flood Relief Fund in Bombay. Everyone who was anyone in the industry, including the very reticent Lata Mangeshkar, turned up for the Shivaji Park event on 26 September 1975. After the formal event at the park was over, the actors rode down the streets in trucks, urging their fans, who had gathered in great numbers, to donate. That Parveen rode with Kabir, and not Danny, for the cause immediately became the talk of the town. Until that morning, there had only been rumours about the end of one relationship and the beginning of another. The same evening, Parveen was in the audience, cheering Kabir on at the opening night of *The Vultures*, the English adaptation of Vijay Tendulkar's play *Gidhade*. Directed by ad man Alyque Padamsee, the drama had Kabir playing an alcoholic, self-destructive man.

A young Kabir had discovered and fallen in love with acting while studying at Nainital's Sherwood College. His passion for the art had neither subsided nor wavered all through his time at St Stephen's College, Delhi. While still a student, Kabir had begun freelancing as an announcer for All India Radio and hosted *Mirror of the World*, a montage of global current affairs, in the early days of Doordarshan. The world of advertising beckoned after he graduated. Before Benson, Kabir had worked under Padamsee at Lintas. While he was creating commercials for these advertising agencies, he was also roped in to model for brands like Wills Filter Kings.

Before *The Vultures* was staged, Alyque had cast Kabir in the role of Tughlaq in Girish Karnad's eponymous play based on the life of the eccentric Sultan Muhammad bin Tughlaq, who ruled Delhi in the fourteenth century. The play was a runaway success and Kabir Bedi became a household name. Detractors insist, though, that more than his histrionic abilities, it was Kabir's naked derrière and rock-hard abs, on display at the beginning of the play, that might have had something to do with its success. Regardless, it didn't take long for Bollywood to 'discover' him. Director-actor O.P. Ralhan's 1971 thriller *Hulchul* introduced Kabir to the big screen. This was also the film in which Zeenat Aman would make her debut.

After a few middling films, Kabir found success with the dacoit drama *Kuchhe Dhaage*, which also featured Vinod Khanna and Moushumi Chatterjee. It was on the sets of this Raj Khosla film that Kabir met Mahesh Bhatt, who was an assistant director at the time. Neither man could have guessed at that point how closely linked their personal lives would become, but professionally they clicked immediately. When Mahesh turned director with the ill-fated *Manzilein aur Bhi Hain*, he roped in Kabir to play the lead. The film ran afoul of the Censor Board of India, which believed that the film 'mocked the sacred institution of marriage'. Kabir stood by his director and friend and they fought for almost two years to get the film to theatres. Unfortunately, the film sank without a trace.

At the time Parveen and Kabir became a couple, she had already been a part of two big Amitabh Bachchan starrers – *Majboor* and *Deewaar* – and had signed films helmed by industry heavyweights like Manmohan Desai and Vijay Anand. Kabir's Bollywood career was taking off, but he was better known for his real and not his reel life. He had also begun to look to the West for work. He would tell *The Hindu* during an interview published on 6 April 2017, 'I realized that if I have to seriously pursue a career in Hindi films, I have to do song and dance. Even though I love song and dance, I didn't want to do it. I realized if I have to be in acting, I have to broaden my horizon.'

In 1973, Italian producer Elio Scardamaglia was looking to make a mini television series based on the locally popular, much-loved literary character Sandokan. Author Emilio Salgari had created the swashbuckling hero, a prince-turned-pirate from Borneo, also known as the 'Tiger of Malaysia', who, along with his trusty lieutenant Yanez of Gomera, fought against the Dutch and British fleets. Kabir explained it in his interview with *The Hindu*: 'As Sandokan was an Asian hero, they [the producer and his team] came to Bombay on their way to ten cities in Asia to find their Sandokan and the first actor they met was me. They needed a tall, athletic, bearded and romantic guy.'

Kabir flew to Rome for the audition and ended up bagging the role. 'Even though I had to spend my own money and fly to Italy for an audition, I wanted to do it,' he is quoted as saying in the 29 December 2015 issue of *Mid-Day*. 'Because even then, I knew how to recognize an opportunity. That's a skill. It [the opportunity] could come in any way; even a conversation with someone could give rise to a great opportunity. It was just about taking it. And it took me on a trip around the world.'

The first stop on his journey to the other side of the world was Malaysia. The tropical beaches and dense jungles of Terengganu province were stand-ins for Sabah, Borneo, where the story is set. Protima and the couple's children Pooja and Siddharth accompanied Kabir to Malaysia for the shoot.

It was in the long gap between the shoot and the series première in 1976 that Parveen and Kabir would become a couple.

Unlike Parveen's previous affairs, this one started out messy and fragmented, and it never went on to acquire a more cohesive, balanced form. No matter how hard she tried, she could not bring herself to shrug off the physical and emotional presence of Kabir's previous relationship in their lives. The tangled map of her life with him always seemed to feature Protima and the Bedi children.

About two months after Kabir had moved in with Parveen, Protima gave her first stage performance as a dancer. It was a big moment for her. Keen to share it with the man who had encouraged her to follow her passion, she had sent out a special invite to both Parveen and Kabir. But on the day of the performance, the couple did not show up. The next day, Kabir made some excuse about having been caught up with a shoot, but Protima was convinced it was Parveen who had prevented him from attending the dance performance. 'Later, when Kabir was away, I met Parveen and asked her the same thing,' she writes in her memoir. 'I told her that since Kabir was the father of my children, surely we could share him. But she was very hostile. She snapped that she didn't believe in sharing.'

It was an attitude born of feelings more complex than mere jealousy. Having Protima around played up Parveen's deep-seated apprehension of being abandoned, coupled with the fear that perhaps she wasn't good enough for Kabir. Feeling vulnerable and dreading that he might go back to his wife made Parveen overpossessive and clingy. She even began to resent him for spending time with his children.

In the beginning, Kabir tried his best to placate Protima. 'She feels insecure,' he'd explain to his wife.

'She wanted Kabir only to herself,' Protima writes in her memoir. 'She was paranoid and neurotic. Kabir could not come to Beach House to see the kids, because she would say to him, "I feel insecure if you go near her."'

Regardless of how she felt about Protima, Parveen loved the children and Pooja and Siddharth loved spending time with her as well. While the kids continued to live with their mother at Beach House, they would visit Kabir whenever he was free. Parveen would even take care of the children when both parents were at work and she did so quite happily. 'They adored Parveen. I am grateful to her for having looked after my kids every time I was away from Bombay. Even now, I send them every second day to see their father and Parveen,' Protima would tell *Stardust* during an interview published in March 1974.

After Protima's unannounced visit to Parveen's house, the two women never met again. As the weeks turned into months, everyone got used to the new normal. The one thing that continued to rankle, though, was the fact that Kabir and Protima had only separated, but were not divorced. Now, Parveen began pressing him to make the split legal. When he broached the subject with Protima, though, she refused to divorce him. 'Parveen was the right thing to have happened to him at the right time, but marriage was different. I knew she would not have made the ideal wife for him, and I told him so,' Protima writes in her memoir.

When Kabir failed to persuade his estranged wife into agreeing to a divorce, Parveen asked her secretary Ved Sharma to get Protima to sign the documents. But Protima would not budge from her stance.

When asked about the possibility of divorcing his wife and marrying Parveen, Kabir was very matter of fact about the logistics of his complicated family life. 'A marriage that does not exist should be ended in law. Certainly, I think a divorce will take place,' he said during an interview for the same *Stardust* March 1974 issue.

Parveen, on the other hand, was less forthright and even a little coy in her response to the same query from *Stardust*. 'My present is filled with a sense of fulfilment,' she said. 'I've really been lonely for such a long time and I needed somebody to understand what I am feeling. I've always met people who've shared just one or two common interests with me. I wanted somebody to get "through" to me, to share my feelings while watching a sunset – somebody I could feel very, very together with. I needed a man with whom I'd be able to face the world together. I've found him in Kabir. And I'm happy and not worried about the future.'

Although the beginning of their relationship had been far from perfect, Parveen and Kabir didn't care. They didn't allow the baggage he had brought into their equation to weigh them down. When they stepped out together, they looked picture-perfect, with Kabir effortlessly filling the role of dutiful, doting boyfriend and Parveen hanging on to every word he uttered. The two were in a state of romantic bliss. There were no disagreements; they wanted to spend all their time with each other and constantly gushed about how much in love they were. Kabir was so smitten that for *Stardust*'s regular feature 'My Favourite Things', he responded to every question with Parveen's name. He described the relationship as 'the most intensely beautiful experience of my life'.

'With Parveen and me, I think it is a case of two very lonely, very beautiful people finding each other at the right time in their lives,' he would say in their first-ever joint interview to *Stardust*, for its February 1976 issue.

Parveen, for her part, said during the same interview that 'it's like all my wishes were granted all at once'. 'Kabir is everything I've always wanted my man to be. So it's obvious why I chose to become his woman.'

A new partner with children represented big changes in Parveen's life. Subtle changes were apparent in her home too, reflecting Kabir's tastes and sensibilities. A Bulbul Singh painting found a place on the living room wall, while an intricate Tibetan thangka hung on another wall. There was also a wooden chest in the living room, with drawers clearly labelled with each of their names. There were some aspects of her life, however, that Parveen was not keen on changing. While she remained insecure about Protima's constant presence in Kabir's life, Danny continued to be a part of hers. Even after they had broken up, the former couple continued to see each other and not just on the sets of films they were still shooting together or at parties they attended.

'We still lived in the same building and Kabir and Parveen would often land up in my house. Kabir and Protima were friends; so maybe Parveen thought that I would be okay socializing with them,' Danny says.

Only he wasn't.

'I finally had to tell them that it was weird for me to see my ex with another man. I might not seem "evolved", but I couldn't pretend that was normal. I think Kabir understood what I meant,' he adds.

For a few months, Parveen kept her distance from Danny. She couldn't stay away from him for too long, though. When he started dating eighteen-year-old Kim Yashpal, who went only by her first name, Parveen was curious. Instead of taking the elevator straight to her fourth-floor apartment, she began to get off on Danny's floor.

'She knew all the servants in the house. So they would let her in and she behaved like a mother hen. Parveen would want to know everything from what was cooked for dinner to whether Kim had been visiting,' Danny recalls.

To make sure that his new girlfriend didn't feel threatened by the presence of his ex, Danny made it a point to reassure Kim that 'there was nothing any more' between him and Parveen.

This was the mid-1970s and the 'television revolution' was still a few years away. Even the idea of watching films at home was a distant dream. On a trip to Hong Kong, though, Danny had bought himself a VCR (video cassette recorder), along with about forty to fifty VHS (video home system) tapes. Paying a hefty import duty for the same was, in those days, worth the bragging rights of owning this piece of cutting-edge technology. It immediately made him an integral part of an informal club of VCR owners in the city. Since there were no video libraries at the time, people would exchange cassettes among themselves.

Danny was used to friends dropping in to watch a film, but remembers that 'Parveen being Parveen would drop in even when I wasn't at home'. 'I would come back from a shoot to find her sitting in my bedroom and watching a film. By this time, Kim had become used to Parveen being around. She'd treat Kim like a younger sister. Parveen would ask her to sit with her and watch a film. Then, suddenly, she'd start bossing her around and ask Kim to make her some tea. Eventually, Kim told me that she couldn't handle Parveen's constant presence.'

It was time for Danny to have another conversation with his ex-girlfriend about boundaries in relationships.

'I explained to her that she was ruining my new relationship. She understood and apologized and immediately she asked if she could come over on Saturday.' He laughs at the memory.

Danny had reached a point where he didn't know how to explain to Parveen that she wasn't welcome any more.

'I felt like she was taking me for granted. So I asked Kim to sit in with me and be firm with Parveen. We explained to her that she had to ask Kim if it was okay for her to come over. Finally, I think she understood. After this, Parveen would call Kim and sweetly ask, "Darling, can I come over?"'

Now, on one front Parveen struggled to keep Kabir all to herself, while on the other she was yet to come to terms with the fact that someone else had replaced her in Danny's life. In both scenarios, there was really no malice from her. She didn't bad-mouth Protima or Kim. If Parveen felt insecure about Protima, it was only because she didn't think she was interesting enough to retain Kabir's attention. With Kim, she didn't want to 'steal' Danny, but couldn't understand why their relationship had to change at all. At some level, Kim understood this. Even when Danny wanted to put an end to Parveen's regular visits, his new girlfriend would tell him, 'It's fine; she's sweet. Let her come.'

It was around this time that Mahesh Bhatt would briefly enter Parveen's life as Kabir's director and friend. Their paths were crossing for the first time since B.R. Ishara had introduced them to each other on the sets of her first film, *Charitra*. There's an odd incident from this period that Mahesh remembers.

'I had come back from the [Osho] Ashram in Poona and was sharing my experiences in the quest towards moksha with Kabir, and Parveen was listening. While I was talking, I saw her slowly gravitate towards Kabir. It seemed like she was curling up within herself and soon she was holding Kabir. I thought maybe the intensity of my experiences was making her shrivel up. But I didn't give it much thought, because I was so caught up in sharing my experiences.'

When it was time for Mahesh to leave, Parveen remained sitting on the low sofa in her drawing room as Kabir walked him to the door.

'Kabir said to me, "Why would you do what you did?" I had no idea what he was talking about. All I had done was share an episode from my quest. Obviously, there was something in my way of conversing that destabilized her,' Mahesh reasons. 'Kabir mistook it to be some kind of pass that I had unwittingly made. I might have gone to Rajneesh and had LSD, but the fact remains that certain dictums were still there and one of them was that you didn't look at your friend's girl.'

Baffled by the peculiar turn the situation had taken, Mahesh stopped dropping by at Parveen's to visit Kabir.

Their personal lives may have been far from perfect but to the world, Parveen and Kabir were the golden couple – strikingly good-looking, talented, successful and in love.

When two stars come together, the public gaze is omnipresent and the odds are always stacked against them. There are competing careers and inflated egos to balance. Add to this volatile mix the ghosts of past relationships, personality flaws and untreated mental health issues and the ground is always going to be shakier than usual. So it would be with Parveen Babi and Kabir Bedi.

12

In early 1976, a pop culture phenomenon swept across Europe. *Sandokan*, a six-part mini-series, had premiered on Italy's public national broadcaster RAI (Radiotelevisione Italiana) in January. By the summer of 1976, the show had been telecast in multiple European countries, including Spain, what was then West Germany and the former Federal Socialist Republic of Yugoslavia. The sweeping saga of adventure and romance set against the backdrop of a kingdom's freedom struggle captured the imagination of the continent. Streets in cities across Europe would become deserted as people hurried home to watch the show's prime-time weekly telecast.

At the centre of this drama set in the Far East was, of course, Sandokan, the legendary prince-turned-captain of the fierce pirates of Mompracem. In his bestselling books centred on this character, author Emilio Salgari described his dashing hero as tall, rugged and devastatingly attractive, with long hair, a beard and cold black eyes. At six foot three and blessed with movie star looks, it was almost as if Kabir had been born to play the smouldering Sandokan. He was clearly more eligible for the role than his predecessors – the ludicrously miscast Ray Danton and body builder-turned-actor Steve Reeves.

Kabir nailed Sandokan's swagger and the vulnerability underlying his virile charm. But even before the show was telecast, he had acquired instant heartthrob status across Italy, thanks to his exotic looks. In the weeks following the premiere on 6 January that year, Kabir was invited to Italy for a round of promotional events. He asked Parveen if she would like to join him. She was, of course, very happy to do so.

She had no way of foreseeing that this would mark the beginning of the end of her relationship with Kabir, though they still had a few good months left with each other.

Their first port of call was Rome.

Parveen and Kabir's flight landed at the Leonardo da Vinci Fiumicino International Airport on a freezing winter morning. Later, Parveen would tell confidantes that she 'lost' Kabir even before they had deplaned. On the tarmac were hundreds of screaming fans who had turned up for one glimpse of their beloved Sandokan. Parveen believed that even before they left the warm comfort of that plane and stepped out into the chill, Kabir had been swept away by his own hype.

He, of course, remembers those heady days with greater fondness. 'Parveen saw streets filled with mobs waiting to get into my hotel. There was utter chaos and confusion and every

With Kabir Bedi during their trip to Italy

magazine had a *Sandokan* cover,' he recalls. 'She was with me, so we were constantly being photographed by the paparazzi. There were lots of appearances – television and radio – every station in Italy wanted to interview me. I'd be doing an interview every thirty minutes, day after day. It was very exhausting.'

Apart from Rome and Florence, the *Sandokan* promotional tour took the couple to towns big and small all over Italy. There was even a stop at Turin, the home town of Emilio Salgari. There were fan meets at hotels, printing presses and even auto factories.

'At factories, people would just abandon their production lines and surround us in large numbers,' Kabir says.

After the Italy tour was over, he was invited as a state guest to what was then the Federal Socialist Republic of Yugoslavia.

'It was a fairy tale,' he remembers. 'There were motorcades from the hotel, blaring sirens, banquets in these European-style halls with huge chandeliers and people welcoming us everywhere. It was the same kind of popularity that *Sandokan* had in Hungary [then known as the Hungarian People's Republic] and Czechoslovakia [formerly, the Czechoslovak Socialist Republic]. It was a huge success. It was wonderful to share that journey [with Parveen] and go to all these wonderful places, meet all these marvellous people, eat all the wonderful food, be wined and dined by film stars and statesmen.'

Parveen was by his side through it all.

'She accompanied me to all my engagements and she enjoyed it as well. She was a film star too and understood the value of crowds and fans who loved you,' Kabir says.

It didn't take long for the glamorous couple to become paparazzi favourites. From the Colosseum in Rome to the Fiat factory in Turin, they were photographed everywhere, which also meant that they were featured in every newspaper and magazine, including *Gente*, one of Italy's biggest celebrity magazines at the time. The *TV Sorrisi e Canzoni*, a popular TV guide, even did an elaborate photo shoot with Parveen and Kabir at the Lake Palace, Udaipur, after they had returned to India in February that year.

This wasn't Parveen's first heady experience of drawing adoring crowds, but it was certainly different. For once, she wasn't the centre of attention. The crowds, the press, the dignitaries – they were all there for Kabir. Headlines screamed 'Kabir causes a traffic jam', 'Kabir, the Italians' heartthrob', 'Kabir waving to the thousands of fans outside his hotel'. Not since her days in Ahmedabad, when she would follow her first boyfriend Neville Damania and his mega popular band Purple Flower everywhere, had Parveen gone through the experience of being on the periphery while the spotlight was on someone else. While she was madly in love with Kabir, the very thought of being sidelined – no matter how much he tried to include her in all his activities – was triggering negative feelings within her. Even as Kabir revelled in the wild, unexpected success of *Sandokan* and his newly minted pin-up status, Parveen had begun to feel insecure.

After a few whirlwind weeks in Europe, Kabir returned to Bombay, having decided that he needed to head West.

'It was a life-changing experience for me. I realized I had to move on from India and make my career abroad,' he explains.

It helped that he had already been signed on for his next international production to play another much-loved Salgari character – Emilio di Roccabruna aka the Black Corsair – in the film *The Black Corsair* (*Il corsaro nero* in Italian). Like Sandokan, the Corsair was royalty-turned-pirate, out for vengeance. These stories of the Black Corsair were set in a milieu located at the other end of the world – the Caribbean – during the golden age of piracy in maritime history. In the action adventure, Kabir was paired, yet again, with his *Sandokan* co-star, French actress Carole André, and was directed by Italian hit-maker Sergio Sollima.

Both Kabir and Parveen, however, needed to first fulfil their professional commitments back in India. The moment they returned, they ensured they were on their respective sets to complete as much of their work as possible before July 1976, when Kabir had to report to Colombia to shoot *The Black Corsair*. Instead of staying on in Bombay and concentrating on her own work, Parveen gave precedence to her need to be by Kabir's side and accompanied him to Colombia. During the shooting of the international film, the couple lived in a beautiful beachfront house in the Colombian port city of Cartagena.

Meanwhile, their absence from Bombay was so deeply felt that the city's gossip columnists, who had earlier carried stories of their favourite Bollywood couple working out – he in briefs and she in a bikini – now began coming up with accounts of them getting married in Colombia. So persistent was such talk and so widespread its effect that even film star Rajesh Khanna, who was shooting *Chalta Purza* with Parveen at the time, could not help asking her about the wedding rumours when they met. Her flat denial of there being any truth to the tales prompted Khanna to respond [according to the *Free Press Journal* of 19 September 1976]: 'I told Bhappi Sonie [the director of *Chalta Purza*] that you hadn't. I know that you aren't in a hurry to get married.'

✿

A lot would change, however, between Parveen's first and second trips to Italy.

Parveen's decision to follow her man wherever his career and success took him understandably became a cause for worry for Parveen's manager Ved Sharma, who had worked tirelessly in the background to make sure that she stayed in the big league. In three short years, she had gone from being a college girl in Ahmedabad to one of the best-known faces in the country, and Ved had played an integral part in her journey as an actress. His inborn tenacity and single-minded devotion to Parveen ensured that he lost no opportunity in promoting her strengths and her value to every producer and director in the industry. Of course, his career was intrinsically intertwined with hers and he certainly stood to gain from her success, but this was the era when star secretaries were genuinely invested in their actors and fiercely loyal to them.

When she broached the subject of following Kabir out of Bollywood, Ved was obviously taken aback. Parveen was the bigger star of the two. He couldn't understand why someone as successful as her would want to pack up and leave, turning her back on a career that was flourishing. Having known Parveen closely for some years, Ved was aware that once she had made up her mind, she wouldn't listen to reason. But he wasn't one to give up without a fight. He knew there was one person in her life that Parveen would listen to, no matter what – Danny.

'One day, Vedji landed up at my home,' the actor remembers. 'He came to me, huffing and puffing. He told me that Parveen wanted to leave the industry and the country. She was going to leave with Kabir, who had become a big star in Italy and signed a few films there. He wanted me to talk her out of this.'

Danny agreed to Ved's suggestion and the duo went upstairs to Parveen's home for the much-needed intervention.

'I tried to convince her, but Parveen didn't listen,' he says. 'She said she was fed up and didn't want to work any more. She thought films were "silly". She even blamed it all on me, because I had introduced her to world cinema and shown her good films.'

Changing tack, Danny reminded her about all the success she had enjoyed in recent years.

'I tried explaining to her that it was the wrong time for her to leave. Her career was going so well. She had signed three-four films with Amitabh Bachchan and had a few hits to her name.'

When she wouldn't budge from her stand, Danny and Ved tried to persuade her against cutting off all ties with films.

'We suggested she could keep coming back to do a few films every year and then go back. Just so she didn't completely give up her career.'

But Parveen had made up her mind and refused to listen to any reasonable alternatives.

※

Back in 1976, *Time* magazine, the international weekly, probably had no more than a handful of regular readers in Bollywood. But that summer, everyone began talking about the 19 July issue of the European edition. Spread across seven pages, the issue's cover story, titled 'Asia's Frenetic Film Scene', examined the prolific film industries across the continent. At the time, film industries from Japan to the Philippines and, of course, India churned out 'five times the annual output of US films and almost twice the number of Western Europe's product'. The article focused on the cornucopia that was Asian cinema – from Hong Kong's Kung Fu films to Bollywood's song-and-dance masala fare – and was peppered with photos that included a film still of Shabana Azmi standing on Shashi Kapoor's back and a behind-the-scenes shot of Akira Kurosawa directing *Dersu Uzala*.

More than the article, though, it was the choice of cover girl that made news in India. Though Parveen wasn't interviewed for the article, she reigned on the cover. Dressed in a black bustier decorated with strings of pearls, her long, lustrous hair cascading down her creamy shoulders, Parveen looked every inch the siren, with her heavily kohled eyes and cherry-red lips.

In the section about the Indian film industry, *Time*'s then India correspondent James Shepherd reported, 'Stars are not only born in a night, but burn out in a night. Producers consider themselves lucky if they wind up a picture with enough money for a new car, a new mistress and a bottle of scotch.'

Understandably, it raised quite a furore in the industry. 'What scotch?' fumed the late Yash Chopra in an interview to *India Today* for its 31 July 1976 issue. 'I don't drink. And who has *time* for mistresses?'

This wasn't the only controversial part of the cover story. There were enough statements by reigning superstars that raised eyebrows.

Rajesh Khanna is reported to have told the magazine, 'Here I am, playing a king in the morning, a painter in the afternoon and a beggar at night. But one of these movies is likely to click and keep me in business.'

If that wasn't bad enough, Raj Kapoor exacerbated the situation by saying, 'Indian actors are like taxis. You pay the fare and they'll go anywhere.'

The overall tone of the section on Indian films was that Bollywood is rubbish, but Satyajit Ray is brilliant. Obviously, no one in Bombay liked that. Directors were upset over the article's condescending tone, producers were furious about being left out and film stars were livid that instead of them, 'an up-and-coming starlet' was on the cover of the magazine.

In his autobiography, *The Best Mistakes of My Life*, actor – film-maker Sanjay Khan takes credit for Parveen landing the cover. 'Ironically and coincidentally, I had been instrumental in Parveen being on the cover, because Gerald Clarke, [*Time* magazine's] associate editor, had asked me to recommend an Indian actress, and I had named Parveen,' he writes.

When asked about it by *India Today* for their 15 October 1976 issue, Parveen had purred, 'Sweetheart, I didn't try for the *Time* cover; these things just happen to me.' Apparently, *Time* had spoken extensively to Shashi Kapoor and had asked photographer Jehangir Gazdar for photos of his co-stars. 'So Jugnu [as Parveen called Gazdar] took photos of Zeenat, Shabana and me and, well, *Time* chose me!'

The *Time* piece described Parveen as 'another (un-Westernized) local Valkyrie, who is as soft and clinging as Benaras silk'. It went on to say, 'Parveen, India's fastest rising new star, is working simultaneously in 20 movies. Fans are particularly fascinated by Parveen because of her candour about her private life; she has publicly admitted that she has had two lovers. Some social critics claim that such behaviour has only encouraged the young to jump into bed with each other.'

As someone who had pored over old issues of *Time* while she was teaching herself English in Ahmedabad and now made regular trips to bookstores across Bombay to buy issues of *Time* and *Life* magazines, Parveen was well aware of the importance of this cover. That July, when she left for Colombia with Kabir for the shoot of his international film *The Black Corsair*, her self-confidence was soaring. After a few blissful weeks in sunny and scenic Cartagena, she returned to Bombay with a stronger resolve to leave the city with Kabir.

The iconic cover of Time *magazine featuring Parveen*

'It was the *Time* magazine cover that did the trick,' Ved Sharma would share with *Star & Style* in its 16–29 October 1981 issue, a few years later.

Parveen called Girish Shukla, a still photographer she had first met on the sets of *Charitra* years ago. They had been friends since and he had become one of her favourites for photo shoots. Though she was usually quite happy about Shukla taking creative control of a photo session, this time she had very specific ideas.

'She wanted to build a portfolio, keeping in mind Hollywood aesthetics. These were the photos that she wanted to circulate among agents and studios in the West,' the photographer says.

She spent days poring over copies of the international edition of *Vogue*. With the pages of references she had collected, Parveen then narrowed down on the looks she wanted. Though she didn't deviate too much from her personal style of hair left loose and 'natural' make-up, Parveen shared her vision for the shoot with her regular hair and make-up team, comprising Irene and Bharat Godambe respectively.

'It was a very glamorous shoot,' Shukla recalls. 'Parveen had gotten some very Western dresses. She had been so involved in the shoot that she even picked out the props. She wanted the look to be very modern and opulent. I remember Parveen got along a tiger skin from Feroz Khan's home for the shoot.'

At the end of the day-long shoot, Parveen knew that she had the kind of photos that would grab an international film-maker's attention.

Before leaving for Europe for the second time that year, Parveen tried to complete as many films as she could. Among them was Manmohan Desai's perfect storm of comedy, action and drama – *Amar Akbar Anthony*. The film starred Amitabh Bachchan, Vinod Khanna and Rishi Kapoor in titular roles, with Parveen Babi, Shabana Azmi and Neetu Singh playing their love interests.

Parveen played Jenny to Bachchan's Anthony. Before casting for the film, producer-director Desai had been looking for someone who shared a great chemistry with his leading man and was just right as the anglicized Jenny who had returned to India after studying abroad. He was shown scenes from *Deewaar* where Parveen and Bachchan had appeared together.

At the time, Parveen's career was going through a lull. After the huge success of *Deewaar*, she had pinned all her hopes on Vijay Anand's thriller *Bullet*, opposite Dev Anand. The film misfired, as did her three films opposite Randhir Kapoor – the 1976 releases *Bhanwar* and *Mazdoor Zindabaad*, and *Mama Bhanja* in 1977. Also dead on arrival was *Rangeela Ratan*, the 1976 film she starred in opposite Rishi Kapoor. It was just when Parveen desperately needed a hit Desai called, offering her a role opposite the reigning superstar of the time.

Desai's son Ketan remembers his father offering to meet Parveen at a venue convenient for her.

She apparently told him, 'Protocol demands that I come to you. Apart from the fact that it's you and that Amitji is there in the film, meeting you [in] itself will be an experience. Also, money is not a criterion at all.'

Her words immediately endeared Parveen to 'Manji', as the film-maker was fondly called by the industry.

It didn't take long for the seasoned crew to fall under the actress's spell.

'She was so well mannered and courteous,' Ketan Desai says. 'She was impeccably behaved with everyone from the spot boy to the producer. What was incredible was that she remembered the names of everyone she interacted with on the set. In a day, she was probably going to three different sets and it was the same everywhere.'

Amar Akbar Anthony was one of the biggest films in production at the time and stories about Parveen from the sets helped to cement her reputation as a consummate professional. Ketan Desai remembers a lunch break that was cancelled for some reason. This would have sent most actors and their staff into a tailspin, but not Parveen. All she did was shrug and say, 'It's okay, we don't come here to eat. It's not a lunch party.'

Parveen's on-set behaviour was reflected in the conduct of her entourage.

'We just never had any problems ever with her staff, which again is very unlikely for a film set,' Ketan Desai says. 'Parveen never complained about anything and her staff followed her lead.' In the film, a bodyguard, Zebisko, shadows Parveen's character. The part was played by Yusuf Khan, who was cast less for his acting experience than for his impressive biceps, which he would keep flexing throughout the film. In one scene, Jenny is leaving to meet Anthony, when Zebisko blocks her way at the door.

'After manhandling her for a bit, Yusuf was supposed to push her into a room and she falls on the floor,' Desai recounts. 'He pushed her so hard that Parveen went flying into the room and hurt her head. It was a great shot, but even after Dad called "Cut", Parveen kept sitting on the floor, holding her head. Everyone rushed to her. Yusuf kept apologizing and Dad offered to cancel the shoot, so she could go to a doctor. [But] All Parveen was interested in was whether Dad got the shot and if it looked real. That tells you the kind of artist she was. Even though she was in pain, she went out of her way to put Yusuf at ease.'

෴

As the date of Parveen and Kabir's departure drew near, Ved Sharma began refusing film offers for the actress and even returned some signing amounts for films that hadn't gone on the floors.

'Before she left, Parveen called all of us and told us that she was leaving with Kabir. She wanted us to move on to other clients,' remembers Bharat Godambe, who had started working with Parveen while he was an assistant to the legendary make-up artist Pandhari Juker.

The world saw a very upbeat Parveen in the weeks leading up to her imminent departure from India with Kabir. Behind closed doors, though, it was a different story. The actress was venturing into the great unknown and that brought with it a familiar, but crippling self-doubt. She clearly remembered how she had felt during their last visit to Italy. It was Kabir whom everyone was focused on and she was left standing on the margins. The fear of rejection predictably spurred a barrage of negative thoughts which, in turn, led to feelings of resentment, jealousy, anger, hurt and distrust.

There were dark days when Parveen would lash out at Kabir. And he dealt with it as best he could. This wasn't the first time he had seen a side to Parveen the world knew nothing about. Earlier that year, during the *Sandokan* promotional tour in Europe, she had been overwhelmed by a whirlpool of emotions that her sense of isolation and self-doubt had triggered.

Decades on, Kabir is, understandably, reluctant to delve into specific incidents. 'The person you're looking at looks the same, but they're not the same,' he says. 'It's like something else has entered them; their brain starts malfunctioning. Of course, it leads to depression... of course, it leads to tears... of course, it leads to scenes... of course, it leads to all sorts of complications. And you deal with that as best you can, but it's not easy.'

On the night the couple finally flew out to Europe, Kabir's friend Mahesh Bhatt was at Bombay airport to see them off. 'I remember they were moving away, lock, stock and barrel,' he says. 'It was a late night flight and she was there. They were both already dressed for Europe. There was a kind of sadness about her, plucking herself from here and going away. But she was Kabir's girlfriend and they were in love. He was a star in Italy and there was a glorious future; so she went.'

When Parveen moved from Ahmedabad to Bombay, she had left behind family and friends to build the life she wanted. In 1976, she left behind that very life and career to follow the man she wanted to be with. This was the first time she would be leaving the film industry.

13

Before setting up base in London, Parveen and Kabir spent some time in Rome. The idea was for them to interact with the who's who of the Italian film industry.

In an interview to *Filmfare* for its 23 December 1977–15 January 1978 issue, Parveen observed: 'I met several eminent film personalities like Franco Zeffirelli, Federico Fellini and Bernard Bertolucci. All very interesting people with their own eccentricities. Like Fellini has this thing about not travelling. He does not go out of Rome. He was making a film on Casanova, who was born in and lived in Venice. And though Venice is in Italy, Fellini had a set erected in Rome. Zeffirelli is a typical European aristocrat, very sophisticated, very polished. He has an eye for beauty. I also met Elsa Martinelli – very bubbly; she is not beautiful, but there is something in her which is striking.'

In the late 1940s, as Europe struggled to rise from the rubble of the Second World War, Hollywood studios began shifting production to the continent, focusing, particularly, on Rome and London for the inexpensive labour and high subsidies on offer. *Quo Vadis*, a 1951 film starring Robert Taylor, Deborah Kerr and Peter Ustinov, was the first big Hollywood blockbuster to be shot completely in Rome's Cinecittà Studios. It was followed by films like the Gregory Peck and Audrey Hepburn starrer *Roman Holiday* (1953), *Ben-Hur* (1959) featuring Charlton Heston, and *Cleopatra*, the 1963 mega film that would set off Richard Burton's love affair with Elizabeth Taylor. These feature films were the highlights of a period that lasted well into the 1970s and was referred to as 'Hollywood on the Tiber'.

It was also during this phase that the Italian film industry was perceived as the gateway to Hollywood, with Gina Lollobrigida being the hottest Italian export, along with Sophia Loren. According to Humphrey Bogart, Lollobrigida's first Hollywood co-star, the Italian bombshell made 'Marilyn Monroe look like Shirley Temple', the child star who was seen as a symbol of angelic innocence. Bogart's remark had substance. For 'La Lollo', as Lollobrigida's fans affectionately called her, was one of the biggest sex symbols of the 1950s and 1960s. Having famously turned down a seven-year exclusive offer from the eccentric actor, director and business tycoon Howard Hughes, the Italian actress had gone on to star opposite some of America's most important leading men: Errol Flynn, Rock Hudson and Frank Sinatra.

As luck would have it, a manager from Air India, who knew Parveen and Kabir, organized a dinner for them with La Lollo. It was going to be a private affair – just the four of them at a swanky Roman restaurant. It promised to be a memorable night. And it was, but for the wrong reasons.

At the dinner, a newly single Lollobrigida had eyes only for Kabir. All evening, she showered her attention on him, completely ignoring Parveen. La Lollo's acerbic wit was just as famous as her voluptuous figure and her ongoing feud with her rival Loren. And Parveen was to get a taste of it when the Italian sex bomb finally acknowledged her presence.

'It was almost the end of dinner when Gina turned to Parveen and said, "And you, my dear? What are you doing? Following the star?",' Kabir says, recalling the details of that evening. 'Parveen was no pushover. She was very bright and quick-witted. So she replied, "No, my dear. I am with my man, because I have a man."'

Before Lollobrigida could retort, Parveen turned to Kabir and suggested, 'Let's dance.'

On the dance floor, she told him quite clearly that she didn't want to spend another moment watching the Italian star fawn all over him.

'I didn't know what to do,' says Kabir. 'Gina was one of the biggest names in international cinema, but Parveen wanted to leave. She said to me, "I'm leaving. The rest is up to you, whether you want to stay or you want to leave." I told her that she was putting me in a very difficult situation, but she said, "That's your problem. I'm leaving. I don't like this woman." Parveen wasn't wrong; Gina had snubbed and disparaged her.'

When they returned to their table at the end of the song, Kabir told Lollobrigida, 'I'm terribly sorry. We've got to leave.'

The Italian actress suggested they stay and finish their meal, but Kabir knew it made sense for them to leave before the evening took an ugly turn.

That evening with Gina Lollobrigida would leave Parveen feeling more anxious and insecure. In an interview that was carried in the April 1983 issue of *Stardust* a few years later, Kabir empathized with Parveen's situation at the dinner: 'Having been quite a successful actress in her own right, Parveen couldn't reconcile [herself] to the fact that she had been dismissed off [sic] as just a hanger-on.' It didn't take long for feelings of hopelessness and despair to completely consume her. 'She would seldom talk and most of the time was lost in her own thoughts. I was there to help her out and tried my level best to cheer her up.'

Not all her meetings with Italian film heavyweights were unpleasant, though. Danny remembers a midnight phone call he received from an ecstatic Parveen.

'I got worried when the phone rang so late in the night. Parveen sounded so happy. She had met Carlo Ponti, the famous Italian producer who had films like *Sunflower, Doctor Zhivago, Two Women* and *Zabriskie Point* to his credit. Ponti was also Sophia Loren's husband. Parveen told me that Ponti came up to her somewhere and said that he was interested in making a film with her.'

To Danny, this seemed like the big break that could catapult her on to the international stage.

'Ponti had famously discovered Sophia Loren. I thought Parveen had that oomph, like Sophia or Gina Lollobrigida, to make it in Hollywood. If Ponti introduced her, I told her that she'd definitely become a star.'

Danny doesn't know what happened after this meeting with Ponti, because Parveen didn't call him again for the next few months.

'The next time I heard from her, Parveen told me that Kabir and she had moved to London.'

It was in a beautiful multi-storey townhouse, overlooking the spectacular River Thames between the Albert and Battersea Bridges in the heart of historic Old Chelsea, that the couple set up their home in London. This was one of the city's most prestigious locations, with stunning river views and easy access to nearby parks and the buzz of King's Road. It was to be their base before Parveen and Kabir took off for Malaysia to shoot their first international film together – *La tigre è ancora viva: Sandokan alla riscossa!* (The Tiger Is Still Alive: Sandokan to the Rescue).

In the months they had spent in Rome, Parveen had failed to get a foothold in the film industry there.

'I know that Dino De Laurentiis [producer of films like *Serpico*, *Death Wish* and Ingmar Bergman's *The Serpent's Egg* who, along with Carlo Ponti, was considered one of Italy's most powerful producers] asked to meet her, but nothing came of it,' Kabir muses. 'The fact that she'd been on the cover of *Time* should have led to a flood of offers, but it didn't. These things depressed her.'

This was around the time when the cast of the next Sandokan production was being put together. Kabir proposed that Parveen be cast as Princess Jasmine, the film's main romantic lead. Carol Levi, his agent at the William Morris talent agency, signed her on as a client to negotiate for projects on her behalf. After the dates of the shoot had been finalized and all the details worked out, Parveen was signed on.

Kabir assumed that being cast in the new Sandokan film could serve as her big break; after all, that's how he himself had been introduced to the West. But the signing did little to lift the deep fog of depression that Parveen was now engulfed in. 'Nothing seemed to cheer her up,' Kabir would share with *Stardust* for its April 1983 issue. 'She was a far cry from the bubbly exuberant Parveen I knew. So I asked her if living abroad was going to have such a terrible effect on her, what was the point in continuing her stay?'

This one question finally pushed Parveen over the edge. Her self-worth was already fragile and Kabir's words seemed to shatter it. 'She seemed to think that I had rejected her by asking that question,' Kabir told *Stardust*. 'And nothing I said or did after that could change her belief that this was, indeed, the end of our relationship.'

A little more than three months after they had settled down in London, Parveen told Kabir that she wanted to return to Bombay.

'One day, she told me that she wanted to go back to have more time to think,' Kabir observed. 'She promised to meet me in Malaysia, where we were supposed to start *Sandokan II*.'

At the time, he thought it was a good decision for Parveen to return to Bombay. Being back in the city where she was recognized as a star, surrounded by people she knew and loved, seemed like the perfect cure for what he thought was a temporary funk. He hoped that the trip home would lift her spirits and she'd join the *Sandokan II* shoot with the much-needed boost to her flagging confidence.

Parveen, though, had no intention of going back. Before she booked her tickets to return home, she had called Ved.

'She asked me whether she would be welcomed back home. "Yes, of course! Come back at once. Your AAA [*Amar Akbar Anthony*] is a hit!" I screamed over the telephone. There were good offers waiting for her and producers who still wanted her,' he is quoted as saying in the 16–29 October 1981 issue of *Star & Style* magazine.

Though Parveen had told her staff, including Ved Sharma, to move on to other clients, he hadn't. And now he was delighted to know that she was coming home.

The night before Parveen left London, she called Danny. It was yet another midnight call. The tone of this conversation was very different, though, from the one they had had while she was in Rome.

'She was howling on the phone,' he says. 'She said that she wanted to come back home. I asked her what [had] happened, but she was uncontrollable and I couldn't make out half the things she was saying. She gave me the details of her flight and I promised that I'd pick her up at the airport.'

A little more than twelve hours later, as rain lashed the runway, Parveen returned to Bombay after her year abroad. As promised, Danny received her at the airport. She looked nothing like her glamorous self. Her eyes were red and her face puffy, as if she had spent the entire time on the flight crying.

'I took her to her home; her mother was there waiting for her to return. In all the years I had known her, I had never seen Parveen in such a state. She just kept howling. I couldn't calm her down. She was a complete mess. At one point, she was crying so much, she started trembling,' Danny recalls.

All through the night, while she was hysterical, Parveen would share confidences with Danny that sounded unbelievable. 'She said that she was expecting a child and that Kabir [had] forced her to get it aborted,' he recounts. 'I didn't believe her, so I tried to tell her that she was imagining this, but she stuck to her story. She kept repeating, "I have broken up with him and I don't want to see his face again."' After a long pause, he continues, 'I've never told anyone this, because I realized she was unwell and this was a figment of her imagination. I didn't confront Kabir about this either and we've never spoken about it.'

Eventually, he gave her a sedative so that she could sleep.

Danny still believes the entire story was the outcome of Parveen's delusional interpretation of reality, seen through the prism of her mental illness.

The following day, in an effort to lift her out of her depressive state, he brought up the topic of her career and reminded her of what a big hit *Amar Akbar Anthony* had turned out to be.

'I told her to rest for a while and let Vedji find work for her,' he says. 'I knew people would sign her immediately, because there were very few actresses who could carry off the "modern" look. Apart from Zeenat and her, there was nobody else. I told her to finish the two films she had left incomplete before leaving for Europe and to do it with sincerity. The industry should know that she's come back and is working hard.'

Danny understood that in the film industry, memories were conveniently short and it wouldn't take long for film-makers to forget that Parveen had just upped and left, inconveniencing many of them by throwing their plans into disarray.

One of the first films the actress would sign after returning to Bombay was Manmohan Desai's action drama *Suhaag*. Encouraged by Danny's pep talk, she had made a call to Desai, who had directed her in *Amar Akbar Anthony*.

The film-maker's son Ketan, who had assisted him, says, 'She told Dad that she was back and if there was any role for her, she'd want to work with him. Dad was going to start shooting *Suhaag*. He told her not to worry and that he'd carve out a role for her.' This was very unlike his father, Ketan Desai insists. 'My dad would rarely say something like this; for him, the film always came first. He'd only give roles to heroines based on merit.'

What made Manmohan Desai bend his rules for Parveen was the fact that he had really enjoyed shooting *Amar Akbar Anthony* with her. She was, moreover, so keen on being a part of his next Amitabh Bachchan–Shashi Kapoor starrer that she even offered to work for free. The film-maker, of course, wasn't about to take her up on that offer, but he immediately got his writers to accommodate Parveen in his film by shoehorning into the script a brand-new character – Anu – as the love interest for Kishen, the character to be played by Shashi Kapoor.

Within a few months of her sudden departure from London, Parveen was back in the English city, dancing to Laxmikant and

Pyarelal's chartbusting 'Teri rab ne banadi jodi' in Hyde Park, along with Amitabh Bachchan, Shashi Kapoor and Rekha.

By the end of 1977, Parveen was well and truly back where she belonged – on the sets of a Hindi film. It helped that in interviews she talked often about her renewed focus on her work. In the 23 December 1977–15 January 1978 issue of *Filmfare*, she was quoted as saying, 'I am devoting all my time to my career now; as much time as is demanded of me. I get my scenes and lines in advance and I read up and prepare at home for the day's scenes. And I am getting greater satisfaction from work now.'

Ved Sharma was delighted to see how focused Parveen was on her work once again. Every morning, when he landed up at her home in Kalumal Estate, she would be poring over a script or rehearsing her lines. These were encouraging signs. 'I could feel her added enthusiasm and interest in her work,' Ved said in an interview to *Star & Style*, published in its 16–29 October 1981 issue.

He upheld his promise of getting her offers and, soon, Parveen was on a signing spree. If there was a big-budget film going on the floors towards the end of 1977, chances were that she was a part of the cast. Consider the 1978 family drama *Aahuti*, co-starring Rajendra Kumar, Shashi Kapoor and Rakesh Roshan; Yash Chopra's 1979 disaster drama *Kaala Patthar*, where the actress was part of an ensemble cast comprising Amitabh Bachchan, Shashi Kapoor, Shatrughan Sinha and Neetu Singh; B.R. Chopra's 1980 action thriller *The Burning Train*, where Parveen's co-stars were Dharmendra, Hema Malini, Vinod Khanna, Jeetendra and Neetu Singh; Manoj Kumar's 1981 opus *Kranti*, where the director-actor's stellar role was complemented by an ensemble cast that included, apart from Parveen, Dilip Kumar, Hema Malini, Shashi Kapoor and Shatrughan Sinha; Manmohan Desai's 1982 film *Desh Premee*, in which Amitabh Bachchan, in a dual role, was supported by an entire array of co-stars like Hema Malini, Navin Nischol, Shammi Kapoor, Sharmila Tagore and, of course, Parveen Babi; and Kamal Amrohi's 1983 release *Razia Sultan*, where her co-stars were Dharmendra and Hema Malini.

This was an era when the industry judged an actress's popularity on the basis of the leading men she was working with. Parveen had films opposite Rishi Kapoor, Shashi Kapoor and Vinod Khanna. More significantly, she had been cast opposite the reigning superstar Amitabh Bachchan in three important films. It couldn't get better than this.

With Parveen's diary jam-packed with dates for films she had been signed on for in Bombay, she didn't think twice before deciding that she wasn't going to shoot *Sandokan II* with her now ex-boyfriend Kabir. She had completely got over the lure of working in the West. More importantly, she wanted to have nothing to do with Kabir, the man for whom she had been ready to give up her flourishing career just a few months earlier.

About a month before she was to report for the shoot in Malaysia, Parveen called Carol Levi, the agent she shared with Kabir, and backed out of the film. 'This not only came as a big blow personally, but it was an even bigger let-down professionally,' Kabir would tell *Stardust* in an interview that was carried in its April 1983 issue. 'My credibility was at stake, because it was I who had suggested Parveen. And shooting couldn't start on time, because no major Italian heroine would have agreed to do the role at such a short notice of twenty days.'

Eventually, British-born actress Teresa Ann Savoy was signed on to play Princess Jasmine.

Parveen and Kabir's relationship had begun amidst a scandal. Now, nearly three years later, it had ended just as dramatically.

14

'Parveen—Protima, the two women who loved and lost Kabir Bedi' screamed the headlines in the September 1977 issue of *Stardust*.

The actress's return from London without her partner had set off a race between journalists for the 'tell-all' interview. Even though it had been over two years since Kabir's marriage to Protima had ended, the relationship triangle that connected the former couple with Parveen retained the sense of smoky intrigue associated with it, along with the fascinating lore it had spawned. From the point of view of the media, this was a story with great potential, involving three beautiful people, a failed marriage and a live-in relationship that had imploded. There were a lot of tantalizing questions yet to be answered about Parveen and Kabir's break-up.

The actress had bucked expectations by not going public with her side of the story. Regardless of what she was sharing with those close to her about her final days with Kabir, she had chosen to take the high road while speaking to the press. The end of their relationship, she maintained steadfastly, was 'by mutual choice'. Though she had readily followed Kabir to Europe, Parveen now maintained that she couldn't have stayed away for too long because of her mother.

'I could never have settled abroad with Kabir, because I feel responsible for my mother whom I have called to live with me now,' she declared in an interview to *Stardust* for its

September 1977 issue. 'Perhaps, in the past, with my great need of independence, I overlooked the fact that my mother is dependent on me. She has nobody but me. I couldn't desert her at this stage of her life and leave India forever, since there's not much chance of Kabir coming back here.'

The dichotomy between Parveen's public persona and her private one is interesting. Away from the spotlight, she found it hard to hide her bitterness over the break-up. In fact, for years afterwards, she would pinpoint the moment she knew she had lost Kabir to his success – the first time they landed in Rome and faced a horde of screaming fans. In print, though, she came across as more forgiving.

'I'm sad, but not bitter,' she would insist in that same *Stardust* interview. Over and over, she reiterated that she didn't 'resent his [Kabir's] success', quickly adding, 'but I do admit that it changed things for us. Our lifestyles weren't right for each other. To be with him, I'd have to follow him around all over the world. As a woman, I have my ego, my pride. I could never become a man's tag!'

Parveen's need to be treated as an equal and with respect was a leitmotif through all her public statements following the break-up, including the one she gave to *Stardust* at the time: 'I did realize that the whole scene had become different for Kabir. Don't forget I'm in the same game myself. I know what the scene is really like. I also know the scenes behind the scenes. It's not that I don't understand that Kabir is now exposed to all sorts of new experiences, in terms of glamour and women. I've seen it for myself, that all those females out there are ready to throw themselves at him. And if Kabir gets attracted to anyone, I could hardly blame him. Yet I wouldn't be able to take everything from him. Surely I can't be expected to sit back and be treated like a doormat? Kabir is not a flirt by nature. But he's not immune to women.'

She made it clear that she wasn't prepared to just sit back and watch women throw themselves at the man who had been her partner.

There was no question of marriage being the key to resurrecting her relationship with Kabir. Two years had passed since he'd walked out of his marriage with Protima, but the two still weren't divorced.

'I would never have gone into a marriage with Kabir just to keep him by my side,' Parveen insisted during her interview to *Stardust*. 'It's true that I did want our relationship to be on a permanent footing but I wanted a normal, secure relationship, not a bondage for Kabir and me. If we were to marry, it would be because it's the natural thing to do, and not because it's a solution.'

As far as Bollywood was concerned, Parveen was the bigger star of the two. That she had given up her career to follow her man had put her in the league of the ideal, self-sacrificing Indian woman. She didn't see herself as one, though.

'He's the kind of man who, when he once sets his mind to do something, does it,' she said during the interview. 'His woman either has to adjust to him or part from him, before she reaches the stage where she does become a liability to him. I did exactly that. I've let Kabir [be] free, because this is the time when he has to make the best of his career without any hassles. I don't say it's sacrifice on my part; I'm not that big a martyr.'

Though Parveen was trying to put up a brave front, it was obvious that this was 'the most intense and ultimate crisis' in her life.

'I'm happy our parting was as beautiful as our love,' she would tell *Stardust*. 'Kabir saw me off at the airport and that was the only time in our relationship that we really fooled ourselves. We didn't say our goodbyes. Instead, we said the usual "See you soon", though both of us knew that we would never be together in that way again. We cheated ourselves; otherwise, it would have been impossible to go through it. Still, making the decision was the most painful part. Once it was made, one felt too numb to feel the pain.'

Having returned from abroad to find one of her films – *Amar Akbar Anthony* – doing well in the theatres and with roles in at least half a dozen big-banner films, Parveen was able to maintain a semblance of normalcy and control over her life. 'It's because I have my work that I don't find myself in such a vulnerable position today,' she would acknowledge to Stardust. 'It keeps me occupied during the days and at nights... Well, I have my books to go to bed with! Jokes aside, I'm not looking for anything particular in life (least of all, a man!) at this stage. In fact, I'm not certain as to what is particular at this moment. I've decided to just flow, to go along in life from day to day.'

The world saw Parveen as a vulnerable young woman coming to terms with heartbreak after being dumped by a man for whom the lure of fame had been a more potent force. She had never shied away from talking candidly about her life and she wasn't about to turn circumspect now. As is usual at the end of any relationship, everyone who knew the former couple ended up picking sides. With Kabir in a different country and unable to present his perspective and Parveen ready to share details of their time together, it wouldn't take long for him to be branded the villain of this story. This particular narrative was further cemented about a year later, when Parveen had her first, very public, mental breakdown.

15

Within six months of returning from her sabbatical, Parveen was back in the race for top billing in the industry. Film trade pundits believed that Raj Kapoor's much-awaited *Satyam Shivam Sundaram* would catapult Zeenat Aman to the numero uno position among actresses. Hema Malini, who had been reigning supreme for some time, had begun refusing films because she was pregnant and wished to reduce her workload. While Rekha's career was yet to take off, Neetu Singh was almost exclusively working opposite her then boyfriend, later husband, Rishi Kapoor. This opened up a world of opportunities for Parveen and she signed half a dozen big-banner films during this period. This sudden rise in her popularity, that too after she had left the industry for quite a few months, surprised everyone. But it didn't take long for film-makers to start talking about the reasons why they were clamouring to sign her on.

Among the film offers Parveen accepted after her return from London was *Chamatkaar*, opposite Rajesh Khanna. This Pramod Chakravarty-directed film was, in fact, one of several for which Ved Sharma had been obliged to return the signing amount when Parveen decided to give up her career in Bollywood and leave for foreign shores with Kabir. The actress had advised Chakravarty and the film's producer Babu Mehra to go ahead and cast someone else in her role, because she wasn't sure if she'd want to continue her career in films in Bombay. Unaccustomed to such courtesy and consideration, the makers of *Chamatkaar* were completely bowled over. Almost a year later, the film was still waiting to be

Parveen on set – her colleagues always described her as being quiet and diligent at work

made. When Parveen returned to Bombay, Chakravarty made sure he didn't miss the opportunity, and immediately signed her on again.

The casting announcement that took the industry by surprise, however, was Parveen's inclusion in the star-studded line-up for Manoj Kumar's *Kranti*. Even by the multi-starrer standards of the 1970s, *Kranti*'s ensemble cast was considered to be in a league of its own. Apart from Parveen and Manoj Kumar, the period film featured Dilip Kumar, Shashi Kapoor, Hema Malini, Shatrughan Sinha, Sarika, Prem Chopra and Madan Puri. The film's casting made news for many reasons. Not only had Manoj Kumar brought his idol Dilip Kumar out of his five-year-long hiatus with this film, but he also cast Parveen as the quintessential '*gaon ki gori*', an avatar she had not been seen in before.

Stardust roped in the actress to interview Manoj Kumar for its October 1977 issue. During the conversation that ranged from his interests in directing to the patriotic themes of his films, Parveen asked him the question that everyone had on their mind, 'Why did you select me for *Kranti*?' He paused, before replying, 'My wife saw a song of yours in a forthcoming film and she liked it.' Manoj Kumar couldn't remember which song this was, but clearly it had made an impression on him as well. 'For me, a glance, a gesture, a close-up is sufficient,' he told his actress-interviewer.

༄༅༅

An unexpected story was added to the lore of Parveen's comeback on the sets of B.R. Chopra's *The Burning Train*. A strapping, barrel-chested, bald white man landed up at the mahurat of the film. In his pocket was a rolled-up copy of *Time* magazine, featuring Parveen on the cover. The man was the Australian expat Bob Christo, who went on to have a very successful Bollywood career as a henchman to the main villain in films.

Before he landed in Bombay, Christo had worked as a civil engineer in Vietnam, modelled for an African beer, built the sets of Francis Ford Coppola's 1979 epic war film *Apocalypse Now* and even run an escort service. It was during his stint with the Special Air Service (SAS) regiment in Salisbury, the capital of Rhodesia (now the Republic of Zimbabwe) that he found an old issue of *Time* magazine that someone had left behind on his bed. He leafed through the magazine, looking for more pictures of the actress featured on the cover. Along with another photo, he found the article on Bombay's thriving film industry. He was intrigued. Christo kept the magazine in his briefcase. As he puts it in his memoir, *Flashback: My Life and Times in Bollywood and Beyond*, he 'hoped that I'd meet that lady soon'.

A few months later, in August 1977, Christo found himself stranded at Muscat airport, without a work visa for Oman. He was told that it would take three weeks to process his papers; during that period, he would not be allowed entry into Oman. 'I saw a big map on the wall of the arrival lounge and went over to get my bearings,' Christo writes in his memoir. 'After some scrutinizing of the map, I realized that Muscat was not far from Bombay. I still had that *Time* magazine in my briefcase. I immediately decided that I'd go to Bombay and try to meet Parveen Babi.'

Once in Bombay, Christo started hanging out at a teahouse near Churchgate station. Within a few days, regulars there had all heard the story of the crazy Australian who had landed up in the city to meet Parveen Babi. Fortuitously, it was at the same teahouse that he would meet Zuber Khan, a cameraman, who told him about a mahurat taking place the following morning that featured Parveen herself. The film was B.R. Chopra's *The Burning Train*, and the location Bombay Central station. When they reached the bustling location, Khan directed Christo to stand in front of a pillar, away from the film crew that was setting up for the first shot.

'After about fifteen minutes, a lady stopped in front of me and said, "Hello, I am Parveen Babi,"' the Australian writes in his memoir. 'I looked at her for a moment and then answered, "You're not Parveen Babi!" Pulling the *Time* magazine out of a pocket, I pointed at it and said, "This is Parveen Babi." The lady laughed and retorted, "In the magazine, I'm in make-up and full get-up. Normally, I don't wear make-up when I am not working. Now, before the mahurat shot, I'll have to go for my make-up first."'

Christo quickly apologized and told Parveen the whole story, starting from the moment he had found the copy of *Time* magazine in Rhodesia to meeting Khan, the cameraman who had got him to the mahurat.

'I've been admiring your beauty. Ever since I read this magazine, I've wanted to meet you personally,' the Australian told the actress.

She smiled at him politely and thanked him for all the compliments, before moving away.

A few hours later, even before the mahurat shot had been taken with the film's stars – Dharmendra, Hema Malini, Vinod

Khanna, Neetu Singh and Parveen – everyone on the set was familiar with the story about the big white man and his fascination for Parveen Babi that had brought him all the way to Bombay. By the end of the week, this story had spread across the industry.

On the surface, it looked as if Parveen's life was back to normal. Her days were spent juggling multiple movies, memorizing lines, sitting patiently for hair and make-up, and learning dance moves. On the sets, she was cordial and incredibly hard-working and at parties she was fun and interesting.

If you had looked closer, though, you would have noticed the cracks.

Almost immediately after Parveen's return to Bombay, she flew to Calcutta with the whole cast for a special screening of *Amar Akbar Anthony*. After the screening was over, the stars greeted the fans in the theatres. The plan was to engage in a small meet-and-greet, but the crowd was just too large and unruly to handle. As the fans surged towards the front where the actors were waiting, the latter were quickly evacuated from the auditorium through a back door.

'Before we could get to the cars, we spent a few minutes in a very small, dim space between the hall and the exit,' Manmohan Desai's son Ketan remembers. 'Amitji, Rishiji, Neetuji were all there. Parveen was right next to me. We were all very tensed [sic], because the crowd seemed to be out of control. Suddenly, I felt Parveen's nails digging into my forearm and she started almost chanting, "Let me go." She looked so afraid.'

Without waiting for an all-clear from the limited security staff there, Ketan Desai pulled the terrified actress out of that small room towards the waiting cars outside.

'I put Parveen in the first car I saw. Her entourage quickly followed her and I told the police that was present to quickly get her to the hotel. I didn't know what it was, but I felt like there was something wrong,' he explains.

Later that evening, when Desai went over to see how she was doing, all Parveen kept repeating was, 'They'll trample all over me. They'll kill me.'

A few months later, the actress was on location in the picturesque hills of Ooty, shooting for Rakesh Kumar's *Do aur Do Panch*. The director had been keen on casting Hema Malini and Rekha opposite Amitabh Bachchan and Shashi Kapoor, but things didn't work out with Rekha. So Parveen was roped in to play Anju in the buddy comedy. Key members of the cast and crew, including Parveen and the director, flew from Bombay to Madras (now Chennai) and were then driven to Ooty in a convoy of five cars. While passing through the jungles of Mudumalai, the director saw someone selling coconuts.

'It had been a long drive and it seemed like a good place to stop,' he remembers.

Kumar and Parveen stood on the side of the road, drinking out of the coconuts and chatting about nothing in particular. Suddenly, a huge herd of elephants appeared not far from where they stood. Everyone was transfixed seeing the majestic beasts up close.

'The coconut seller told us to not be scared and that the elephants weren't dangerous,' Kumar recollects. 'Everyone else went back to their conversations, but I noticed that Parveen was trembling with fear. I held her hand and tried to calm her. That's when she whispered to me, "They will attack me first."'

Kumar couldn't really figure out why Parveen was so terrified and, fortunately, the herd ambled away soon after.

It would take two years for *Do aur Do Panch* to be completed and the director remembers yet another incident involving Parveen that took place close to the end of his shoot and left him confused.

'Parveen always seemed like she was on the edge, always tense,' he says. 'And she would be chain-smoking, which was something that I didn't like.'

Kumar assumed that in the course of filming, he had got to know the actress well enough to be able to talk to her about her addiction and persuade her, perhaps, to give it up.

'One night, after pack-up, I took her aside and we started talking,' he recalls. 'I told her to disconnect from things and people who made her so stressed that she smoked so much. I think I jokingly said that if I saw her smoking, I'd slap her.'

Kumar didn't give this conversation much thought. All the more because Parveen hadn't seemed to mind him taking the liberty of bringing up the topic.

A few days later, Ved asked Rakesh Kumar if he had reprimanded Parveen.

'Apparently, she had a nightmare and told her maid that I am going to kill her,' the director recalls.

He didn't know how to react to the situation.

'I really thought Ved was joking,' he now says. 'When I realized he wasn't, I recounted the exact conversation I had had with Parveen. I really didn't think it would become such a big deal. I only had her best interest at heart.'

The director wanted to apologize to Parveen, but Ved told him not to bother.

Kumar and Ketan Desai were among the many beyond the actress's inner circle who remembered these stray encounters they had had with her between her return to Bombay in 1977 and her first publicly reported breakdown two years later. Apart from the fact that very few had any knowledge of mental illness in those days or were aware of the ways it could manifest itself, most people who came in contact with Parveen brushed aside all their concerns, because she seemed 'so normal' much of the time.

'Apart from these two instances,' Rakesh Kumar reflects, 'Parveen was always so courteous and soft-spoken. Everything I had heard from other directors about how professional and punctual she was turned out to be true. I used to start shooting at 7 a.m. on most days throughout the thirty-day schedule. She would be ready with full make-up by 7.30.'

Ved tried to explain away the actress's behaviour as the outcome of a heavy workload and very little food, for during her time in Rome and then London, Parveen had become obsessed with the need to lose weight and become slimmer. As a result, she was always on a diet. As Ved would tell *Star & Style* during an interview published in its 16–29 October 1981 issue, 'She had this slimming obsession – she used to scan foreign magazines and try out the diet and advice given there for maintaining a trim figure. Very often, I'd see her eating nothing, except a few slices of fruit. I think rigorous dieting, coupled with an overload of work, began to play havoc with her health. When one is physically weak, one becomes mentally weak too. I saw her cracking up gradually.'

Meanwhile, the rumour mills had already started churning with tales of Parveen's supposed love life. After all, she was single for the first time since she had chosen a career in films. While she wasn't in the market for a relationship, it didn't take long for speculations to start in that direction. And the first person she was linked to was her former love – Danny.

Everyone loves a love story and there are few developments more romantic than a former couple getting back together. It didn't take long for this kind of wishful thinking on the part of film industry watchers to turn into rumours and spread far and wide. In a cover story for *Stardust*'s March 1978 issue, Parveen picked Danny as one of 'the men she desires'. His name featured along with those of illustrious personalities like Salvador Dali, Ingmar Bergman, Ravi Shankar, Anwar Sadat and Paul Newman, as one of the 'thirteen celebrity turn-ons, with more to them than just their bodies'.

Parveen was generous in her praise of Danny. 'He is genuinely nice. All these years I've known him, never once have I felt or seen him wanting to harm anybody intentionally; it's a refreshing quality. There is nothing complicated about him. There's a child-like spontaneity in him.'

Danny, for his part, had made statements like 'no man can be indifferent to Parveen Babi, least of all Danny', while she was still seeing Kabir. It seemed as if there were some residual feelings there. It didn't help that Parveen and Danny continued to be neighbours and the actress had, once again, become a frequent visitor to his home. In her fragile state, she evidently saw Danny as her emotional anchor.

This complicated the actor's life somewhat, as he was still in a relationship with Kim.

'Once again, the relationship with me got complicated and she started depending on me too much,' Danny says. 'It was the same situation all over again and she was there at my house all the time.'

As for Kim, the sight of Parveen in Danny's house again was, obviously, quite a shock.

Unlike the old days, when Kim had seemed to adapt well to the other woman's constant presence in Danny's life, she wasn't quite so accommodating this time around.

'Kim really began thinking that something was going on between Parveen and me,' Danny says, but is quick to clarify that their eventual break-up years later had absolutely nothing to do with Parveen.

Much like him, Kim was very discreet about their personal life. So when a journalist from *Stardust* asked her about the possibility of a romance being rekindled between Danny and Parveen, she laughed.

In the magazine's May 1978 issue, Kim is quoted as saying: 'I mean, Parveen comes back, minus Kabir, and begins visiting Danny and that's it; people start saying, "Poor Kim, what'll she do now?"' As for the whispers of her feeling threatened by Parveen's frequent visits, Kim said firmly, 'I'm sure of myself and I am sure of Danny. So what if Parveen drops in on Danny on her way up and down? Most times, I am around too. We've even played Scrabble together. So, no, I don't feel that my love or life is threatened by Parveen Babi.'

It was believed that one of the reasons why Kim was so secure in her relationship with Danny was that he had taken it forward by inviting her to meet his family in Sikkim. It was no secret that Danny was a very traditional man and this was seen as a big step for his future with Kim.

Parveen too was very clear that she had no romantic interest in Danny. 'He is a swell guy and I'll never stop liking Danny,' she told *Stardust* in an interview that was carried in its May 1978 issue. 'But there's no question of getting involved with him once again. You can't have the same intensity twice.'

But no matter how much the three people involved in this imagined love triangle tried to quash the rumours circulating about them, the stories simply refused to die. What people didn't know yet was that there was already a new man in Parveen Babi's life.

16

The first time Mahesh Bhatt met Parveen on the sets of B.R. Ishara's *Charitra*, he was intrigued. Only, at the time, he was more interested in his cricketing idol Salim Durrani. During the next five years he would regard Parveen as no more than 'Danny's or then Kabir's girl', as he puts it. Their paths often crossed – they were a part of the Juhu Gang, and Mahesh had worked with both Danny and Kabir – but their interactions were always fleeting. They were aware of each other's existence, but only at the periphery of their consciousness. Both were leading very full lives that needed every bit of their attention.

'She was a gorgeous girl; not much of a talker,' Mahesh recalls. 'She was cautious and had an affected or cultivated style of talking. I could see [that] behind the demeanour there was somebody else.'

The then thirty-something director, who had debuted with *Manzilein aur bhi Hain* a year after Parveen's launch, didn't think much of her films either.

Yet, just before Parveen's departure for London, Mahesh had transitioned from being a mere acquaintance to someone who would eventually become a friend because of a shared interest. In the 1960s and 1970s, the new-age trend had introduced the West to a plethora of spiritual philosophies and movements. Mystics like Jiddu Krishnamurti, Meher Baba, Rajneesh (later known as Osho) and George Gurdjieff had emerged as dominant personalities on the world stage. Closer home, the disillusioned in Bollywood had also begun to look for gurus to offer them a clearer spiritual vision and guide them towards better living.

By the mid-1970s, both Vinod Khanna and Mahesh Bhatt had become followers of Rajneesh, who encouraged them to explore Jiddu Krishnamurti's books and attend his talks, both at the JJ School of Arts and at the home of India's 'tsarina of culture', Pupul Jayakar. By the time Mahesh met U.G. Krishnamurti, he had gone through quite a few spiritual gurus and still hadn't found what he was looking for.

'I met UG when I was going through a spiritual wasteland, when I went to ashrams like people go to brothels or bars – to seek comfort,' he was quoted as saying in the 21 June 2009 issue of the *Telegraph*.

It was Mahesh who would introduce his spiritually inclined friends in Bollywood to UG. On one occasion, Kabir was one of the many invited for the latter's talk and Parveen accompanied him to the event. The couple had been regulars at Jiddu Krishnamurti's talks in Bombay and Parveen considered herself a 'JK-ite'. UG made it quite clear that he wasn't a fan of JK's teaching, but he succeeded in instantly captivating the actress.

'Parveen found him [UG] very fascinating,' Kabir remembers. 'He was a man who lived with utmost simplicity and there was a certain glow around him. UG was very different, because he had a very cut-and-dry view of the world. His wasn't a message of hope. His message was, "There is no hope. You are what you are. You have to view things as they are, for what they are – unsentimentally. Be realistic and understand the true nature of things."'

'After spending about two hours with him, Kabir and I took our leave,' Parveen reminisced in 'The Confessions of Parveen Babi', a cover story she wrote for the 29 January–4 February 1984 issue of the *Illustrated Weekly of India*. 'UG stood on the balcony, waving goodbye. As we were getting into the car, UG observed to Mahesh, standing beside him, that my relationship with Kabir [would] not survive.'

While UG was uncannily accurate in his forebodings about the fate of Parveen and Kabir's relationship, even he couldn't have predicted that he'd play an important role in the actress's life and in her relationship with Mahesh.

※

Born out of wedlock to a Shia Muslim mother and a brahmin father, Mahesh Bhatt grew up craving the legitimacy of a conventional family. His formative years were spent playing cricket, being mesmerized by movies and selling everything from car fresheners to nuts and bolts during school vacations. While he was still in school, Mahesh met and fell in love with Lorraine Bright (she changed her name to Kiran later), a student at the Bombay Scottish orphanage. They married when Mahesh was just twenty and their eldest daughter Pooja was born a year later.

After completing school, Mahesh made ads for brands like Dalda and Lifebuoy before he started assisting Raj Khosla, the director of *Mera Gaon Mera Desh*. The release of his directorial debut was stalled by over two years and the two films that followed – *Vishwasghaat* and *Naya Daur* – didn't work at the box office either. It was during this difficult phase in his career that Parveen came back into his life.

It started with one phone call.

When Parveen began rebuilding her career after her return from London, she had started reaching out to old friends and acquaintances. Mahesh Bhatt was one of them. She invited him over to her Kalumal Estate home to 'catch up with life', as she put it.

'I was a married man in my twenties,' Mahesh recalls. 'I was struggling and my movies weren't doing well; travelling from Mahim to Juhu was an expensive affair.'

Yet, there was something that compelled him to visit Parveen.

That evening, Mahesh began seeing her in a new light. 'There was this gloom around her,' he recalls. 'This was a woman that truly belonged to the space where she lived; that space where she was solitary. She was beautiful and she was desolate.'

The last time he had met her, Parveen was living with Kabir. They were a couple and she was following him to greener pastures. Like everyone else who had known them as a couple, Mahesh was curious about what had gone wrong with their relationship, but he refrained from probing.

'It was obvious that she didn't want to talk about what had happened,' he observes, 'so I never asked her about it. We didn't talk about any of her past relationships either. I always believed that if a person doesn't want to talk about something, it's their privilege. Just because you're related emotionally to someone, you don't have the right to open every closet in their mind.'

Mahesh's visit to Parveen's home was meant to be a casual one. They were just two acquaintances spending time with each other for the first time without distractions coming in the way. With every turn of the conversation, they got to know each other better. They discovered commonalities, exchanged stories and shared secrets. Sunset was followed by the glow of twilight. As evening descended, the sky was littered with tiny, sparkling stars. The hours passed and it was late, but neither Parveen nor Mahesh noticed.

At some point during the evening, Parveen placed a vinyl of Farida Khanum's *'Aaj jaane ki zid na karo'* on the turntable. As the ghazal played on a loop in the background, Mahesh felt the shift in mood.

'That evening started off [with] two friends catching up,' he acknowledges, 'but the conversation kept getting deeper and the silences got comfortable. The attraction between us was palpable.'

At the back of his mind, Mahesh kept reminding himself that he had a wife and a daughter waiting for him at home. He might well have been a follower of the free-thinking spiritual guru Rajneesh for some time and influenced by his unconventional views, but he realized that releasing himself from the stranglehold of the value system he had grown up with was not easy.

'I might have parroted the whole narrative of free love, but I was held back by morality,' he confesses.

Reluctant to test his resolve further, Mahesh got up to leave. Parveen stood up as well. But she didn't follow him to the door. 'It was a long corridor from the living room to the main door,' he remembers. 'I was almost at the door when I realized that Parveen hadn't come to see me off. Just as I opened the main door, I heard her call my name.'

He turned around and walked down the corridor for the last time that night. The door to Parveen's bedroom was open.

'She was lying there on the bed, waiting for me. There was complete silence, because there was no need for words any more.' The film-maker describes this night as the one that 'completely played havoc with my already devastated life that was going nowhere'.

⁂

For a while, to Parveen, her relationship with Mahesh seemed very different from the ones she had been involved in before. For the first time ever, she found herself in what could be described as a clandestine relationship. Kabir had also been a married man when he started seeing Parveen, but his was an unconventional, open marriage, as it were. Mahesh, on the other hand, was believed to be in a stable, loving marriage. As a result, when rumours about their involvement started swirling, Parveen resorted to a lie instead of openly declaring their relationship.

'Mahesh Bhatt is not the new man in my life,' she announced to *Stardust* in its July 1978 issue. 'All through this, he has been my friend. And he still is. And there is a difference between a friendship and a relationship. I don't want to comment any further, because I don't want to start a controversy.'

Parveen was anxious for the public's focus to remain on her work and not be diverted by her love life, and she went the extra mile to hammer home the point.

'I've started believing that there is a time for work and there will be a time for love,' Parveen was quoted as saying in the July 1978 issue of *Stardust*. 'Though I've realized that the kind of love, the kind of relationship I seek is too much of a dream. I expect everything to be smooth and to go right in a relationship with my man. As long as I don't find such a relationship, I don't want to compromise at least in this one area of my life. When it happens, I'll give (it) a thought. Until then, I'll concentrate on my work, not as a substitute, but because it's what I've willingly decided to do and do it well.'

Deep in her heart, though, Parveen hated being secretive about her new relationship. Well-known scribe and former editor of *Savvy* magazine Bharathi S. Pradhan remembers spotting them at a movie theatre in the early days of their relationship.

'There had been whispers about Parveen and Mahesh, but there was no confirmation,' Pradhan acknowledges. 'I was going towards the box office to buy myself a ticket when I saw them. They quickly hid behind a pillar. A few seconds later, Mahesh emerged from behind the pillar and came over to say hello, while Parveen stayed "hidden".'

That Mahesh wished to keep their relationship under wraps was evident in the fact that he always went back to his family at the end of the day, regardless of how much time he had spent with Parveen. It did occur to her that going public would mean the end of his marriage and she'd have Mahesh all to herself. Having to share her man, as she saw it, brought all her latent insecurities to the fore.

'It started to become tough to keep a lid on things,' Mahesh says in retrospect. 'I wasn't in a position to play ducks and drakes all the time.'

Eventually, he bit the bullet and told his wife Kiran about his affair with the actress, and about six months into his relationship with her Mahesh moved in with Parveen.

From the time Parveen had debuted in Bollywood, the focus had always been on her unconventional lifestyle and she felt it was time for a shift in the narrative.

'I want to make good as an actress. I work from seven in the morning till eleven in the night and when I come home, all that I want to do is sleep,' Parveen told *Filmfare* for its 16–31 December 1978 issue. 'I have no time for nor interest in parties or get-togethers any more.'

Most of her films were multi-starrers and while she acknowledged that she didn't have pivotal roles in them, she was determined to prove her acting credentials.

'In a multi-starrer, you may have to share the footage with so many others, but you can make a mark if the role is good,' she said in the same interview.

In the big-banner films that Parveen acted in, she had some interesting roles lined up – a gypsy girl in pre-Partition India, a modern housewife pining for her husband's attention, a newspaper journalist, a pop singer and a confidante to the only female ruler of the Delhi Sultanate.

Among her co-actors, Parveen's most frequent collaborators were Amitabh Bachchan, Shashi Kapoor and Hema Malini. The first film Hema and Parveen were signed on for was Kamal Amrohi's passion project *Razia Sultan*. By the time the opus hit theatres in 1982, it had been in the making for about a decade, of which seven years had been devoted to its shooting. The film had 'Dream Girl' Hema in the role of a lifetime – playing the thirteenth-century queen Razia Sultan. Dharmendra played her Abyssinian slave general Yakut and Parveen essayed the part of Khakun, the queen's ravishing lady-in-waiting.

The film is remembered for N.B. Kulkarni's lavish sets and Bhanu Athaiya's costumes and, of course, for being the colossal failure that it was at the box office. What still provides fodder for discussion, even now, is an unlikely moment of homoeroticism between Razia and Khakun during the song 'Khwab ban kar koi aayega'. Sailing in an opulent swan-shaped boat that serves as a bed, Khakun is singing a sexually charged lullaby to Razia. As the queen's eyes glaze over and her toes tingle while she dreams of the dashing Yakut galloping on a horse, Khakun leans over to caress her face. An oversized white plume covers their faces, suggesting a kiss and the women steering the boat go wide-eyed and giggle.

In the book *Hema Malini: Beyond the Dream Girl* by Ram Kamal Mukherjee, actor Vijayendra Ghatge, who played one of Razia's suitors, Malik Ikhtiar-ud-din Altunia, says, 'Well, there was a scene between Hemaji and Parveen Babi, which had a hint of [homosexuality]. After the film was released, the press and public did talk about this scene and I still remember that. Years later, when the film was shown on Doordarshan, this particular scene, followed by a solo song sequence by Parveen Babi, was cropped. I really don't know whether Razia was a lesbian or not. I guess Kamal Saab would have been the right person to answer this question. But I would also like to say that both Hemaji and Parveen did a fantastic job. It was aesthetically done. In a way, Hema-ji deserves kudos for having the guts to do that scene.'

Hema smiles at the memory of shooting the sequence for the lilting 'Khwab ban kar koi aayega'. 'I thought it was a very sweet song,' she observes, 'but Dharamji [Dharmendra, her husband] would always say, "What is this rubbish song?" Parveen would laugh and say that Dharamji was being jealous. What Kamal Amrohi had told us about the song was that these girls lived in a harem, so this kind of a relationship between two girls was very natural. Obviously, he didn't want to show much, so he put that big feather there. When we were shooting that scene, I had no clue what it would look like on screen. We were just told that I would be lying down and Parveen comes close to me and covers our faces with the feather. It was only later when I saw the scene on screen that I realized what it looked like. Though I think Parveen was a lot smarter about things like this. She must have figured it out much before me.'

Among her contemporaries, Hema was known to be quiet and aloof, but not around Parveen.

'She was much younger than me, but I never felt uncomfortable around her. It was easy to talk to her. I remember, other heroines wouldn't interact much and I wasn't very outgoing either. I was very friendly with Parveen. If we had Shashi [Kapoor] and

Amitabh [Bachchan] on the set, it meant that we were all laughing all the time. Those two fellows were complete jokers,' she adds.

Their friendship grew from the shared experience of shooting one film for seven years. 'We used to joke about how long it was taking to make *Razia Sultan*,' says Hema. 'After shooting the last scene of a schedule, we'd say, "See you after a year to shoot the next scene."' Their future interactions might have been limited to the sets of the six films they would eventually shoot together, but Hema still has fond memories of sharing her homemade lunch with Parveen and talking about skincare routines.

'We never really talked about her personal problems,' Hema says. 'Though Parveen would ask me for advice on how to deal with pushy producers. She'd tell me that they were demanding too much and she didn't know how to deal with them.' There was one incident, though, on the sets of *Kranti* in late 1978 that cemented Hema's bond with Parveen. A fight sequence between the Anglophile Rajkumari Meenakshi (played by Hema) and Surili (with Parveen in the role) from Bharat's (Manoj Kumar's) army of freedom fighters was being filmed in Rajkamal Studios.

'We were fighting with swords and the fight master in the background was shouting, "Hit her with force." I don't know what happened, but both Parveen and I messed up our timing and I hit Parveen with my sword,' Hema remembers. 'Parveen's finger started bleeding. I was so upset, I started crying.'

She was, in fact, so distraught that eventually Parveen had to try and calm her down by saying, 'Don't worry, Hemaji, it was my fault.'

The film's leading man and director Manoj Kumar remembers feeling squeamish when he saw how much Parveen had bled from her injury.

'I went inside Parveen's make-up room to check on her,' he says. 'She laughed and said, "Don't worry, I am fine. I have a lot of blood in me." She came back to shoot the next day.'

Like the directors and producers whom Parveen had worked with earlier, it didn't take long for Manoj Kumar to be bowled over by Parveen's work ethic.

'For the song "Mara thumka badal gai chal mitwa", I wanted Parveen to imitate Bhagwan Dada, but she wasn't getting the steps,' he recalls. 'My son Kunal showed her the steps and she rehearsed with him for hours, until she was perfect. When we were shooting the scene where [the character she plays] is being molested by Manmohan, she made no fuss about anyone watching or her clothes [being in disarray]. She would have to stand in water for hours for the scenes next to the waterfall. She'd be shivering in the water, but never complained.'

When not in front of the camera, Parveen was just as easy-going. 'She was completely unlike the heroines of those days,' the actor–film-maker remembers. 'She had no demands. She wouldn't even ask for a chair or an umbrella when it was very sunny. She never asked for any special food. If there was no plate at the lunch table, she'd use her roti as a plate, put a little sabzi on it and eat standing. That's how no-fuss she was.'

Although *Kranti* did not release before early 1980, photos from the sets had started circulating soon after the film's first schedule ended in 1978. It triggered a puzzling shift in how the industry saw Parveen. There was suddenly a lot of buzz around her sex appeal. Both she and her contemporary Zeenat Aman had been seen as the epitome of 'bold' – both on and off the screen – but it was commonly held that the latter exuded greater sex appeal. All it took was photos of Parveen in a tight choli with a plunging neckline and a short ghagra to tip the scales in her favour.

In the same way that the press had built up her 'bohemian' image, reams were now written about this 'new' Parveen. To begin with, she had resolved to refrain from smoking on film sets. She conversed in Hindi more often than she had earlier. Instead of shrugging off discussions about her characters with journalists by using the standard line 'I am playing the heroine,' Parveen now went into detail about her roles. To industrywallahs, these were all signs that the actress was finally serious about her career. She wasn't an outlier any more. She belonged.

For the first time since comparisons between the two actresses had been set off, it seemed as if Parveen just might get ahead of

Parveen in a light moment

Zeenat. Except for the success of *Don*, 1978 had been a disastrous year for the latter, with two big films – Raj Kapoor's *Satyam Shivam Sundaram* and Krishna Shah's ambitious Hollywood-Bollywood co-production *Shalimar* – opening to virtually empty theatres. Parveen was still riding high on the success of *Amar Akbar Anthony* and, predictably, film-makers had all queued up to sign her on.

Parveen found comparisons with Zeenat Aman, an actress she wasn't interested in competing with, odious. Being referred to as the 'poor man's Zeenat Aman' did not go down well with her.

'I am not competing with her,' she was quoted as saying in the May 1979 issue of *Stardust*. 'You can't base your career on competition. You can't decide that you're going to be better than so-and-so, because that person is going to keep changing and improving. All you do is improve on your own, to be one better than what you were.'

Parveen was quite categorical about her intention to push herself to do better and she had no ego standing in the way when it came to asking film-makers to cast her in their productions.

'Every producer has about four five alternatives [for their cast] when he plans a project. It's up to him to make his choice,' she said in the same interview.

She understood that building connections in the industry helped get more work, but she wasn't someone whose behaviour was driven by what she could gain out of deliberately cultivating people.

'Nobody in the industry is stupid enough to let anyone take them for a ride, no matter how much *chamchagiri* [flattery] he/she does,' she went on to say. 'If people feel that I say the right things about the right people, it's because that's how I feel about them.'

When Hema Malini's mother Jaya Chakravarty decided to co-produce her first film, adding Parveen to the cast was a given. Both Hema and Mrs Chakravarty were very fond of her and there was a role in the film that she was perfect for. The film was Vijay Anand's *Ek Do Teen Chaar*, which probably had the most ambitious cast of the time – Dev Anand, Dharmendra, Shashi Kapoor, Rakhee, Hema Malini, Rishi Kapoor, Tina Munim, Amjad Khan and, of course, Parveen Babi. The invite for the film's mahurat held at Mehboob Studio on 3 October 1978 proclaimed *Ek Do Teen Chaar* to be 'the biggest Hindi film in the world'. The glittering mahurat shot had Dev Anand surrounded by Amjad Khan and his goons, his female co-stars strung up in chains and Dharmendra and Shashi Kapoor attempting a daring rescue. The shooting of the film was stalled midway, however, and *Ek Do Teen Chaar* never made it to theatres.

Such eventualities weren't exactly unheard of at the time. Films could be abandoned midway for a host of reasons or an actor could be replaced overnight after being cast in a particular role. Being unceremoniously dumped from a film was, in fact, an unpleasant reality that actors had to face more frequently than they would have liked. This was, after all, an era during which superstar directors ruled and actresses, in particular, were believed to be easily replaceable. How one reacted on losing a film to a rival left an indelible impression and had far-reaching consequences.

It's fairly well known that Yash Chopra had replaced Parveen for a role she had been originally cast in – the one that Rekha eventually essayed in *Silsila*. This wasn't the first time the director had done so just days before shooting was to begin. Immediately after the success of *Deewaar* in 1975, Chopra had wanted to work with Parveen again and signed her on for his next – *Kabhi Kabhie*, a generational love story. But on the very day of the mahurat, he decided that the actress 'wouldn't look good with Chintu [Rishi Kapoor]'.

'The next day, Chintu was to go to Paris, so I wanted to do the mahurat in Raj Kamal [Studio],' Chopra recalls in his biography *Yash Chopra: Fifty Years in Indian Cinema* by Rachel Dwyer. 'I was looking for Parveen to tell her she was not in the film. She took it sportingly. In the evening, she came to my home and said, "Yashji, don't avoid me, you must have thought it best."'

As the actress left, she requested Chopra to call her if he ever had a suitable role for her. Neetu Singh was eventually cast opposite Rishi in *Kabhi Kabhie* and the film, when it released in 1976, was a runaway success. Two years later, when Chopra was putting together the cast for *Kaala Patthar*, he immediately thought of Parveen.

☙❦❧

The second time Parveen Babi met UG, she found herself helping the spiritual leader and his Swiss companion Valentine de Kervan find a place to stay in Juhu. She also spent a lot of time with him. One evening, while UG was reading her palm, he told her that there'd be another break in her career.

Parveen was taken aback.

'I needed another break in my career like I needed a hole in my head,' she wrote in her cover story for the *Illustrated Weekly of India*. 'I was still struggling to recover what I had lost when I had walked out on my career to follow Kabir.'

The thought that she might lose everything she'd been working so hard for initially made Parveen anxious, but eventually she convinced herself that she was merely anticipating setbacks when there was scope for none.

'Producers were happy with me, audiences liked me – so why should there be a break? I didn't need it, I didn't want it and I was determined not to have it. I examined every logical and rational possibility – the future of my career looked sound,' she wrote.

Instead of worrying about UG's casual prediction, Parveen began focusing on his spiritual lessons. When she wasn't shooting for a film, she spent all her free time listening to his discourses. It was UG's no-nonsense approach to spirituality that struck a chord in her. Unlike most other gurus who promised nirvana or offered hope for a better life, UG urged those who flocked to him to stop chasing what they regarded as enlightenment and get on with their lives, instead.

'He hated the term "enlightenment",' Parveen wrote. 'His main message of purpose seemed to be to dissuade people from their search for the utopian concept of the state of enlightenment. He said nobody was going to find it, because that state of being does not exist.'

When the weather in Bombay became unbearable for UG, he decided to visit Mahabaleshwar, a quaint hill station about six hours from the city. Parveen and Mahesh, along with three of UG and Valentine's European friends, accompanied him. The group rented a small house in the hills. Those eight days were a blissful period for Parveen – helping in the kitchen, taking long walks outdoors and engaging in longer conversations that ranged from divinity to showbiz gossip.

By the end of this visit, UG had found a special place in Parveen's life.

'Every time I met UG, I liked him a little more,' she revealed. 'There was something about him that made him very trustworthy. Somewhere deep within myself, I felt here was a man I could trust, who could not take advantage of me in any manner. I also felt that if UG betrayed my trust, then there was nobody worthy of trust in this world. It was a very extreme emotion to feel, but I felt it strongly.'

UG had become one of the most important people in her life.

17

It would seem as if Parveen was going through a near-perfect phase at this point. She had found love and had an impressive line-up of films to boot. Among the big-ticket movies she was filming were Kamal Amrohi's *Razia Sultan*; Manmohan Desai's *Suhaag* and *Desh Premee*; B.R. Chopra's *The Burning Train*; Ravi Tandon's *Khud-Daar*; Manoj Kumar's *Kranti*; Yash Chopra's *Kaala Patthar* and Ramesh Sippy's *Shaan*. Parveen put the number of films in her kitty at twenty, while Ved Sharma mentioned that she had signed thirty-five films between 1978 and 1979. This is typical showbiz hyperbole, of course, and the correct number probably lies somewhere in between.

Like fellow 'masala' films director Manmohan Desai, Prakash Mehra had also signed on Parveen for multiple films – *Jwalamukhi*, *Laawaris* and *Namak Halaal* – in one go.

'He had heard that Parveen was a good artist, who was very cooperative. Once Prakashji liked an actor and had built a relationship with them, he'd repeat them in his films,' says Sushil Malik, Mehra's assistant.

All his three films that featured Parveen Babi were launched in 1979 on Mehra's birthday – 13 July. The scripts for these films were more or less ready and the films themselves were expected to release with a gap of six months between them. This was a financially feasible arrangement for the production house, with the crew being paid a monthly salary, instead of a 'per film' fee.

Laawaris was being made under the Prakash Mehra Productions banner, while the film-maker's friend Satyendra

Pal Chaudhary had undertaken to produce *Namak Halaal*. For *Jwalamukhi*, a new production house was floated under the name of Mehra's brother Babboo.

For the launch of the three films, small segments were shot for each. The mahurat shot for *Laawaris* was the famous, emotionally charged confrontation scene in a cave, which appears just before the film's intermission. Here, Amitabh Bachchan tells Parveen Babi (later, Zeenat Aman, with whom the film would be reshot), '*Laawaris woh gandi naali ka kida hota hai...* (An orphan is like a worm from a dirty drain...).' The mahurat scene for *Namak Halaal* was shot on the same day at Hotel Holiday Inn, followed by the shoot at Hotel Centaur for *Jwalamukhi*, which was slated to be the first of the three releases.

In between takes

As the actress took charge of her career and, by extension, her life, it was obvious that she was trying to bring about some necessary changes. 'I could not go on being the way I was. I had to change. Part of it was consciously done, part of it was natural and part of it happened due to the new circumstances. I may not be deliriously happy about it, but I am not unhappy either,' she was candid enough to admit during her interview for *Stardust* that came out in its May 1979 issue.

She went on to claim in that interview that she had become more responsible in every aspect of her life from financial matters ('Whenever I am free, I try to sort out my papers and taxes...') to her relationship with her mother ('Previously, I would let weeks go [by] without calling her. Now I ring her up every Sunday...').

She realized, of course, that there were sacrifices involved and she would have to exercise self-discipline and rein in her natural spontaneity to some extent, but that was a small price to pay for the benefits that came with the changes.

'I know I can never go back to being what I was,' she declared during the *Stardust* interview. 'I am different today, and I will be even more different tomorrow – maybe better, maybe worse – who knows? But one can't go back.'

꘎꘎꘎

The early days of Parveen and Mahesh's relationship were exhilarating and full of passion. She may have been considered one of the most glamorous women in India – 'Parveen could really stop a room when she entered,' says Rauf Ahmed, veteran journalist and former editor of *Filmfare* – but at home, she was devoid of the usual trappings of a movie star. A beauty on screen, Parveen looked even better scrubbed clean and without make-up. When she wasn't shooting, her long hair would be coated in coconut or olive oil and bundled up in a messy bun. Her home, intimate, comfortable and fuss-free, was Parveen's refuge from the glitz and pressures of Bollywood.

'On a normal day, she'd stay at home and cook for us,' says Mahesh. 'She'd spend hours poring over issues of *Architectural Digest*; she was obsessed with interior decoration.'

Parveen idolized Mahesh. She thought he was the most talented and intelligent man she knew. She was generous, not just with her compliments and her undivided attention, but also with money. At the time they were together Mahesh was going through a phase of deep financial distress. Parveen showered him with gifts. On her shopping trips, she would always buy something for him, to the extent that the few friends she still had suspected Mahesh was sponging on her. They weren't the only ones who secretly held this opinion and both Parveen and Mahesh were painfully aware of it.

One of the first trips the couple took out of Bombay was to Switzerland.

'She felt it was the only way she could be with me, without the press hovering over her starry life. It was not very respectable to be attached to a man who was a nobody, a boyfriend you couldn't flaunt,' says Mahesh.

The plan was for the couple to spend some time with UG Krishnamurti at his chalet 'Sunbeam' in Gstaad, Switzerland, before travelling on to London.

Their first trip together was meant to strengthen their relationship, bring them closer. But quite the opposite happened. During this trip, the initial feelings of attraction that had drawn Mahesh and Parveen together and promised to develop into a deeper level of intimacy began to wear off. Mahesh had started noticing annoying habits and shortcomings in her that he had overlooked or ignored during the year they had been together. These were, undoubtedly, little hiccups, but increasingly Mahesh began to feel that perhaps he and Parveen were mismatched.

UG too must have noticed some element of strain in their relationship that led him to conclude it wouldn't last. One afternoon, while they were sitting in the garden of his rented chalet, he brought up the issue with Parveen. Though he insisted that this wasn't a prediction he was making about her future, but merely hazarding an 'educated guess' as to how her relationship with Mahesh might turn out, it made a deep impact on her and filled her with a sense of foreboding. She simply couldn't get it out of her mind.

'No! I did not need a third broken relationship in my life,' she wrote later in her article for the *Illustrated Weekly of India*. 'I had already been through two and that was quite enough. How I wished I could brush aside UG's comments and forget about them, but I couldn't.'

The income gap between Parveen and Mahesh had always cast a shadow on their relationship as a couple, but now this divisive issue began taking a serious toll on it. While they were in Gstaad, Mahesh wanted to buy a gift to take back to his daughter, but 'I didn't have money', he says. He asked UG for a small loan.

'UG being UG gave me the money in front of Parveen,' Mahesh elaborates. 'She was surprised and asked him why he was giving me money. He told her that I wanted to buy something for my daughter, so "he naturally doesn't want to take the money from you".'

This really upset Parveen.

'She saw it as an indication that I wasn't committed to her in the relationship.'

No matter how much he tried explaining that he couldn't possibly live off her, Parveen just wouldn't understand his predicament. Eventually, they moved on from the tricky subject, but the fault lines in their relationship had cracked open.

From Gstaad, Parveen and Mahesh travelled to London.

'We were sharing a plush apartment that she had paid for,' Mahesh says. 'It was beyond my imagination to afford a place like that.'

Once again, money became a bone of contention. He remembers a particularly bitter argument over a restaurant bill. In those days, a restriction was in place over how much foreign currency an Indian national could hold. It was a common (though illegal) practice at the time to get money transferred through a hawala transaction.

'We were supposed to meet the Englishman who used to keep her money, for dinner,' Mahesh explains. 'He was supposed to hand over her money. As the evening was coming to an end, Parveen started giving me money under the table to pay the dinner bill.'

Mahesh reveals that he was confused. He couldn't understand what was going on. Parveen was trying to be discreet, but their English dinner companion sensed what was going on and the situation became even more awkward and embarrassing for Mahesh. Eventually, the bill was paid and the couple left for their apartment.

'Parveen was enraged,' Mahesh recalls. 'We had a huge fight about it. I told her that it was her money and she should have paid the bill. I couldn't understand why she felt the need to pretend. It was demeaning [for] me.'

Their recurring differences over money forced Mahesh to recognize Parveen's need to keep up appearances. From the time she was a little girl in Junagadh, she had hidden behind a façade of perfection. Her choices were always informed by what people expected of her. Through her years in Ahmedabad, she had grown up to be 'the bohemian girl' and that was the image with which she had arrived in Bombay. It probably wasn't a calculated move to begin with, but it had certainly made it easier for her to go through life without having to reveal her real self – the one with flaws – a person others might not take to.

'There always was this conflict between the "posturing" her and the "real" her,' Mahesh explains. 'This side to her was what separated us ideologically. Staying true to myself was the mantra that guided my life and this kind of posturing was a huge turn-off for me. I was not very impressed by her views and ideas and she could see that.'

It wasn't just the fights that made him uneasy. He had started noticing little signs that disconcerted him. Parveen hated being alone and developed an intangible fear of odd things around the house. She would get Mahesh to check inside cupboards and the space under the bed on several occasions.

Parveen's growing fears weren't restricted to just inanimate objects though, and she'd begun reading into people's words and actions and looking for hidden meanings.

While they were at UG's Swiss chalet, the spiritual teacher once again offered to read Parveen's palm.

'He wasn't some kind of fortune-teller, but people thought he was clairvoyant, while UG did it more as a joke,' says Mahesh.

While reading the actress's palm, UG told her that 'there's a break in her fate line, so she'd get marooned somewhere'.

'It was meant to be a joke,' Mahesh explains, 'but it stayed with Parveen.'

A few days later, when they were in London, he woke up one night and discovered that Parveen was missing from the bed they shared. He went looking for her and found her sitting near a lamp in the living room, staring at her palm.

'This became her defining image for me,' he says.

It was an image that Mahesh recreated in *Arth*, the film he based on his relationship with Parveen. 'In the film, Smita Patil [who played Parveen] sits and keeps looking at her palm.'

Their vacation abroad marked a tipping point in the actress's relationship with Mahesh and it would never regain its original footing. Parveen's insecurities had begun to drive a wedge between them, particularly when they were manifested in her distrust of him.

'Even after I had moved in with her,' observes Mahesh, 'Parveen suspected that I still went to see my wife. I didn't, but she'd wait by the window for me to come home. And sniff my clothes after she thought I had gone to sleep.'

Mahesh would recreate these moments of erratic behaviour in his 1982 film, *Arth*.

⊚⊰⊚

The disturbing changes that were taking place within Parveen's mind began showing up once she was back at work as well. Among the first to notice them were members of her staff. Bharat

Godambe, who had been doing her make-up almost every single day for seven years at a stretch, remembers days when the actress would be completely withdrawn. In the process of applying layers and layers of make-up on her face, he'd notice tears welling up in her eyes.

'She wouldn't talk to anyone. If we tried to engage her in conversation, she'd look at us blankly. She'd cry and smoke cigarette after cigarette,' Godambe recalls.

As soon as she was called on set, though, a weak smile would replace the tears.

'She'd go out on the set and shoot a romantic scene or a song. Everything would seem normal. But then she'd return to the room and it was the same thing again,' Godambe says.

While Parveen's life seemed vibrant and full of promise on the surface, her inner journey was becoming a slow descent into hell.

18

Having returned home from his holiday in Europe with Parveen, Mahesh couldn't ward off the feeling of impending doom growing inside him. There was a sense that something wasn't right, something that he couldn't quite put a finger on. He felt as if his world was about to crumble around him and it wasn't a state of mind he was familiar with.

Unable to cope with it, he reached out to his friend and actor Uday Chandra, who suffered from paranoid schizophrenia.

'He took me to Dr S.M. Lulla's clinic in Lamington Road,' Mahesh remembers.

The doctor was one of Bombay's foremost psychiatrists and head of BYL Nair Hospital's psychiatry department.

'I told him I was having a strange feeling about the unorthodox life I was leading, along with the cumulative strain of my career not doing well,' says Mahesh.

Dr Lulla explained to him that he was probably just stressed and prescribed some medication to help him sleep.

Once Mahesh had found a way of coping with his anxiety, his life with Parveen went back to normal. They would wake up together on most mornings; she'd go off to shoot multiple shifts in studios across the city, while he tried to get his next film off the floor.

'She'd usually wake up before me, put on her dressing gown and go outside to get her hair and make-up done for the day,' he recalls. Before she left for the day, she'd walk into the bedroom to give Mahesh a kiss. 'She'd be fully made up and have rollers in her hair; I could feel the paint on her face,' he says.

One overcast July morning in 1979, Parveen woke up as usual and stepped out to get ready for a day of shooting for director Prakash Mehra's *Jwalamukhi*, in which she had been cast opposite Shatrughan Sinha. Mahesh was still in bed, drifting in and out of sleep. When Parveen tiptoed back into their bedroom, he was expecting his daily peck. Instead, she whispered that they should not have any conversation outside their room. Before he could react to her words, she had left.

It was a day Mahesh is unlikely to forget, for his life as he had known it would change forever.

When he came home that evening, Parveen's mother, who was visiting, answered the door with an anxious looking Ved Sharma standing in the background.

'*Munna, dekh...Parveen ko kya ho gaya* (Son, look... something's happened to Parveen),' Jamal told him.

'I couldn't understand what was happening,' says Mahesh. 'It was all very ominous. The atmosphere in the house was charged. The servants' body language had changed.'

He walked into the house and headed straight for their bedroom.

'Here she was, curled up on the floor like a beast in one corner of the room,' he says. 'She was still in her film costume. She was holding a knife; it was the knife she used at the breakfast table.'

Mahesh slowly walked towards her. Before he could sit down next to her, Parveen whispered to him, 'Shut the door.' When he sat down close to her on the floor, her delusions came tumbling out and the source of her fear was revealed.

'They tried to kill me,' she told him. He asked who was trying to kill her.

'Amitabh Bachchan,' she replied, urging him to lower his voice, lest he be overheard. 'The room is bugged,' she went on. 'You don't know; you are an innocent man. They are going to drop a chandelier on me.'

Though he had had no past experience of dealing with someone in the middle of a psychotic episode, Mahesh was the only one in Parveen's life who recognized that evening that there was something seriously wrong with her.

'As a child, I had seen a south Indian actor named Ranjan in our neighbourhood,' he recalls. 'He was said to be a victim of schizophrenia and that was my only reference.'

That night, Parveen didn't sleep. Neither did anyone else in the house. Throughout, she kept muttering that Amitabh Bachchan was trying to kill her. At some point, she started claiming that her manager Ved Sharma was also involved. As morning broke, Jamal, Ved and Mahesh got into a huddle to try and find a solution. Parveen was expected to report for work in a couple of hours. She had multiple films on the floor at the time, including *Kranti*, *Jwalamukhi*, *Shaan* and *Biwi O Biwi*. Yet, she was clearly in no condition to step out of the house, let alone face the camera. During the night, Mahesh managed to piece together the events of the day that had apparently tipped her over the edge.

Parveen was expected on the sets of Prakash Mehra's *Jwalamukhi* for a 2 p.m. shift. They were to shoot portions of the song 'Kabhi tumne kisi ko phaansa' with Kader Khan and Bindu, who were playing parents to Parveen's character in the film. Also involved in the shoot were Shatrughan Sinha, the love interest, and Ram Sethi, who played the person Parveen's character was getting engaged to.

'We were shooting at Hotel Centaur, near the airport,' Sethi remembers. 'Shatru was the hero. In the scene he jeopardizes the engagement and throws me in a swimming pool. There was a small stage next to the pool where we were shooting.'

There was also a short scene with a few dialogues that had to be canned before the song was shot.

Two hours had passed after call time and there was still no sign of Parveen. In an industry where actors are perpetually late, this wouldn't have been a big deal, but Parveen had built a reputation for being punctual. When she finally reached the hotel at around 4.30 p.m., Prakash Mehra was keen on quickly shooting the short scene before they started filming the more elaborate song sequence.

'This was a scene that had only Kader Khan and me with Parveen,' Bindu recalls. 'The problem was that Parveen couldn't remember the dialogue. Parveen used to be so good with dialogues that we couldn't understand what was going on. Retakes used to be expensive and after the fourth or fifth take, Prakashji started getting angry. The angrier he got, the more nervous Parveen got and ended up making more mistakes.'

The situation reached a point where Mehra finally gave up and cancelled the shoot for that day. Parveen ran out of the hotel in tears and got into her car. Her staff's response to this development was purely based on muscle memory – always follow and protect the star. They jumped into the car along with her and brought her home. They had little understanding of what was going on, because there was no external manifestation of her illness. But Parveen's mind was in disarray.

In 'The Confessions of Parveen Babi', referred to earlier, the actress described this breakdown with chilling candour.

'One day, I was sitting in my make-up room with full film make-up, when I noticed that my skin had lost its lustre, my foundation had turned dark on my face. I felt deep fear in the pit of my stomach. That was the beginning of my nightmare. For the next two days, I tried desperately to continue working. I kept on reporting for work in that condition, suppressing and controlling my fear, until finally one afternoon, in the middle of a shot, the fear took over. I became frantic. I ran out of the stage, sat in my car and reached home. Every muscle in my body was shivering. My eyes were bulging out with fear. I was feeling sick, panic-stricken and I lay huddled in my bed. From then on, things only got worse'.

꧁꧂

Ved Sharma began making the necessary calls to explain Parveen's absence from the sets. He informed those concerned that she wasn't well, but chose to keep the details of her ailment vague. He promised that she'd be back at work in a day or two.

With dialogues being written on the set and directors deciding what they wanted to shoot only once they got there, film-making then wasn't as structured as it is today. A certain flexibility was always maintained in shooting schedules. Not too many directors were, therefore, miffed with Parveen for taking some days off from work. After all, it was just a matter of a few days, as Ved had assured them.

The next step was to get Parveen the necessary treatment. Unfortunately, Mahesh was the only one at home who realized that she urgently needed psychiatric help. 'But I was alone. I had no status in her life. I was not a credible entity in the industry. I had no rights as a boyfriend or anything. Her mother and secretary were there to make those decisions,' he says. There was some talk about getting Dr Lulla to see Parveen, but it led nowhere. It didn't help that Jamal thought her daughter was possessed.

Over the next few days, it became clear that Parveen was not going to get better on her own. She made the servants at home open up the air conditioner in her bedroom to look for electronic bugs. She had not eaten or changed out of her clothes for days. She'd walk across to the young Malayali couple who lived on the same floor and ask if she could sleep in their home, because there was something wrong in hers.

'It was just never-ending,' says Mahesh. 'One day, she said, "They'll kill me at six o'clock." So when it was past six, I pointed out that she was still alive and unharmed. She said, "No, it's not today; it's tomorrow six o'clock." And this would continue until another delusion took over.'

It was clear by now that Parveen was convinced that Amitabh Bachchan was out to kill her. Slowly, she began believing that everyone around her – including Ved Sharma, her cook Burma, her mother and, eventually, even Mahesh – was colluding with Bachchan to harm her. When Mahesh tried to reason with her, asking why he, of all people, would want to kill her, Parveen replied that 'they' had kidnapped his daughter Pooja and were holding her for ransom. The only way for Mahesh to save her was to give in to 'their' demand of killing the actress.

'I went to Pooja's school, Petit, in Bandra that day and asked her if she could do something for me,' Mahesh recalls. 'I told her Parveen's not well and asked her to come with me to Parveen's house. I had to hide this from her mother. Pooja must have been about six years old at the time and she still clearly remembers that day. I brought her to Parveen's straight from school. She was still in her uniform. Parveen spoke with Pooja and even gifted her a bottle of Fidji perfume from among the many on her dresser.'

After Pooja had left, Mahesh asked Parveen if she was convinced that his daughter was safe and not being held to ransom in a bid to have the actress killed. To which she retorted with her distorted logic, 'They've let her out only for some time to convince me [that no attempt was being made on her life].'

Mahesh realized that he needed an ally to get Parveen the necessary help. He reached out to Danny and called him over to Parveen's for dinner.

Danny recollects the three of them sitting after dinner and having either liqueur or brandy. There were some silver-lined conch shells on the sitting room table and he commented on the use of these shells in the monasteries of Sikkim. 'I picked it up and blew it, and suddenly she freaked out. I asked her what happened. Then Mahesh took me to the other room and explained to me — that was the first time I came to know that she wasn't well,' says Danny.

'I got to know a lot of things, like how Parveen thought that there was poison in her food, so she made others taste her food,' Danny says. 'Parveen usually slept with a hard pillow and one day, her mother bought her a new, soft pillow to use. She tore up the pillow, because she thought there was a knife hidden in it and that her mother wanted to kill her.'

Seeing how fearful and suspicious she was of everything around her, Mahesh had an inkling that Parveen would react adversely if he got doctors to visit her at home. Therefore, Danny's apartment became the venue for all conversations relating to her treatment.

'I took Kim into confidence and told her what was happening with Parveen and not to tell anyone about it,' Danny says. 'So the only people who knew the truth about Parveen's illness were Vedji, Mahesh, Kim and I, and we kept it a secret. Doctors would be called to my house. They said this was a case of schizophrenia. We'd have meetings to discuss the medicines and treatment that could be given, but eventually it didn't work.'

A severe and debilitating mental illness, schizophrenia is often mistaken for manic depression or bipolar disorder, but is quite different from both. Unlike the other forms of illness, it isn't mood-altering, but it does hamper the ability to think rationally. Manic depressives can continue working and functioning efficiently, as has been the case with Vincent Van Gogh, Stephen Fry and Francis Ford Coppola, all icons in their respective fields. Schizophrenia, however, weakens the mind, slowly making it waste away. Among its most famous victims was John Nash, the brilliant mathematician and Nobel Prize winner for Economics on whose life the Russell Crowe starrer *A Beautiful Mind* is based.

However intelligent or insightful one may be, schizophrenia affects the way one thinks, feels and behaves. Fear and delusions can cloud the mind to such an extent that one risks losing all touch with reality. Imagine having a chorus of angry, disembodied voices shouting at you. Or being trapped in a nightmare you can't wake up from, with bizarre, terrifying, jumbled images clamouring inside your head. Parveen was now living this never-ending nightmare.

'Have you ever wondered what it is like to function in life, distrusting everything and everybody?' she wrote in the *Illustrated Weekly of India*. 'Slowly, one by one, I lost trust in everybody and everything around me. We trust most of the things and people around us without questioning. We trust the food we eat, the water we drink, the air we breathe. We trust basic modern amenities like phones, air conditioners, fans, not to mention doctors, medicines, family, friends, most of the world and most of humanity. It is impossible to function in life without trusting. And that is precisely what happened to me. I lost trust in everything and everybody, including my mother and my boyfriend.'

※

For reasons that aren't difficult to fathom, the select group of people who knew of Parveen's condition actively discouraged visitors from coming to her home. On the rare occasion that the actress spoke to someone on the phone, she sounded 'normal'.

'One moment, she'd be trembling with fear; the next, she could carry on a regular conversation with someone on the phone and then go back to being terrified,' observes Mahesh. 'People outside just wouldn't believe that there was something wrong with her.'

One of the few persons other than the family who managed to see Parveen in the middle of this psychotic phase was Jyotsna, her friend and former roommate from Ahmedabad. In town for a play, she tried to call Parveen at home, but no one answered the phone. One afternoon, she was passing by her friend's apartment and decided to drop in. If nothing, Jyotsna reasoned, she could leave a note with the housekeeper Maggie so that Parveen would know she was in Bombay.

'I rang the doorbell a couple of times, but no one answered,' Jyotsna recalls. 'I could make out that there were people inside, but no one opened the door. Eventually, Maggie opened the door slightly and quickly stepped out. She whispered, "*Madam bimaar hain* (Madam's unwell)." I must have looked very confused, because the next moment she opened the main door and pulled me in.'

As the two were walking towards the kitchen, Parveen stumbled out of her bedroom.

'Who is it? Don't open the door. He is standing there with a knife,' she warned, sounding completely manic.

'She also looked haggard,' Jyotsna remembers. 'I had never seen her like that. She was wearing a maroon gown; her hair had come loose from her plait and her skin looked patchy and dirty. She couldn't stand, so she was leaning against the wall.'

When her eyes finally focused on the visitor standing in the kitchen, she recognized her old friend.

'It's you,' she observed, adding, 'I thought someone had come to kill me.'

Jyotsna was bewildered. She couldn't understand what she had walked into.

'Why would anyone want to kill you?' she asked Parveen.

Maggie, who was standing close to Jyotsna, signalled to her that she should avoid questioning the actress or challenging her absurd claims. But at that moment, Mahesh walked out of their bedroom and gently guided Parveen back to the room. Jyotsna followed them in and so did Maggie, carrying a bowl of soup for Parveen. Mahesh took the bowl and started to feed her.

Parveen turned towards Maggie and said, 'You taste it first.'

Mahesh, Jamal and Maggie had been through this routine a few times in the past and were used to it, but Jyotsna couldn't stop herself from asking why this was necessary.

'The soup is poisoned. People want to kill me,' Parveen explained.

Maggie finally gave in and had a spoonful. Only then did Parveen accept the bowl and agree to have the soup.

While she was doing so, Jyotsna took in the odd tableau before her. Except for the soft sounds of Parveen eating, the room was unnaturally silent. Almost as if the people there were holding their breath in anticipation of the next outburst. After she was done, Parveen wanted to sit in the drawing room, but was too weak and unsteady on her feet to make it there on her own. So Mahesh carried her there. Once installed in the drawing room, Parveen curled up in a foetal position. When Jyotsna finally sat down next to her, the actress shared her delusions of being in danger yet again.

'You don't know what I am going through,' she murmured. 'I can't eat or drink anything. I can't stand. People are trying to kill me.'

Many years later, Jyotsna would watch Mahesh Bhatt's telefilm *Phir Teri Kahani Yaad Aayee* and be reminded of the unnerving afternoon she had spent in Parveen's home.

Having seen and heard everything she had since she entered her friend's house, Jyotsna still could not decide how to react. Eventually, she left. But she couldn't stop thinking about Parveen, about how she seemed to have 'gone mad'. There was such little information about mental health issues at the time that one couldn't really blame Jyotsna, or anyone else for that matter, for entertaining such thoughts. The common perception at the time swung between the extremes of 'normalcy' and 'insanity'. There was no in between. And if you were, indeed, afflicted, you were bound to either spend the rest of your life in a state-operated mental asylum or as a homeless wanderer.

※

While Parveen continued to suffer, film-makers had begun to lose their patience and their temper.

'I still remember those days – they were a nightmare,' Ved Sharma told *Star & Style* for their 16–29 October 1981 issue. 'The doctors couldn't state definitely how soon she would recover. It could be a week, it could take months. I was in a quandary. What could I tell the producers? Should I tell them to wait or not to wait? They kept insisting on meeting her personally, but I knew she was in no condition to see anyone. I refused to let them in. Some of them abused me. But I was adamant. All I wanted was that Parveen should get well.'

Propelled by the success of *Sholay*, director Ramesh Sippy had kicked off *Shaan*, yet another mammoth multi-starrer with Sunil Dutt, Amitabh Bachchan, Shashi Kapoor, Shatrughan Sinha, Rakhee, Parveen, Bindiya Goswami and Kulbhushan Kharbanda. A lavish set had been erected at Film City for the shooting and Parveen's illness was holding up what was already turning out to be a difficult and expensive film. Then there was

Kranti, which had already been in the making for over a year, not to mention the three Prakash Mehra films – *Laawaris, Namak Halaal* and *Jwalamukhi* and a dozen others.

Ved still didn't know how long it would take for her to recover sufficiently to start shooting again. By now, the press had also started sniffing around. So he bought himself some time by telling everyone that Parveen was down with jaundice and should be back on set in a month's time.

Mahesh, in the meantime, was trying everything he could to get her the treatment she urgently needed. Weeks had passed since the first night of her breakdown and there was no hope of recovery in sight.

'Apart from Dr Lulla, there was another doctor in Vile Parle who would come to treat her,' he recalls. 'Medicines had to be administered through Parveen's food or she wouldn't take them. After a point, she started forcing her mother to eat the food, because she thought her mother was trying to kill her.'

The traditional route of psychiatry and oral medication was obviously not working. The next available procedure, Mahesh was told, would involve the administration of electric shocks.

※

With U.G. Krishnamurti in Bombay, Mahesh took Parveen to meet him at director Vijay Anand's home in Pali Hill, Bandra.

One piece of advice that UG gave the actress was to immediately leave the city.

'I told him I didn't have the courage to travel alone,' Parveen wrote in the *Illustrated Weekly of India*. 'He said, "Courage will come." Unfortunately, I did not follow his advice. I could not. I was so full of fear that I could not imagine from where "the courage will come"! I discussed with him whether I should accept medical help. Doctors had been brought in, but so far I had refused to take any medicines. I distrusted both doctors and the medicines. He said it should be entirely my decision.'

On their way home after meeting UG, Parveen jumped out of the moving car, because she was convinced that there was a bomb in the vehicle.

'I had to run after her and drag her back to the car. People thought we were fighting and that I was abusing her,' says Mahesh. It didn't take long for this news to reach the press. The narrative that was built, both in the press and in Bollywood was that drug addiction and a promiscuous lifestyle had contributed to Parveen's mental breakdown.

It was only after about two days that she finally agreed to take the pills prescribed for her.

'I swallowed a handful of tablets without having any trust or faith in them. I felt so weak, I could hardly get up from my bed – medicines slowed me down, but they did not bring back the trust I had lost,' Parveen wrote. 'UG would come to visit me whenever I called him. He would ask me not to be afraid and time and again assured me that nothing would happen to me, that he would personally protect me.'

But she had already retreated to a dark place in her mind where these assurances made no impression.

Everything Parveen felt at the time was intensified a thousand times over in her mind. In her article she describes an episode that not merely offers an insight into what she was going through mentally, but also highlights how crucial UG's presence was in her life:

> One day, I myself experienced something quite inexplicable and extraordinary. I had just finished a hot cup of tea at UG's place and I began to feel cold and my legs felt weak. It was not the ordinary feeling of cold or weakness. I identified those sensations in my body as loss of life. Yes, I was losing life from my body, starting from my legs. I was dying! As absurd as it sounds, it did happen to me. UG asked me to go home. He put a shawl around my shoulders, shook my hand and said, 'Goodbye.' Mahesh took me to the car. I couldn't walk. I was reeling, as though drunk. I had no control over my legs; Mahesh was literally dragging me

to the car. I was in panic — I was dying! I collapsed in the car. I could not believe I was dying! Halfway to my home, I felt as though my stomach had turned into a suction pump and was drawing all the air out of me.

We reached home. Mahesh physically carried me to my flat. They put me on my bed — I lay there flat on my back, my respiratory pattern changed. Instead of inhaling and exhaling, my body only exhaled. So far, I had felt panic, disbelief and I had been fighting what was happening to me. Whatever was happening to me was so powerful that I could not fight it for long. It was taking me over physically and with great speed. I had no alternative but to surrender to it. I surrendered to this great physical force that was draining out the life from me. I mentally came to terms with the fact that this was the end of me. I was dying — I had no choice in the matter — all I could do was die!

Now my entire body from the neck down felt lifeless. The only evidence of life I felt was in my throat—two veins in my throat were still throbbing. I also felt a throbbing sensation in the middle of my throat between the collar bones. I could not move any part of my body except my head. I could still think, see and talk. My mother, Mahesh, my secretary, servants, all stood around my bed, some crying. I wanted to be on the floor, closer to the ground. They lifted me and put me on the ground. I wanted to be fed some water, and I wanted to speak to UG. They fed me some water with a spoon, dialled UG's number, and held the receiver to my ear. I said in the phone, 'UG, I am going.' UG laughed and said, 'Where?' I told him I wanted to see him. He said, 'Can you hold on until seven o'clock? I have some people here.' I said, 'I think I can. I'll see you at seven.'

I lay there waiting — I must have waited about half an hour; the doorbell rang, I knew it was UG. I asked someone to get to the door and looked at the watch. It was seven sharp. I heard UG enter the apartment. He walked through the passage, removed his chappals and emerged into the room I was lying in. At that very moment, I felt a throbbing between my eyebrows, just above the nose, in my pituitary gland. He smiled, gave me his hand and said, 'Get up.' I felt life return to my body. I took his hand and got up.'

In the same account, Parveen acknowledged that people around her 'were going through a different kind of hell'. 'My mother could not understand what was happening to me. Mahesh was incapable of coping with the situation. He seemed more concerned about himself than about me and I could sense it. This made things even worse for me – the nightmare continued. The only time I felt fearless and secure was in UG's presence. I believed that UG was the one person who would never harm or hurt me, and that he had extraordinary powers which could protect me.'

It is important to note that this account dates back to 1984, when Parveen had quit Bollywood. She was living in the US with UG and Valentine for much of the time and her life completely revolved around the guru. Though her relationship with UG was purely platonic, Parveen was repeating the cycle she'd invariably get caught in during her romantic relationships. The man in her life would become the centre of her existence and she saw him as the protector and provider. Prey to that kind of extreme emotional dependence, she probably wasn't the most reliable chronicler of a period she describes as a nightmare.

Meanwhile, there was growing pressure from film-makers who were unconcerned about or failed to understand what Parveen was going through. There was even a prevailing suspicion among them that Mahesh was simply exaggerating the gravity of her ailment. All they were interested in was how soon they could start shooting their respective films with the actress. Being a part of the industry, Mahesh thought it might help if he approached directors himself and shared the truth about Parveen's condition.

'I had to go and convince Ramesh Sippy that Parveen needed therapy and it would take at least eight weeks,' he says.

His candour only made matters worse and he was seen as the villain in the actress's life.

Since Parveen was in no condition to make the right decisions about her treatment, everyone looked to her mother to take charge. The problem was that Jamal, having failed to recognize her daughter's illness as a serious one, was simply looking for respite from the issues triggered by Parveen's ailment.

At this point, Mahesh began to fear that Jamal would agree with the doctors' suggestion that Parveen be given electric shocks.

'So I called UG and he said nobody really knew anything and all they're interested in was to prop her up like a doll in front of the camera. "They aren't interested in seeing Parveen get better. Once their work is over, they'll dump her. If you give her electric shock treatment, that's the end of her. If you really love her, run away from there."'

So, that's what Mahesh did. About three months after Parveen's first breakdown, he decided to take her away from Bombay. Their destination was Bangalore (now Bengaluru), not just because it was far from the demands of showbiz, but also because UG was there at the time.

Taking Parveen from Bombay to Bangalore was an ordeal, however.

'I remember going to the airport manager to get Parveen a wheelchair,' says Mahesh. 'That man sneered at me and said, "You think I'm a Bollywood fan? I know you people are leading a perverse life and this is what the gods have willed on you. There will be no exceptions made."'

Even decades after this interaction, Mahesh recalls shaking his head in disbelief. Despite him showing the airport manager Parveen's medical reports, the man had refused to budge.

'He said to me, "These medical reports can be bought by people like you." That's when I realized how much the media had poisoned the air that even an airport manager was completely biased.'

Despite such obstacles, Parveen and Mahesh managed to board their flight to Bangalore without any further incident. Mahesh, though, was on high alert.

'I was worried. What if she had an episode [when the flight was] mid-air? I kept remembering that time she jumped out of the moving car. If she tried something on the flight, I wouldn't be able to do anything.' Through the whole journey, starting from Parveen's home in Bombay to the time they met UG at Bangalore airport, Mahesh kept telling her, 'We're going to UG, we're going to UG... there's light at the end of the tunnel. UG's there.'

Amrish Puri and Sanjeev Kumar were on the same flight.

'I think they were going for some shoot,' Mahesh says. 'Amrishji came up to speak with us. He was very nice.'

What Mahesh didn't realize, though, was that somewhere along the way from her home to Bombay airport, Parveen had gone from being 'petrified of the journey' to being 'totally devoid of feeling'.

'Since fear and distrust were the only two feelings I had felt for weeks, I became an automaton, a physical being propelled in forward momentum by a force within me,' she wrote. 'My head held itself high and my body became straight and erect – the physical stance of a totally fearless person. I felt some force moving within my stomach, slowly catching hold of it. These past few weeks, I had felt and experienced everything in my stomach. Fear used to start as a physical sensation in the pit of my stomach and used to physically churn the inside of my stomach. I felt as though this force was holding me together. I never again felt "scared to death".'

UG was there at the airport to receive Parveen and Mahesh when their flight landed in Bangalore.

'The minute I saw him, I handed Parveen over to him,' Mahesh remembers. 'It required a more sturdy and sane mind to deal with her.'

19

The moment the flight landed at Bangalore airport, UG took Parveen, along with Mahesh, to the home of his long-time follower K. Chandrasekhar Babu and his wife Suguna on Anjaneya Temple Street in Basavanagudi, a bustling residential neighbourhood in the southern part of the city. Parveen was so frail when she reached that for over forty-eight hours she couldn't step out of the room her hosts had prepared for her in their home. Babu vividly remembers the first few days of hosting their visitors from Bombay.

'Parveen was dressed all in black when she came to our house,' he recalls. 'She got off from the taxi and ran into the house. UG took her straight into her room.'

To ensure their guests' privacy, the couple, along with their young daughters, had moved out of the main house and into an outhouse at the back of the property. UG, Valentine and Parveen occupied the three bedrooms on the upper floors of the main house. The actress's room on the first floor adjoined a glass-covered balcony that overlooked a picture-perfect street lined with temples and gardens. It took Parveen a few days to step out of her shell.

'Change of environment was the solution to my problem,' she wrote in her 1984 cover article for the *Illustrated Weekly of India*. 'I felt secure in this environment. The fact that UG was physically present all the time was my main source of comfort.'

Mahesh, in the meantime, had returned to Bombay. 'On October 16th, UG weaned me away from her and told me, "It's a dangerous cocktail, you and her. And if you love her, leave her." That's the day the relationship ended. I returned [to Bombay] and picked up the pieces of my life,' says Mahesh.

As the paranoia that had taken hold of her loosened its grip, Parveen's eyes lost their vacant look. Her smiles were warm once again. Every day she was taking baby steps towards being a functioning person. 'I no longer locked doors and windows,' she wrote in her piece for the *Illustrated Weekly of India*. 'I went out for short walks with UG, met people freely and trustingly, started eating proper meals and was able to sleep soundly and peacefully. The difference between my condition in Bombay and my condition in Bangalore was astounding.'

Within a fortnight, it seemed as if she had recovered. The homebody that she was at heart, Parveen unconsciously gravitated towards the seemingly mundane life of her hosts.

'She'd come to our part of the house and spend time in the kitchen with me,' Suguna recalls fondly, adding, 'she'd cook with me or play with my daughters.'

In the mornings, she'd help Suguna pack lunch for Babu. Once he left for work, Parveen would play with their two-and-half-year-old, while Suguna finished her chores around the house. Even as she grew comfortable with her hosts, the actress continued to feel uneasy when other disciples came to listen to UG's discourses.

'She'd either quickly run up to her room and stay there while there were other people in the house, or she'd come to the outhouse to spend time with us,' Babu says.

Parveen's faith in UG was so unshakeable that her fear and mistrust of doctors appeared to disappear in his presence. He called in Dr H. Narayan Murthy, an old friend and head of clinical psychology at the National Institute of Mental Health and Neuro Sciences (NIMHANS), to treat Parveen.

'UG insisted that Parveen see Dr Murthy and take the medicines that he prescribed [for] her,' says Babu. 'The doctor felt that UG's presence in her life was helping Parveen.'

For probably the first time in her life, the actress was diligent about taking her medicines, but not necessarily because she believed they were helping her to recover. 'I rested a lot,' she wrote in the *Illustrated Weekly of India*. 'Though the fears had disappeared completely, I still had a lot of recovering to do physically. I had grown extremely weak. My voice had deteriorated. Most of my nerves and my brain cells had to heal. UG would, from time to time, transmit some energy through my palm and assure me that I could recover completely. At that time, I strongly felt that it was UG's energy and not the medicines that were helping me.'

With every passing day, Parveen settled into her life in Bangalore, far from the bright lights of Bollywood. She'd spend her days reading or writing. When she stepped out of the house to go for a walk, take a motorcycle ride down M.G. Road or watch a film, she'd wear big sunglasses to avoid being recognized. No one in the neighbourhood realized that one of the most popular faces in the country was living in their midst.

'If anyone recognized her and asked if she was Parveen Babi, she would just laugh and say, "Oh my gosh! You think I look like her?" People would get confused and leave her alone,' Suguna recounts with a laugh.

While it seemed as if her life had completely changed during those weeks, the one thing that remained a constant was her addiction to nicotine. In those days, there was only one shop in all of Bangalore that sold Dunhill, the brand Parveen smoked.

'I would go to this one shop on Brigade Road to buy cigarettes for her all the time,' Babu recalls.

༺❁༻

A little more than a month after she had first come to stay in Bangalore, Parveen was happy and healthy once again. There was some talk of her returning to Bombay, but she refused to leave Bangalore. That November, UG planned a trip to Kodaikanal, a pretty town in the hills of Tamil Nadu, about ten hours by road from Bangalore. Both Valentine and Parveen were to accompany him. Mahesh flew in from Bombay to join them on this month-long trip. The plan was for them to travel from Bangalore to Mysore, then Ooty, with a three-day stopover in Wellington, before proceeding to Kodaikanal.

In his book *U.G. Krishnamurti: A Life*, Mahesh compared their stay in Kodaikanal to 'a page from Dante's Inferno'. UG was suddenly taken ill and his condition was so grave that he couldn't eat for over three days and eventually even stopped drinking water. To make matters worse, Parveen also refused food and water. She locked herself up in her room and refused to come out.

'It was, perhaps, a sympathetic response to UG's condition,' Mahesh wrote in the book. 'The damp, cold, wet weather added to our discomfort.'

One night, UG was in such acute pain that he started talking about dying.

'Looking at his friend Valentine, he said, "It looks like the time has come for me to go,"' Mahesh records in his book. 'To this, Valentine remarked, half-jokingly, "UG, I don't think it is practical to die in a place like this, at a time like this." UG burst into laughter.'

Miraculously, UG started feeling better that night. Even so, the group decided to cut short their stay in Kodaikanal and, a fortnight after leaving on their road trip, were back in Bangalore.

Meanwhile, in Bombay, Ved Sharma was facing the ire and exasperation of film-makers on a daily basis.

'Parveen had signed nearly thirty-five films by the middle of 1979, most of which were halfway through [filming],' he told *Star & Style* for its 16–29 October 1981 issue. 'While Parveen was packed off to convalesce, it became a daily routine for me to answer phone calls and [listen to] abuses.'

In the initial weeks of her illness, Ved had warded off film-makers and the press by saying that the actress was down with a nasty bout of jaundice. Everyone had believed him, because there seemed to have been an epidemic of jaundice in the industry that summer. Amitabh Bachchan and Hema Malini had also been indisposed and the shooting of films like *Shaan* and *Kranti* had been held up as a result. Parveen was a part of both these films. When she didn't return to the sets and wasn't seen at any film events, wild rumours about her began floating around. They included conjectures that Parveen was pregnant and had taken time off for an abortion, that she had become a drug addict, that Mahesh's wife Kiran had assaulted her. *Filmfare* even carried a short piece on how the actress had eloped with a sixty-year-old south Indian doctor and that director Vijay Anand had given away the bride.

One of the first publications to write about Parveen's mental illness was *Stardust*. The 'Scoop of the Month' for its December 1979 issue declared that 'Parveen had cracked up'. According to the two-page article, her break-up with Kabir had 'left Parveen in a dizzying vacuum. She was like an object hurtling aimlessly through space.' Mahesh Bhatt, the one man she leaned on for solace, was already married. 'She lived with the uncomfortable truth for months, and what happened was, in a way, inevitable.'

The narrative spun by the magazine portrayed Parveen as 'a girl with a broken heart' and supported the idea that 'being unlucky in love had pushed her over the edge'. This is, in fact, what most people in the industry still believe. Even today, the stigma of mental illness is so deeply entrenched that most of the actress's colleagues and old friends don't mention her condition at all. Few realize or acknowledge that Parveen had suffered from a severe and debilitating mental illness, which left her incapable of thinking logically. Victims of schizophrenia describe a psychotic episode as one during which they hear disembodied voices clamouring in their heads. This experience, coupled with unimaginable fear and mistrust, makes it impossible for them to distinguish reality from fantasy, to manage normal emotions and make decisions. Blaming Kabir's ambition and, perhaps, callousness towards Parveen or Mahesh's marital status as the triggers for her illness would be taking the easy way out. Genetics and brain chemistry were contributing factors as well, but few were knowledgeable enough to understand that.

All the film-makers who had cast Parveen in their productions were losing money every day that she wasn't shooting. Ramesh Sippy had a set worth lakhs standing at Film City. Manoj Kumar had had to cancel an outdoor schedule and the makers of *The Burning Train* were waiting to finish dubbing. Among the big-budget films that were stalled because of Parveen's unavailability were Rahul Rawail's *Biwi O Biwi* with Randhir Kapoor and Sanjeev Kumar, Ravi Tandon's *Khud-Daar* with Amitabh Bachchan and Narendra Bedi's *Taaqat* with Vinod Khanna.

As 1979 drew to an end, Parveen had been away from films for nearly six months. Directors and producers were justifiably agitated. Many requested the Indian Motion Pictures Producers Association to step in and find a solution to the problem. But there was little that its then president G.P. Sippy could do; his own film *Shaan* was also delayed because of Parveen's absence and no one could force an actress, who was clearly unwell, to start working.

Directors were left with limited choices. If they hadn't shot substantial segments of their films with Parveen, they could replace her. Rahul Rawail had barely completed four days of shooting for *Biwi O Biwi* when Parveen fell ill.

'They were mostly scenes with Sanjeev Kumar. We had only shot an entry and exit with Parveen,' Rawail recalls.

Raj Kapoor, who was producing the film, flew down to Bangalore to meet with Parveen. She gave him the go-ahead to replace her and Poonam Dhillon was signed on in her place.

Manmohan Desai hadn't started shooting for *Naseeb* and cast Reena Roy in the role that had been initially offered to Parveen. *Khud-Daar* was Anwar Ali's maiden production and though they had barely shot two days for the film, he was reluctant to replace Parveen. The biggest setback was for films like *Shaan* and *Kranti*. Their makers had already shot so much footage featuring Parveen that the films couldn't be completed without her.

The pressure on Ved Sharma was mounting and he could turn to no one but the actress's mother Jamal for help. The duo decided to fly down to Bangalore in an attempt to reason with Parveen and, perhaps, bring her back to Bombay to complete her pending films. But it wasn't a happy reunion between mother and daughter. Jamal had little or no understanding of Parveen's mental condition. In her typical brusque manner, she commanded her daughter to return immediately to Bombay and finish her pending work. Parveen refused point blank and told her mother that this wasn't a conversation she was prepared to engage in. That's when things turned ugly.

'Her mother started abusing and attacking UG,' Babu recalls. 'She said that he had taken Parveen away and was brainwashing her. Jamal was clearly frustrated, because Parveen refused to even look at her or talk to her properly. UG kept telling Parveen to speak with her mother, but she wouldn't listen. "She's your mother, after all," he told Parveen. Jamal left our house so angry that she was still shouting and abusing in the street. Parveen's manager Ved Sharma kept trying to pacify her.'

Eventually, though, the actress gave in and decided to begin working again.

'I started to meet my producers and the pressure for me to get back to work started to mount,' she wrote in her cover story for the *Illustrated Weekly of India*. 'I began with dubbing a few hours a day. Slowly, as I grew stronger, I prepared to get back to my career and to pick up the various lost threads of life. Everybody, especially those connected with me professionally, seemed pleased with my decision.'

The first film Parveen resumed work for was B.R. Chopra's *The Burning Train*. She had finished shooting, but needed to dub for her scenes. There was one scene in the film where her character Sheetal is distraught, because her son Raju is trapped in a fire. UG believed that Parveen wasn't emotionally well enough to dub for this scene. But once she started dubbing, she breezed through it.

UG wasn't particularly happy about the actress's decision to get back to films. 'He felt it was the tension and the pressures of a show business career that were responsible for my breakdown,' wrote Parveen. 'Now that I knew I was genetically susceptible to this illness, it would be foolish for me to put myself in exactly the same situation once again. He pointed out to me that there was always a possibility of a relapse with this particular illness.'

Memories of the nightmarish experience she had lived through because of her ailment were still fresh in Parveen's mind. 'Relapse' was a word she didn't want to dwell on. Now that she was feeling better, she wanted to be optimistic and not live in fear. Having broken up with Mahesh, she had distanced herself from the life that UG wanted her to leave behind. But she couldn't think of giving up her career. She knew she had commitments that she had to fulfil.

On 22 December 1979, about six months after she had fled from the set of *Jwalamukhi*, Parveen returned to Bombay. This was the second time she was coming back to the city, hoping to pick up the pieces of her career and her life. Once again, she was alone. The difference this time was that being aware of her genetic predisposition to mental illness, she didn't know if she could trust her mind or control her behaviour. No matter how much she tried to convince herself and people around her that she didn't want to live in fear of another psychotic episode, apprehensions lurked somewhere in the deep, dark recesses of her mind.

20

It was on 15 January 1980 that Parveen returned to a film set after a hiatus. The film was *Shaan*. On a lavish set that had been created in Film City, director Ramesh Sippy eased her back into the process of shooting. For most of the day, he filmed simple reaction shots of Parveen that had been pending from the film's previous schedule. She was required to emote in response to situations that had already been filmed with her co-stars. The actress was quiet and distant, but between 'Action!' and 'Cut!' she seemed like her old self. If anything, she had lost weight and looked refreshed after her six-month sabbatical.

With Amitabh Bachchan in a scene from Shaan

Once the reaction shots were canned, it was time to shoot the film's title track 'Pyaar karne wale', which is also when Sunita, the character played by Parveen – a singer who turns out to be a con artist – first appears on screen. In a shimmering silver gown with a plunging neckline and billowing sleeves that highlighted her sensational figure in all the right places, the actress looked every inch the 'glamazon'.

Since she wasn't, even at the best of times, a particularly good dancer, choreographer P.L. Raj gave her very simple steps to execute for this song. Sippy shot both the title track and the climax song 'Yamma yamma' during this schedule. The choreography for the latter required a lot more effort and skill from Parveen than she was able to muster. If one pays close attention today to her moves in the song as she dances to R.D. Burman's chartbusting tune, it is quite obvious that she isn't in her element. Not only are her movements mechanical, the actress looks tentative and unsure in the song. Parveen was still dealing with the aftermath of her mental breakdown, but those around her on the sets of *Shaan* misinterpreted her lack of ease as laziness or apathy towards her work. In an article for the 7 December 1980 issue of the *Free Press Journal*, the film's director clarified that though he bore her no grudge for the delays in his shooting schedule caused by her illness, he 'was upset when I discovered that on her return a punctual and professional actress like Parveen Babi had lost interest in her work'.

Bindu, who had been on the sets of *Jwalamukhi* on the day Parveen fell ill, also featured in *Shaan*'s title track as a princess whose diamond necklace is stolen during the song. So did Amitabh Bachchan, Shashi Kapoor, Bindiya Goswami and Johnny Walker, along with at least a hundred junior artists or 'extras', as they were called then. Bindu and Parveen were sharing a make-up room, because another one wasn't available.

'When we met on the first day, I asked her how she was feeling, because everyone knew about her breakdown. She told me that she was well and was looking forward to shooting again,' Bindu recalls.

With her Shaan *co-star Bindiya Goswami*

It was when she wasn't in front of the camera that Parveen seemed to be different.

'When we'd be in the make-up room, it was obvious that there was something wrong,' Bindu notes. 'I'd be talking to her and it would seem like Parveen was not all there mentally. She kept tuning out of conversations. Or she'd look through me, like she couldn't see me. It was very odd behaviour for someone who used to be very friendly.'

Shaan was the first film in which Bindiya Goswami was cast with Parveen. She had heard stories about 'this cool senior' from her sister Pearl, who had stayed in the St Xavier's hostel in Ahmedabad at the same time as Parveen was there. And she turned out to be just as warm and friendly as Bindiya had imagined.

'We had a lot of scenes together and these were all big song sequences. We'd normally end up shooting only two or three scenes a day, so there was a lot of waiting around in our make-up rooms,' she says.

When they started shooting for *Shaan*, the two actresses instantly gravitated towards each other.

'She treated me like a kid sister,' Bindiya recalls. 'We would discuss diets and make-up. My sister Pearl would bring make-up by Mary Quant and Rimmel from abroad and the three of us would sit and try them out. Parveen was lovely and so friendly.'

When she returned after her sabbatical, though, there was an obvious change in Parveen's behaviour.

'She didn't interact that much with anyone, including me,' Bindiya observes. 'She would be quiet and withdrawn. She was just very focused on finishing her scenes and leaving.'

Her co-stars weren't the only ones who noticed the change in Parveen. Journalist Bharathi Pradhan was on set during this shoot. In an article for the 8–21 February 1980 issue of *Star & Style*, she describes the actress as ghost-like and 'nervously avoiding conversations as she rested her head on the table as if to shut everyone out'. 'Amitabh strides in and the clowning begins. He gapes at Parveen and play-acts at putting his head on the table too. She looks up with a weak smile,' Bharathi writes.

The split-level glass-restaurant set was one of the most expensive ever created especially for the film. As Asha Bhosle's voice echoed, Parveen shuffled around, pulling the characters played by Bachchan, Kapoor, Bindiya and Bindu to the dance floor that was lit from below. In between takes, Bachchan continued to joke around in the hope of lightening the atmosphere on set. The film was four months behind schedule and Sippy was focused on completing it as soon as possible. He had already lost time, with too many actors falling ill. To compound Sippy's problems, Mazhar Khan, who was making his debut in the film, had injured his arm just days after he started shooting.

The director had pegged the film's budget in the region of ₹5 crore, a considerable sum at the time. Not only was *Shaan* extravagantly mounted, but the makers would also lose a great deal of money because of delays and scheduling conflicts. Apart from its eight main characters, the film also had an extensive supporting cast that included, apart from Mazhar Khan and Bindu, Sujit Kumar, Helen, Padmini Kapila and Katy Mirza. It was no surprise that coordinating the dates of all the actors had been a nightmare for Sippy and his production team.

'*Shaan*, at times, because of the need to have so many stars together, became an impossible movie to make,' Sippy wrote in his article for the *Free Press Journal*, just days before the film's release.

※

The early days of Parveen's return to Bombay were tense and chaotic. Now that she was back in the city, producers were breathing down Ved's neck to get her dates. He had given priority to the makers of *Shaan*, *Kranti*, *Taaqat* and *Jwalamukhi* and allocated dates to them between January and March. Parveen, though, wasn't mentally fit to shoot back-to-back scenes as multiple shifts demanded. Even though everyone in her inner circle, including her mother and Ved, had witnessed her in the throes of a psychotic episode, she didn't fit the conventional image they had of an 'insane' person. The breakdown that had occurred six months ago had been dismissed as an unfortunate 'phase' triggered by excessive hard work. And now that she was back at work and seemed to be fulfilling her commitments, there was no way that she could still be ill, they concluded. In their minds, there was no good reason for her not to get back to firing on all cylinders.

There was UG, on the other hand, who was also in Bombay at the time and constantly warning Parveen about the possibility of a relapse manifesting in another attack. Every time she saw him, he'd bring up the topic. This was highly disturbing for Parveen and shook her. Given her faith in UG, she believed he could never be wrong.

'I certainly did not want to go mad again,' she wrote in her cover article for the *Illustrated Weekly of India*. 'UG's warnings grew so intense that they almost became threats. The possibility of the relapse became a certainty. I didn't know what to do. How do I avoid going mad again? UG suggested I give up my old way of life entirely.'

The idea of abandoning the life she had made for herself in Bombay terrified Parveen. She saw her career and relationships as fundamental to her identity.

'The question that bothered me the most was what to do after walking out on my past. I could see nothing certain, like a different career or some other job – or anything for that matter,' she wrote in the same article.

Then there were her professional commitments. Producers stood to lose lakhs if she didn't complete the films she had signed.

'I really did not wish them any harm, financially or otherwise,' she wrote in her article, referring to her producers. 'But if at the same time, continuing with my career meant going mad for certain, then what was the right thing for me to do? Should I continue with my career to save my producers or discontinue it to save my life?'

Eventually, Parveen decided to complete all her films, with as many breaks as she could take in between.

Much to Ved Sharma's dismay, she decided to take her first break in March, less than two months after her return to Bombay. Parveen told him she needed a month off, and for her first holiday of the year, Parveen accompanied UG and Valentine to Bali, Indonesia. UG was a no-frills traveller and this was the first time Parveen experienced what it would be like for her if she quit show business. She didn't like it.

'I felt awkward and uncomfortable, even in my relationship with UG. I didn't know what to do with myself. I began to miss the glamour, the glitter and the hectic pace of the old life.'

For the first time since she had met UG, Parveen's belief in him was beginning to falter. She began to question his importance in her life and her place in his.

'Why was UG frightening me all the time with such a possibility [of a relapse]?' she wrote in her cover story for the

Illustrated Weekly of India. 'Was he using that threat to control and to manipulate me? Why did he want to help me, in particular? I thought maybe he was a little in love with me, or I thought Valentine was growing old, and I, with my financial assets and my circumstances, was the ideal person to replace Valentine.'

Parveen couldn't dismiss these questions that arose in her mind. With all that doubt and negativity swirling around within her, she spent almost all her time in Bali locked up in her room.

Meanwhile, back in Bombay, this holiday completely threw off the schedule Ved had drawn up for Parveen and the film that bore the brunt of her absence was Prakash Mehra's *Jwalamukhi*.

Mehra had to cancel his March schedule and Ved couldn't supply him with fresh dates because Parveen was part of five other films, schedules for which had been fixed over April and May. 'I had even accepted the money for that schedule and felt terribly guilty,' Ved was quoted as saying in the 16–29 October 1981 issue of *Star & Style*.

When Prakash Mehra heard that Parveen was holidaying in Bali instead of allotting him the days he required to finish shooting his three films, he was furious. Mehra was convinced that her illness was nothing more than a concocted tale.

In fact, many directors and even some of Parveen's co-actors suspected she was faking ill-health. Most expressed their views off the record, but not Prakash Mehra. He had initially signed Parveen for three films – *Jwalamukhi*, *Laawaris* and *Namak Halaal* – and shooting for all of them had begun just before she took ill. In fact, she had been shooting for *Jwalamukhi* on the day of her breakdown.

'I think Parveen Babi is a hoax,' *Stardust* quoted Mehra as saying in its June 1980 issue. 'Her illness is [a] hoax. She is a liar and a cheat. Her only intention is to ditch her producers and leave the country. She did it before, when she left the country with her boyfriend Kabir Bedi. She not only made a fool out of me, but the whole industry.' He insisted that Parveen's illness had cost him about ₹25 lakhs and he would have to write off the loss. 'Why does she have to do all this *natak* [drama] to leave the industry?' he said, lashing out at the actress. 'If she wants to quit, she can do so gracefully. Many heroines before her have left the industry, but they did it decently and not in a third-rate manner.'

Mehra wasn't above using intimidation to get her back on his sets.

'I was the one who approached the income tax officers and warned them that she was fleeing from India,' he went on to tell *Stardust*. 'They made her sign an affidavit saying that she couldn't leave India. If she thought she could get away scot-free, she was highly mistaken.'

Mehra's anger was justified, if not his actions. After all, he had waited patiently for six months for Parveen to return and three of his films were simultaneously held up. Ved Sharma tried his best to ensure that Parveen didn't lose out on all the films she had signed with Mehra, but eventually he had to get her to give the director permission in writing to cast someone else in her place. Mehra immediately started shooting *Jwalamukhi* with Reena Roy. The scenes that had already been shot with Parveen had to be redone. 'The song that we were shooting when Parveen left was reshot on a pre-existing set at Seth Studio,' says Ram Sethi, one of her co-stars. 'The concept for the song had to be changed because there was no [swimming] pool in the studio.' Mehra also brought in Smita Patil for *Namak Halaal* and Zeenat Aman for *Laawaris*.

By the end of May 1980, Parveen had completed the bulk of her work on *Shaan* and *Taaqat* and resumed work on films like *Razia Sultan*, *Kaalia* and *Kranti*. During this period, she'd had two releases – *Do aur Do Paanch* and *The Burning Train*. Both films barely made a ripple. The pressures on Parveen, though, showed no signs of easing. She had hoped that her month-long stay in Bali would help her unwind, but the suspicion that UG didn't have her best interests at heart had taken root in her mind. She spent most of her stay on the idyllic island imagining hundreds of scenarios, where the one man she depended on was plotting against her. When she resumed shooting, film-makers were threatening to sue her and the press was still clamouring to interview her.

In her fragile state of mind, Parveen felt that everyone was out to get her, and she couldn't stop thinking about UG's prediction that she would have another psychotic breakdown. It seemed as if she couldn't get off this crazy train of anxiety and fear. That constricting panic, where she felt weighed down by a sense of doom, seemed never-ending. UG was still in Bombay and when the situation reached a stage that suggested that Parveen's fear and anxiety were going to snowball into another episode, he proposed that she travel to Gstaad in Switzerland with him and Valentine.

Once again, Ved Sharma put Parveen's film schedule on hold, while UG tried to explain to her why her high-pressure career and her genetic predisposition to schizophrenia were a threat to her mental well-being. He hoped that she would use the three-month stay in Gstaad to plan her exit from Bollywood. Parveen left Bombay that summer, afraid she would 'crack up again'.

After a few days in Valentine's picturesque but quiet chalet, however, she found that she was bored. After a week of gazing out at the snow-capped mountains and walking around in the pretty garden, the charm of her relative seclusion wore off.

'In Switzerland, I slept for fourteen hours a day, because I had nothing to do,' Parveen would write in her cover story for the *Illustrated Weekly of India*. 'I kept on waiting for my new life to start – nothing happened. I grew more and more desperate and lonely.'

When she wasn't sleeping, the actress devoured UG's entire collection of James Hadley Chase novels – sixty of them! – went grocery shopping with Valentine and helped her in the kitchen.

It wasn't lost on UG that the actress was just going through the motions.

In a letter written on 6 June to Mahesh in Bombay, UG expressed his reservations: 'I can't say Parveen is really enjoying her stay here. She gives me the feeling that she is kind of bored, listless and lonesome, like waiting for something to happen. If it were not for one dark pit of fear of a crack-up again, she would have certainly gone back to her old way of life. [A] movie career is her life, her heart... What seems to bother her most is that she can't get used to living with uncertainty. By [my] relentless insistence that she [should] burn her boats in Bombay and abandon her old way of life and start a fresh life a new way of life. [It] is something hard for her to do. She is trying hard. She has to learn to live with uncertainty. She has now an opportunity to make a fresh start.'

UG was promising Parveen a better life. Except now that she was far from the angry demands of producers, the pressures of looking perfect and the intrusive queries of journalists, she could only remember Bollywood and Bombay through rose-tinted filters. This was where she had found fortune, fame and love. Racked by the thought that she'd have to be crazy to leave it all for the great unknown, Parveen finally decided it was time to part ways with UG. She was feeling good and looking better. There was no need to saddle her life with someone who was hell-bent on steering her in a direction she wasn't at all keen to explore.

When she asked UG for her ticket to return to Bombay, he made one last-ditch effort to stall her. 'He said I would certainly have a relapse and that it would be fatal for me. I did not listen,' she wrote in her article for the *Illustrated Weekly of India*.

On 27 July 1980, Parveen returned to her home, her friends and her career in Bombay once again.

'I was so happy to be back in my world, where I felt I really belonged,' she wrote. 'I decided to wipe UG and his warnings out of my system and start life anew on a positive footing.'

Publicly, Parveen never denounced UG, but to those close to her, she talked about how he had 'tried to control and manipulate' her life. This marked the end of another relationship that she had counted on. It might not have been the kind of traditionally romantic relationship she had been involved in earlier, but it was one that had mattered to her. And, once again, she was all alone.

21

Parveen's return to Bombay justified Ved Sharma's faith in her. Through everything she had endured, he had always stood quietly in her corner, doing the best he could for her — at times, under the most trying circumstances. He had spent almost a year in damage-control mode – pacifying furious film-makers who had been let down, keeping at bay inquisitive journalists who sensed there was more to the actress's absence from the scene than they had presumed and coaxing a reluctant Parveen to return to work. Many in the industry had advised Ved to stop working for her altogether. After all, there were other actresses he could represent, they suggested, and standing by someone as erratic and unpredictable as Parveen could only hurt his credibility as an able manager. But Ved was steadfast in his loyalty and stayed put.

As soon as his client returned to Bombay, he got down to doing what he did best – getting film-makers to sign her on for their productions and ensuring that Parveen completed all her pending films. But first, he had to make amends to the justifiably irate Prakash Mehra. Apart from the mahurat shots, the director hadn't yet started shooting *Laawaris* and *Namak Halaal*. When Parveen had left for Bali, he replaced her in these films with Zeenat Aman and Smita Patil respectively. In *Namak Halaal*, Parveen had originally been cast to play Poonam, the love interest of the character played by Amitabh Bachchan, while Zeenat Aman was roped in for the role of Nisha, the young singer Shashi Kapoor's character falls in love with.

After Parveen's return from Switzerland, Ved called on Mehra at his house and beseeched the director not to replace her in all three of his films. He promised Mehra that Parveen was well and back for good and that, more importantly, his films would never again suffer because of her. Too infuriated over the trouble he had been put through, the director initially refused to meet Ved, but eventually he gave in and rehired Parveen. In what can only be described as a classic casting switcheroo, Parveen was now cast in Zeenat Aman's original role in *Namak Halaal* and the dates Zeenat had allocated for this film were used for *Laawaris*.

In the story Kader Khan had initially written for *Namak Halaal*, both female characters had been given equal importance. But with Parveen's dates not being available, Mehra would start shooting the scenes that didn't require her character's presence. By the time the film released, her character Nisha's screen time had been reduced to less than twenty minutes and included two songs – 'Raat baaki' and 'Jawaani jaaneman' – that would eventually become superhits. Khan also had to make appropriate changes to Poonam's character so that it would be a more suitable match for Smita Patil's personality and also tweak the main story in order to phase out Parveen's character. Interestingly, the song 'Pag ghunghroo baandh' that was filmed on Amitabh Bachchan and Smita Patil was actually written with Parveen in mind.

According to Mehra's long-time assistant Sushil Malik, the line 'Sangemarmar ki hai, koi moorat ho tum (You are like a marble statue)' was written specifically for Parveen and wasn't an appropriate description of Smita, who had a slightly dusky complexion. 'The song had already been recorded by the time Parveen was replaced, so Mr Mehra had no choice but to use it,' Malik explains.

Mehra wasn't the only director who would rehire Parveen for a film after replacing her with another actress. Manmohan Desai had, in fact, replaced her with Reena Roy in *Naseeb* and with Moushumi Chatterjee in *Desh Premee*. As soon as he heard that Parveen was back to work, however, Desai, who had apparently been unhappy with Moushumi, signed on his original choice again for the same role.

༺✦༻

Parveen was shooting for five films opposite Amitabh Bachchan during this period. Only a handful of people knew the details of her breakdown in 1979, and that she had repeatedly said Amitabh was trying to kill her. Ved was one of them. Now that she was back on sets with her frequent co-star, it worried and surprised him that she displayed no signs of that fear. In fact, Parveen made it clear to Ved that she wanted to do as many films opposite Amitabh as possible because he was the biggest actor in the industry at the time.

The signs of her growing obsession with Amitabh were always there for those who looked closely enough. Jyotsna, one of her oldest and closest friends from college, remembers spending some time with Parveen in Bombay during this period. On one occasion, she accompanied Parveen for a morning shift to Chandivili Studio. 'They were shooting for the "Mach gaya shor sari nagri re" song from *Khud-Daar* that day. Amitabh picked up the steps quite fast but Parveen wasn't a very good dancer and it was taking her time. She was very conscious about not making any mistakes in front of Amitabh so she came home that day and practised harder than she normally would. She wanted to be as perfect as possible,' says Jyotsna.

On another day, during the shoot of *Desh Premee*, when Jyotsna was visiting, Parveen left her friend a little bewildered by warning her not to touch any of Amitabh's things if they were invited into his make-up room at Mehboob Studio. She told Jyotsna that it would make him angry. 'Amitabh was always cordial to me but I couldn't imagine a scenario where he would invite me to his make-up room. I couldn't understand why Parveen felt the need to warn me, so I just laughed it off,' says Jyotsna. And the obsessive behaviour didn't stop there. 'If he was on the set at the same time as her, Parveen would keep asking me if he was looking at her, who he's talking to or what he was doing – all this while pretending to be completely nonchalant and unaffected by his presence,' she recalls.

⊚⊛⊚

The developments of the previous year had tarnished Parveen's image as an approachable and professional actor. While Ved was out making amends with film-makers, the actress focused her attention on the press. Since the beginning of her career, she had been an actor who was on friendly terms with journalists. While she understood how important they were in the ecosystem, she was also well disposed towards them because of her love for books and magazines. Journalists, in turn, were extremely fond of her, because she was candid and always made for good copy. In the twelve months gone by Parveen had shunned them when they visited her movie sets and refused to grant any interviews.

Now that she had resolved to give her career another go, the actress decided that it was time to open up to the media once again. There were only a handful of film journalists at the time and most of them were well known to the stars. Normally, an actor would hold a small press conference if he or she had any important announcements to make. Parveen, however, decided on a more intimate approach. She invited a few journalists home for coffee and a chat. And, as always, she was candid about every aspect of the battle she was engaged in 'to keep her sanity'.

She didn't quite know how to describe her breakdown. There had been no tearing of clothes or screaming in the streets or similar overt manifestations of abnormal behaviour which she and most people around her associated with mental illness. 'I suffered from overriding fear and I myself did not know about it, till it was all over,' she confided to *Stardust*, as quoted in its September 1980 issue. 'It was not a memory lapse, for I remember each and every thing clearly. Why it happened and why it had to happen to me is something I still can't understand.

It is a mystery... Maybe, it was overwork,' she said, 'but everyone in the industry works just as much as me.'

Parveen was quick to quash rumours doing the rounds that her ailment was a hereditary one. While talking about her family in a rare, unguarded moment, during the same interview, she said, 'This was the time when I really wished I had a large family or, at least, a father or a brother who could have taken over my personal as well as my business affairs when I could not function normally. Physically, it was impossible for me to handle things. I was and still am a one-woman show.'

She was quick to credit UG for having helped her through the 'greatest crisis' of her life, as she put it, but indicated at the same time that she was well enough to not need a crutch.

'I could not follow UG forever,' she observed. 'I had to live my life myself. UG cannot live my life for me, just the way I cannot live his life. And now that I am back, I miss him, but I am not lost without him.'

Parveen also responded just as candidly and graciously when asked about the industry's reaction to her illness.

'I don't blame the industry for treating me the way they did. I don't think they have been unfair to me. They did the right thing, when they replaced me in their films. They could not possibly wait forever. After all, big money was involved in all their projects and I was in no condition to work,' she clarified in the September 1980 issue of *Stardust*.

She wasn't even upset at all the unkind allegations Prakash Mehra had levelled against her.

'I don't blame him for lashing out at me,' she said with a measure of understanding. 'The problem is that the industry has not yet understood the nature of my illness and what I went through.'

The important message that Parveen wanted to convey was that she was 'fit to work without a break', but understood that returning to the spotlight after a very public mental breakdown might not be easy. She knew she would be under greater scrutiny than ever before.

'Every action of mine might be interpreted differently by different people,' she told *Stardust*.

Besides, there was the very real possibility that the industry might not give her this third chance.

UG had urged Parveen to change her ways, both professionally and personally, and warned Mahesh that a relationship with Parveen could completely derail his life. Yet, disregarding their spiritual mentor's advice, Parveen and Mahesh had reconnected in the months preceding her brief Swiss holiday.

'We met behind UG's back, though I think he knew that we were meeting,' Mahesh says. 'He even wrote some letters to me about Parveen from Switzerland.'

A few days after she was back in Bombay, Mahesh visited her at her home. There was nothing out of the ordinary about this evening; they had been meeting in secret for a few months, after all.

Mahesh kept trying, without much success, to talk Parveen out of her decision to go back to acting in films.

'I was trying to explain to her that all the stress that stardom brought wasn't good for her. She wasn't interested in this or any conversation,' Mahesh says. 'To distract me, she wanted to make love.'

'Parveen took my hand and led me to her bedroom. We undressed each other slowly. As we lay wrapped in each other's arms, she whispered, "UG or me?"'

Mahesh recalls a long breathless silence in the room, which, according to him, symbolized all her fears of rejection coming true.

'She then played her last card when she whispered "I love you",' says Mahesh. 'She whispered a little louder this time, making sure that I heard her over the drumming sound of the pouring rain. They were just three little words, but the ache and anxiety in her voice betrayed how desperately she needed me to say the same words to her. I did not.'

Mahesh remembers hopping out of bed and pulling his clothes on in a silence that was thick with tension. Then he opened the main door and pressed the elevator button.

That's when Parveen spoke again. '"Baba...," she called out to me,' says Mahesh. 'I didn't reply. I knew her well enough to anticipate that she'd follow [me]. Only I had nothing left to say to her. All I could think of was leaving before she came out. Unwilling to wait for the lift and have her catch up with me, I took the stairs, but Parveen wasn't far behind. She ran down behind me to the floor below. And stopped suddenly. Perhaps, that's when it dawned on her that she wasn't dressed.'

Mahesh remembers walking out into the rain that night and never looking back.

Once again, Parveen found herself utterly alone, nursing a broken heart. This marked the end of her third adult relationship since moving to Bombay. She had been chasing her dream of 'happily ever after' for almost a decade. Every time she thought she had found 'the one' who would make her fantasies come true, life would get in the way. This break-up felt a little different, though. It didn't leave her as dejected as she thought she would be. She did mourn the end of a pivotal relationship, but being focused on her career helped Parveen bounce back quickly.

ಅ⋆ಅ

In showbiz, success helps to gloss over failings of all kinds. This unspoken rule was one of the reasons Parveen did not find it too difficult to make multiple comebacks. It's not as if there weren't other actresses who could have permanently replaced her in the industry, but film-makers were fine with the status quo in her case, because her films continued to work at the box office. Her return to Bollywood after the sojourn in Italy and London with Kabir Bedi had coincided with the runaway success of *Amar Akbar Anthony*. This time around, in the second half of 1980, the industry was abuzz with news about just two films – *Kranti* and *Shaan* – both of which featured Parveen Babi.

What got people talking about these films was not just their star-studded ensemble casts or the fact that their respective directors – Manoj Kumar and Ramesh Sippy – were returning to the big screen on the back of humongous hits. The former had directed four superhit films on the trot, while the latter had delivered three, including *Sholay*. Dazzling sets, thrilling action pieces, chart-topping music, cutting-edge technology (both films were in 70 mm, with stereophonic sound) – there was much that the two films had in common.

More than anything else, it was the single-minded focus and dedication of the two directors that set them apart from their peers. Both films took over 500 shifts (one shift covering eight hours) to complete. Manoj Kumar even admitted that he had shot longer for *Kranti* than he had for all four of his previous films put together. Sunil Dutt alone, credited with a 'guest appearance' in *Shaan*, shot the film for sixty days, a much longer period than the time he had devoted to shooting his other films as a lead.

Both *Kranti* and *Shaan* were launched in the winter of 1977, their release schedules delayed by the indisposition of their main cast. Shooting for *Shaan* was affected when both Amitabh Bachchan and Shashi Kapoor fell ill, while Manoj Kumar had to postpone his shoot for *Kranti* because of Hema Malini's illness. Then there was the six-month delay caused by Parveen's mental breakdown. There were rumours that Sippy had got a body double to wear a special Parveen mask to complete his film.

'Not that I have heard of,' Parveen said, laughing, when asked about it.

The other rumour was about Manoj Kumar abruptly bumping off Parveen's character Surili in *Kranti* to eliminate her from the story, but the director denied it at the time. In the final film, though, Surili is killed just after the interval point.

Shaan was the first to release among these, on 12 December 1980. Though the film opened to packed houses across the country, it was seen as an average grosser because it had been an expensive film to make. *Kranti* released less than two months later and was an instant hit. The success of both the films played an integral part in Parveen's rehabilitation in the industry. Regardless of how little screen time she had in these films, the actress was seen as a 'hit heroine' and that's all the industry needed to forget about her breakdown or the losses the filmmakers had had to incur because of her prolonged absence.

ೂಲ

Towards the end of 1980, Parveen had almost finished catching up with her backlog of films and had started signing new ones. There was an untitled project with Dharmendra for director Vikramjit and Harmesh Malhotra's *Mangal Pandey* that reunited her with Shatrughan Sinha. Director Umesh Mehra was putting together the cast for his most ambitious film, *Ashanti*, inspired by the American television show *Charlie's Angels*.

For the crew of three ass-kicking crime fighters, Mehra cast Zeenat Aman, Parveen Babi and Shabana Azmi. Rajesh Khanna, as Inspector Kumar Chandra Singh, was the Indian Bosley who puts this ragtag team together and Mithun Chakraborty, cast as

With dance director Kamal on the sets of Mangal Pandey

Shankar Dada, was paired opposite Parveen. As expected, the film made news because of its casting. Parveen and Zeenat had been seen as rivals for years, while Shabana's impressive résumé proved that she could hold her own with as much élan in a Satyajit Ray film as in a Manmohan Desai potboiler.

Every other film being made in Bollywood at the time featured a formidable star cast, but there was one film that made news like no other, primarily because of its controversial casting – *Silsila*, Yash Chopra's much-hyped take on love, marital responsibility and extramarital guilt. The director was certain that he wanted Amitabh Bachchan to play Amit, the playwright torn between his marriage and his love, but had to deal with a high-profile line-up of leading ladies who came and went. According to film lore, Chopra's original idea was to cast real-life couple Jaya and Amitabh Bachchan as two people forced into marriage and Rekha as the man's first love Chandni. The problem was that Jaya had 'retired' from films after her marriage. And Bachchan himself wasn't keen on the casting suggested by Chopra, because there were already enough rumours doing the rounds about his real-life relationship with Rekha; if he were paired with her, it would only add fuel to that fire.

This was when Chopra cast Smita Patil to play Shobha, the quiet wife. At some point, Rekha decided not to do the film at all and returned the signing amount she had received. Subsequently, there was some talk of Dimple Kapadia being cast as Chandni, but it went nowhere, because her marriage to Rajesh Khanna was allegedly imploding at the time. So Chopra auditioned Padmini Kolhapure for the role. This didn't work out either. Some suggest that the actress, then fifteen, was too young to play Bachchan's love interest, while others claim that she had scheduling issues, having already allocated dates for Raj Kapoor's *Prem Rog* and Nasir Hussain's *Zamane Ko Dikhana Hai*. Bachchan was, at the time, shooting with Parveen for Tinnu Anand's *Kaalia* and Chopra had enjoyed working with her in *Deewaar* and *Kaala Patthar*. Ved Sharma was called to the director's office and Parveen was signed on for *Silsila*. This was a significant accomplishment for her. A year ago, she had been hiding in Bangalore, struggling to regain control over her sanity, and now a little more than six months after her return to Bombay, she had been cast in one of the most talked about films of the year. More importantly, this was a film opposite a superstar who was well on his way to becoming a legend. Signing a new film with Amitabh Bachchan would send out the much-needed signal to the industry that Parveen Babi was no longer a 'flight risk'. The actress was elated at having come this far, following the serious setback that had threatened to derail her career.

Chopra was supposed to start shooting for *Silsila* in Srinagar on 21 October. Parveen and Bachchan were already there to shoot for *Kaalia*, while Smita Patil and Shashi Kapoor were to fly in from Bombay. Just days before the shoot was to commence, Chopra arrived to spend some time with Bachchan and oversee the shoot for another film – *Sawaal*, starring Waheeda Rehman and Sanjeev Kumar – that he was producing.

'After dinner one night, Bachchan Saab asked me if I was happy with the casting of the film,' Chopra shared in a public conversation with Shah Rukh Khan in 2012. 'I told him I wasn't. So he asked me [what I thought was] the ideal casting. I told him this conversation is pointless, because we were about to start shooting. He pressed, so I told him that I'd want Jaya, Rekha and him in the film. He decided that we should fly back to Bombay the next day and that I should talk to the two actresses.'

His one-day trip to Bombay made all the difference and Chopra finally had his dream cast. All that was left to be done was to tell Parveen and Smita that they weren't going to be a part of *Silsila* any more. During that televised chat, Chopra confessed that he 'couldn't share bad news with people'. So, to spare himself the ordeal of telling the two actresses himself that they were out of his film, he enlisted the help of his assistant Romesh Sharma, who was in Srinagar, to inform Parveen. Shashi Kapoor offered to break the news to Smita Patil.

When Chopra landed back in Srinagar, the first person he met was Parveen. She had finished the shoot for *Kaalia* and was leaving for Bombay as she was no longer required for *Silsila*.

'She came running to me and said, "Yash, you are doing what's good for the film. Don't be afraid of me. I have only one condition – that you owe me a film,"' Chopra recounted.

When he reached his hotel, the film-maker found a lovely letter from Parveen addressed to him.

This was the second time that the director had ousted the actress from one of his films at the last minute. And though there was now a significant gap in her schedule, she took the high road every time she was asked about her views on being replaced in *Silsila*. According to the *Free Press Journal* of 15 November 1980, Parveen reasoned, 'The set-up is now much more saleable than what it was when only Smita and I were in. Yash told me sweetly that he was planning to cast Rekha and hence I would not be required.'

In private, though, Parveen was heartbroken. Actor Ranjeet, who was shooting in Srinagar at the time, remembers her sobbing.

'She had been very excited to start the shoot for *Silsila*,' he recalls. 'It was obvious that she was very upset, but she was also on set; so she had no choice but to continue working.'

Parveen wore a mask of composure and courtesy during her last two days of shoot in Srinagar and even when she bumped into Yash Chopra at the airport on her way out. It was only later, when she returned home, that she could finally give vent to her emotions.

At home, the actress locked herself up in her room and sobbed her heart out. She couldn't understand where she had gone wrong or what she needed to do to persuade Amitabh Bachchan to sign a new film with her. In her mind, her success in Bollywood was entwined with him.

Afraid to leave her alone, her staff quietly sat outside her room that night.

Danny, who was still a friend, had heard about what had happened in Srinagar from Romesh Sharma. He knew how important this film was for Parveen, because she had told him about it on numerous occasions before leaving for Srinagar.

'Amitji was working with her in all the hit films. She thought her existence in the industry was because of him,' Danny explains. 'Even his flops made more money than most other films back then and she was his co-star in most of the hits.'

When he heard that Parveen was back home, Danny reached out to her.

'I tried explaining to her that this was just a film and that there would be others,' he says. 'But she wouldn't listen. She kept saying that Mr Bachchan doesn't want to work with her and that her career was finished.'

It wasn't as if *Silsila* was Parveen's last chance to work with Bachchan. Apart from *Kaalia*, the duo had four more releases, including future mega hits like Manmohan Desai's *Desh Premee*, and *Mahaan*, which had the superstar playing a triple role. While it would be a few years before Parveen actually started publicly accusing Bachchan of attempts to kidnap and kill her, it is possible that this was the time those fears took root in her mind. Her focus now was on being a successful actor, and losing *Silsila* made her assume that her career was at stake. Her mind found connections where there were, perhaps, none. And although replacing Parveen had been Yash Chopra's decision, she chose to squarely blame Amitabh Bachchan for it. Her indignation and hurt over losing the film that had meant so much to her, coupled with hallucinations and delusions triggered by her mental condition, would eventually become a source of crippling fear for her.

22

Bollywood is fickle by nature. Halfway through 1981, the 'Babi boom' had taken over and sent into oblivion the 'Ban Babi' campaign that had been raging the previous year.

The trajectory of Parveen's return was similar to the one that had followed the first hiatus in her career in Bollywood. Only the characters involved were new. This second comeback of hers was, yet again, a testament to the goodwill she had garnered through the years with her natural courtesy and professionalism, the power of Ved Sharma's persuasive networking and the industry's astonishingly short memory.

Umesh Mehra, who was directing Parveen in *Ashanti*, couldn't stop praising her.

'She is one of the most hassle-free girls in the industry,' he told *Stardust* for the magazine's September 1980 issue. 'She is only interested in her role and performance. She doesn't bother about what the other heroines of the film are doing. She doesn't even want to know how long their scenes are or what dialogues they have.'

In a business where actresses were habitually deemed interchangeable, perpetuating deep-rooted insecurity among them and intensifying feelings of rivalry, this was high praise indeed.

'Another thing I like about Parveen is that she makes it a point to be pleasant to everyone,' the film-maker added during his conversation with *Stardust*. 'She gets along with both her co-stars Shabana Azmi as well as Zeenat [Aman].'

Ravi Tandon, who was directing her in both *Bond 303* and *Khud-Daar*, echoed Mehra's words. Only his praise was directed more towards Ved Sharma's almost superhuman ability to schedule and reshuffle Parveen's shoot dates.

'She goes out of her way to oblige her producers,' the director stated to *Stardust* for its September 1981 issue. 'There isn't a single producer who has any complaints about her. Even though she has signed so many new films, Parveen has always managed to give producers the dates they want. And being a thorough professional, she does not please one producer by depriving the other of his dates. She's got everything well planned out.'

Parveen's *Ashanti* co-star Shabana Azmi had a different take on her comeback story, however.

'Parveen is definitely an A-class heroine,' she was quoted as saying in the same *Stardust* article. 'And most of the other actresses in that category are demanding heroine-oriented films these days. Parveen is willing to do the other kind of glamour roles.'

There was some truth to what Shabana had said. Hema Malini had just delivered her first baby; Neetu Singh and Dimple Kapadia had given up their careers in films after getting married. Jaya Prada had just debuted, while Bindiya Goswami had shocked the industry by getting married to actor Vinod Mehra at the age of eighteen. Zeenat Aman was probably the only contemporary of Parveen's who was actively looking for roles that challenged her acting abilities after receiving Best Actress nominations for her performance in *Satyam Shivam Sundaram* and *Insaaf ka Tarazu*.

It was around this time that Parveen too began feeling she could explore her acting prowess further and lend a new dimension to her glamorous image by being open to more meaningful roles. One of the first of this kind that she accepted was in director Esmayeel Shroff's *Dil...Akhir Dil Hai* where her co-stars were Naseeruddin Shah and Rakhee. Then there was Hrishikesh Mukherjee's *Rang Birangi*, opposite Amol Palekar. This was a role originally offered to Rekha, but the director claimed he 'preferred Parveen to Rekha' to play the lonely wife in this comedy. 'The fact

*At the stage in her career when she began exploring
non-glamorous and meatier roles*

that I've signed Parveen opposite such a mature actor like Amol should speak for how I rate the girl as an actress,' Mukherjee told *Stardust* in an interview for its September 1981 issue. 'She is a very intelligent girl, with extreme sensitivity.'

※

Adman and former BBC broadcaster Vinod Pande was putting together the cast for his second film *Yeh Nazdeekiyan*. The idea for the film that dealt with marital infidelity had come from Shabana Azmi. So it was a given that she would be part of the cast. Pande was keen that his London-based friend Marc Zuber, a stage and television actor, play the male lead. But even two months into the shoot, Pande had been unable to zero in on an actress to play the supermodel that Zuber's character, a much married advertising executive, falls in love with.

Shabana advised Pande to reach out to Ved Sharma in order to rope in Parveen, but that meeting never took place and the director's quest for a suitable actress continued.

'On the day we were going to sign someone else, Ved landed up in my tiny apartment-office in Juhu,' Pande says.

Parveen's manager was there to pick him up, because 'Madam wanted to meet' him. He was taken to a bungalow close by, where she was shooting for *Dil...Akhir Dil Hai* with Naseeruddin Shah.

'In between shots, I narrated the story of my film and she immediately said she wanted to do the film. I was in a bit of shock. Everything had happened so quickly that I didn't have a chance to calculate how many days we'd need her for or even how much we could afford to pay her,' Pande recalls with a laugh. *Yeh Nazdeekiyan* was a small-budget film and the director knew he couldn't pay Parveen her market price. Very hesitantly, he broached the subject.

'I explained to her that our budget was very limited. Apart from her, Shabana was the only other known face in the film. I told her that I could only afford to pay her ₹1 lakh.'

At the time, Parveen was making in the region of ₹2 lakhs to ₹3 lakhs per film.

Expectedly, she was taken back, but after a short pause, she accepted the deal. 'Okay,' she told Pande, 'but only for you.'

Before he could celebrate, the director had another admission to make: he could only afford to pay for twelve outfits for her character. Parveen merely laughed when informed about the film's budgetary constraints that would restrict her wardrobe. She told Pande not to worry; she'd get extra outfits made on her own, if she thought she needed them.

But there were more favours he needed from the actress. He had already been shooting for months and needed to shoot a few more scenes at the same location, before the crew left for the outdoor schedule.

'I just needed her for a few hours. It's possible that by this point, she was regretting agreeing to do my film, but there was no harm in asking,' Pande says. 'She agreed to that as well. She said she'd come in when she got breaks between other shoots and also get her own clothes, because we obviously couldn't get anything made at such short notice.'

Parveen had only one condition – she wanted top billing. 'She said, "Munni [Shabana's nickname] shouldn't have a problem with this, because I am senior to her." Shabana was okay, as long as Parveen knew that she was the one who had recommended her for the film, which she did. Everything was signed and we started shooting.'

Pande had heard stories about the ease of working with a cooperative actress like Parveen, but he had dismissed it as showbiz hyperbole. Until this meeting, that is.

'She was just a joy to work with,' he declares.

If Parveen's mental health issues had eroded her confidence or her passion for the work she did, you'd never have known it while talking to her. She was aware, however, that she couldn't push herself as hard as she had before her breakdown. 'The only major regrettable mistake I feel I've committed is pushing myself to the brink, mentally and physically, during the past three years,' she told *Star & Style* for its 9–22 January 1981 issue. 'It doesn't harm only me, but also people around me. Having been ill once and having faced the drastic repercussions, I know what I'm talking about. I've realized that health is one of the most important things in life.'

The first step for Parveen towards changing her perspective on her work as the ultimate priority in her life was examining the compulsions that kept bringing her back to Bollywood to take on the pressures of juggling work in an increasingly greater number of films. These compulsions included her obsessive quest for perfection and her need to be utterly engrossed in her work to the exclusion of all else. 'I'd also realized that the only thing I could depend upon, to a certain extent, was my work,' she told *Star & Style*. 'I had no other direction in life that absorbed me as much as my work. Basically, there was nothing I wanted to do more than work. I need to be consumed totally in anything that I do and nothing absorbed or consumed me then as much as my work.'

She had gradually come to understand that obsession with anything wasn't a particularly healthy inclination. 'An obsessive mind is not a clear mind,' she acknowledged. 'And clarity is the most important factor in all walks of life. I shall strive for a clear mind.'

These interviews, where Parveen talked about her struggles with mental illness and her subsequent recovery, weren't given just for publicity or so that she could occupy pride of place in a magazine. They were also her way of placating directors and producers she had upset by her absence from the industry and sending out the message to all concerned that not only was she well enough to get back to work again, but that she was taking sufficient care of herself to eliminate any risk of a relapse. In reality, though, Parveen was back in work mode, full throttle, her days harnessed again to a punishing schedule.

At the time, a wave of art-house or parallel cinema was tempting mainstream actors to test their acting chops in films that were a departure from the multi-starrer, tear-jerking, song-and-dance-filled masala films they were used to working in. Like some of her contemporaries, Parveen too was looking at pushing her boundaries. *Rang Birangi, Yeh Nazdeekiyan* and *Dil...Akhir Dil Hai* were films that promised to take her out of her comfort zone. 'On each of the occasions when I have come back to the industry, I've returned a better person,' she was quoted as saying in the 21 August–3 September 1981 issue of *Star & Style*. 'The expectations that I have of myself have increased and I intend to rise slowly, but steadily. I intend tapping my full potential as an actress. I refuse to remain mediocre.'

Despite the sobering lesson she had learnt from the consequences of her breakdown, Parveen was pushing herself harder than ever in her ambition to rise above the ordinary. She was on a perennial diet that included mostly lime water or fruits which she consumed through the day. Dance had never been one of her strengths, but the crew of *Meri Aawaaz Suno* insisted that she match her co-star Jeetendra (so agile and light on his feet that he had been nicknamed 'Jumping Jack') step for step in the Asha Bhosle–Kishore Kumar track 'Mehmano ko salaam hai mera'.

In the initial months of Parveen's return to films, Mahesh had lost no opportunity in warning the industry about the pitfalls of signing her on for their productions. Before her breakdown, he and his elder brother Mukesh had announced *Ab Meri Baari* with Dev Anand, Rishi Kapoor and Parveen. But in early 1981, although Parveen was back at work once again, the Bhatts chose to replace her with Rekha. That the film was subsequently stalled and Mahesh moved on to *Arth* is another matter.

In interviews, he tried explaining how Parveen's illness had left her too mentally debilitated to deal with the pressures of stardom and that overworking her could trigger another breakdown. UG had expressed the same apprehensions to Parveen repeatedly, but in private.

If Mahesh's public comments upset the actress, she chose to take the high road while reflecting on them. Speaking to *Stardust*, which quoted her words in its September 1981 issue, she observed, 'He was at a stage when he did not realize the weight his words carried. He was very liberal in sharing his feelings with the world. But his statements could not hurt my career. At that time, it was seemingly beyond repair. Nothing could have hurt it any more.'

Since the night Mahesh walked out of her life, Parveen had decided that she was done with love. She'd been searching for it all her life in vain. Perhaps, she was destined to be alone forever, she told herself. 'My career is all that matters to me today,' she asserted to *Stardust*. 'I have absolutely no personal life. I don't want anything to spoil things now. I've got a chance and I am not a fool to throw it away.'

There were some rumours about a new man in her life – a Britisher by the name of Guy David – but most people who were close to Parveen at the time have no recollection of such a person in her life. In an article published in *Stardust*'s May 1981 issue under the heading 'Parveen's Strange New Foreign Lover', the actress credited David with having helped her through her mental breakdown. She resorted to Bollywood's favourite euphemism 'good friend' to define her relationship with him, adding, 'I met him through a friend three years ago in London. He has a fashion house in London.' While the piece insinuated that marriage was very much on the cards for the couple, there was no subsequent mention of David. It was as if he didn't exist.

There was another relationship, though, that Parveen managed to keep completely under wraps. She had been introduced to Abdul Elah, an Arab from Dubai, by Sanjay Khan's wife Zarine in the early 1970s. A married man and a father, Elah was described by Parveen's friends as being 'medium height, bearded and very rich'. He was instantly smitten. More than Parveen's looks, it was her intelligence that Elah apparently fell in love with.

It's unclear when they went from being acquaintances to lovers, but he says that they knew each other for about seven years. It was a long-distance relationship during which they spent a few days together about four or five times a year. When they were in Bombay, Elah would book a suite at the Sea Rock Hotel and if she visited him, he'd book a plush hotel in downtown Dubai for Parveen and her friends. Elah pampered her whenever they were together. He brought her bottles of the really expensive Tea Rose perfume and lavished gifts on her friends.

When they weren't together, he'd call often.

'Parveen would panic if she had to step out of the house for some reason around the time he was expected to call. And when he was in Bombay, it didn't matter what work she had. She would leave everything to spend time with him. She really loved him, but knew that they had no future, because he was married,' confides a friend, who didn't want to be named.

Elah claims he saw Parveen through her breakdowns. 'At the beginning, she was very loving, but suddenly, something changed [in] her life,' he says. 'I tried to ask [her about it], but she never told me what happened. She wanted to be alone and adopted loneliness. She was a completely different personality.'

As the internal demons Parveen was battling took a firm grip on her life, her relationship with Elah died a natural death.

***

Those years, however, were marked by an important addition to the actress's life – Xerxes Bhathena. A young designer, Xerxes had quit his job at Burlingtons', a store at the Taj Mahal Palace Hotel that was known as the 'Selfridges of the East', in the early 1980s, and was looking to strike out on his own.

'I had made seventeen garments and I went to star homes and had a model showcase the outfits,' he says. 'Hemant Trivedi and his girlfriend used to help me.'

Chance took him to Shabana Azmi's home.

'She loved the outfits, but said they weren't her type. She suggested that I meet Parveen. She even gave me Parveen's home number.'

However, getting in touch with the actress was far from easy. Every time Xerxes called the Babi home in Kalumal Estate, Ved, who answered the phone, fed him the standard secretary line: 'Madam *nahin hai* (Madam's not home).'

'One day, I decided to call in the night,' says the designer. 'There was no way that the secretary would be there at that time. It was a gamble.'

It paid off. Parveen came on the line right away.

'She told me to come over immediately. She had a flight to Canada for which she had to leave home at 1 a.m. and she had nothing to do until then.'

Xerxes rounded up his friends and the model, loaded all the outfits in a borrowed car and drove to Juhu.

'I remember that night so vividly,' he says. 'Parveen was eating mangoes. She didn't offer us anything, not even water. We showed her all the outfits. She didn't say anything. I walked out of her house really dejected.'

The second time Xerxes met the actress was about a fortnight later at Bhalla Bungalow in Pali Hill, where she was shooting for the film *Ashanti*. Shabana Azmi and Zeenat Aman were also there. 'She told me that she was leaving for Hyderabad that evening for a shoot and she wanted a glove dyed black,' Xerxes remembers. 'It was short notice, but I told her that I could do it. Next, she told me that she wanted me to do her clothes for Prakash Mehra's *Namak Halaal*.'

The first complete 'look' Xerxes designed for Parveen was for the 'Jawaani janeman' track in *Namak Halaal*. She described it to him as a take on Donna Summer's disco hit, 'The Wanderer'.

'I immediately said, "Become Donna Summer." I made her a sequinned leotard with a tie at the waist. I had only five days to get the outfit ready. We kept making the outfit tighter. Parveen didn't have much of a cleavage, so I gave her a Gossard bra. This was Parveen's most daring outfit yet.'

From that day on the sets of *Ashanti* until the end of Parveen's acting career, Xerxes was the only designer she worked with. More than that, he became her best friend.

With Xerxes while on a holiday in Srinagar

'We spent almost every single day together,' he says. 'I was with her on the sets, we spent evenings together, talking and watching movies, and we even went on holidays together.'

Xerxes would be by Parveen's side three years later, when she left the industry following her second breakdown. It was the first time he had been present when she suffered a full-blown psychotic episode. But he had already noticed behaviour patterns that, in hindsight, seemed beyond the realm of the 'normal'.

Another chartbuster, 'Raat baaki...', was being picturized on the sets of Prakash Mehra's *Namak Halaal*. In the film, Parveen's character Nisha is coerced into killing Raja Kumar, a rich hotelier played by Shashi Kapoor to whom she has been introduced as a singer invited to perform at his hotel. As Nisha sings '*Raat baaki...*' at a party, masked goons lurk in the shadows. She is so traumatized by the thought of having to kill Raja Kumar that she starts hallucinating in the middle of the song and screams, '*Main tumhe nahin marne dungi*, Raja (I won't let you die, Raja)!' While shooting the song sequence, Parveen began confusing fiction with reality and was terrified by the sight of junior artists dressed as masked assassins walking around the set.

'One night, after we had returned from the set, Parveen called the director home,' says Xerxes. 'She told him that she didn't want to shoot the song any more, because she was going to get killed. She believed that those [masked] extras were going to kill her. It took us some time, but we managed to convince her that she wasn't in danger. I think it was a mild attack, because she was back on set the next morning.'

At the time, the designer had attributed the actress's erratic behaviour to her nervousness about the shoot. Besides, she had put herself on such a rigorous diet for that song sequence that it could well have heightened her feelings of stress.

'She'd have only a bowl of curd three times a day,' Xerxes remembers. 'She did the Jane Fonda workout every day. By the time we shot 'Raat baaki...', Parveen's waist was just twenty-two inches. She had become so weak that she'd faint every other day.'

Bollywood was still a few decades away from being consumed by the fad of achieving a 'size zero' and none of Parveen's contemporaries was driven by the obsession to lose excess pounds. There were no external pressures on her to be thin; the compulsion was hers alone. She was pushing herself to be what she imagined was the best version of herself and in Parveen's mind, this version was a great deal thinner and, hence, sexier than she was. As time went by, she became increasingly fixated on this ideal image of herself that would match her notion of unblemished perfection.

23

Once again, Parveen's star was burning bright.

Like many in the industry, the actress too was trying to make sense of how her career had miraculously received a fresh lease of life after teetering on the brink of total ruin. 'Once you create a star, it's not really easy to destroy [the image],' she would tell the *Free Press Journal* during an interview published in its 13 June 1982 issue. 'And since, in the first place it's not easy to make a star – it costs a hell of a lot of money – people don't want to destroy a star. Also, my professionalism, enthusiasm and hard work were contributing factors [for restoring her career]. After all, people do notice it and appreciate it sooner or later. And, of course, my ability to deliver the goods.'

Parveen was also quick to credit Ved Sharma as an equal partner in the resurrection of her career. 'I am lucky to have him,' she acknowledged during the same interview. 'He has done much more than his job as a secretary demanded.'

Since the actress's return to the arc lights, Ved's job had become doubly difficult. Not only did he now have to convince film-makers that Parveen was a superb actress, ideal for a particular role in their films, but he also had to reassure them that she was well enough to actually complete the film. In addition, he had to serve as a buffer between his employer and the press and manage the narrative of her troubled mind deftly, so that she elicited sympathy rather than hostility or derision.

By mid-1982, however, there were rumblings of trouble once again. Stories were making the rounds of Parveen locking herself up at home and refusing to meet anyone; of film shoots being cancelled; of the actress having fled to an undisclosed location abroad to get away from it all.

Unable to breach the formidable wall of silence Ved had erected around his employer's privacy, inquisitive journalists turned to the one person who had never shied away from sharing news about the actress – Mahesh Bhatt. 'I'd met Parveen some time ago and she'd expressed her desire to see my film *Arth*,' he stated in an interview that appeared in the April 1982 issue of *Stardust*. 'I advised her not to see it, because the film could disturb her very much. She agreed. At that time, she seemed absolutely okay to me. But then, recently, Parveen was shooting for *Ashanti* in Bangalore. An acquaintance of mine informed me later that Parveen had revisited the place where she was put up during her last breakdown. It is a modest apartment where she was recovering under UG's supervision. This time, I believe, she went and stood watching the room where she'd stayed. Perhaps, all the memories came back and they had [an] adverse effect on her.'

Inadvertently, the film-maker added more fuel to all the speculation swirling around the actress by telling his interviewer, 'Parveen's illness is time-bound. It's like a pendulum that sways to one extreme, only to gather momentum and sway right back. With such an illness, the moment the patient is in a state of normalcy for long, you can be sure that the relapse is round the corner. Today, Parveen is on certain drugs. She has to maintain a certain level of these drugs in her system permanently. The moment the drug content in the system falls below the minimum level, she'll be down again.'

By now, Ved was weary of these speculations. Having put in a great deal of effort to ensure Parveen's reinstatement in the position she deserved after all the years of hard work, he was exasperated with these rumours which weren't helping her cause. 'Nothing is wrong with Parveen's health,' he declared to *Stardust* and was quoted in the same issue that carried Mahesh's interview. 'She is reporting regularly for shootings, and is in fact doing double shifts.'

While Ved was incensed by all the negative speculation about Parveen, her own reaction, as always, was measured. She didn't blame journalists for printing the rumours, but she did let it be known that she was very disappointed with people from the industry. 'I know that these rumours are originating from the industry,' she would tell *Star & Style* for its 28 May–10 June 1982 issue. 'Somehow, people have forgotten how to be humane. They seem to take a certain delight in running down a fellow artist. Nobody thinks about how difficult it was for me to come back to normal and what it's like to have to live with fear. How many people have touched insanity and come back to normal? It's so easy to talk, it's really surprising how insensitive others can get.'

Early in her career, Parveen had learnt how it felt to be the subject of idle gossip. She had never paid too much attention to it before, but now there was a very real danger that this whisper campaign against her could cost her her career. 'When I came back after my illness, I had to start from scratch and I've put in a lot of effort and dedication into earning people's trust,' she elaborated during the same interview. 'You know when the trade papers said I was down at the Poona mental hospital, I was here shooting at Natraj, running from pillar to post, completing my shootings. I didn't even go to Poona, whether it's to the hospital or otherwise. They don't know how badly all this can affect my career.' This possibility was increasingly becoming a source of real apprehension for her.

Even though there had been no full-blown episodes lately, Parveen was already living with the anxiety of having another mental breakdown. With fresh rumours circulating in the industry about her condition, her fear was greatly intensified.

The time came when she started believing that everyone was constantly watching her in anticipation of the moment she would falter, analysing her every move to see when she would stumble. Her apprehensions were not completely unfounded.

A female co-star, who was sharing a make-up room with the actress at Mehboob Studio during this period, remembers a day when Parveen wasn't feeling too well.

Preferring not to be named, she confides, 'I think she had an upset stomach. She had made multiple trips to the bathroom we shared. After a few hours, she walked up really close to me and whispered, "Is everyone talking about me? Are people saying that Parveen is sick? Do they know how many times I have been to the bathroom?"'

Parveen's co-star apparently pacified her with the gentle reassurance that no one had noticed how many times she had used the bathroom. But in the days, weeks and even years that followed, this very co-star would share the same anecdote every time the conversation around her turned to speculations over Parveen's fragile mental condition. One of the loveliest actresses of her generation, with a great deal of affection for her afflicted co-star, she still wasn't above a little gossip about her. And, like many of Parveen's contemporaries, she had little or no understanding of her mental illness.

Simultaneously, another, much juicier piece of gossip was doing the rounds: 'Are Parveen and Danny to marry?' It soon took over all conversations and magazine headlines. Danny's relationship with Kim, his girlfriend of five years, was going through a rough patch. She accused him of not spending enough time with her and resented the fact that Parveen continued to be an integral part of his life. She also alleged that he had lost interest in directing *Phir Wahi Raat*, which was meant to be Kim's big debut, after Parveen passed up the opportunity of being a part of the cast. *Stardust* compounded the problem by going so far as to quote an unnamed friend of theirs who insisted that Danny had introduced Parveen as his wife to an acquaintance.

According to the June 1982 issue of the magazine, Kim, who was clearly smarting from what she saw as the end of her relationship with Danny, fanned the flames by speculating about this rumoured marriage. 'I wonder whether their marriage will be a successful one,' she was quoted as saying. 'I doubt if Danny will allow Parveen to work, and Parveen is far from [being] a home-loving bird. All the same, I wish them all the best.'

Fiercely private about his off-screen life, Danny was, justifiably, infuriated. He had been quite open about his earlier relationship with Parveen and even after their affair ended he had continued to be very fond of her. It was unfair, he thought, to have her dragged through the muck, because his present relationship was imploding.

'Kim or someone said that Parveen comes to my house to watch video [tapes] and that she is there all the time... Of course, Parveen and I are friends and do see each other,' he clarified. 'I am not the kind of person who can cut off a four-year relationship totally. I am a nice guy, not one to harbour a grudge against a woman and [plot] revenge, just because she left me for another man. I still feel for Parveen.'

Just in case there were any doubts about the kind of relationship they shared, Danny clarified that it was purely platonic.

'I still care for Parveen the way one human being cares for another. I feel protective towards her the way I feel for old school friends and relatives with whom I have lived for long periods [of time]. Parveen and I understand each other, we are friends, but it is not the same any more. There is no kind of physical contact between us.'

And there was no question of marriage either.

Even as the industry grapevine buzzed with stories about Parveen all through 1982, she was hard at work. She had had a dozen releases in the two years since her return and she was shooting for a dozen more films at the time, including *Mahaan, Bond 303, Tala Chabi, Rang Birangi, Bad aur Badnam, Mangal Pandey* and *Arpan*. Of these, only two – *Mahaan* and *Tala Chabi* (this Raj Sippy film stalled even before shooting began) – had her starring opposite Amitabh Bachchan. They had worked together first in Ravi Tandon's sleeper hit *Majboor* in 1974 and had since been cast together in some monster hits.

With co-star Reena Roy on the sets of Arpan

In all those years, Bachchan and Parveen had been perceived as friendly co-stars; there was never any speculation about a romantic relationship between them. Since her return after the breakdown, Parveen had been single. Suddenly, towards the end of 1982, whispers began doing the rounds of an affair between the two stars. The fact that Bachchan was married or that there was already a rumoured relationship with Rekha didn't seem to succeed in nipping these speculations in the bud. The morning after a Diwali party hosted by Pamela and Yash Chopra, almost everyone was talking about the way Parveen had hovered around her male co-star through the night. Apparently, he was also spotted in the vicinity of Parveen's apartment in Kalumal Estate. Whispers about Rekha supposedly 'looking through' Parveen at social gatherings were seen as further confirmation of the fact that something was brewing between the actress and Bachchan.

There was even a rumour that Rekha had not only 'caught Amitabh and Parveen red-handed above Sumeet [a preview theatre]', but had discussed the incident with some journalists and even called Parveen a 'bloody bitch'.

When asked about it, Parveen shot down these rumours in no uncertain terms. 'With Amitabh, I share a cordial working relationship,' she was quoted as saying in the 13 June 1982 issue of the *Free Press Journal*. 'I deny any other kind of relationship.'

When questioned about the Sumeet incident, she refused to demean herself by name-calling Rekha. 'I am not aware that Rekha has stated anything [of this sort],' she declared in the same issue of the publication. 'But if she has, then I would rather choose not to comment on what Rekha has supposedly said. For I strongly believe two wrongs can't make a right.'

Between April and June 1982, Parveen and Bachchan had three releases – *Namak Halaal*, *Desh Premee* and *Khud-Daar*, while *Mahaan* and *Tala Chabi* had also been announced. The immediate assumption was that Parveen's male co-star was promoting her because of their affair. 'The only film I have signed opposite Amitabh lately is *Tala Chabi*,' she told the *Free Press Journal* during the same interview. 'And if they have signed me, it's not because Amitabh is in the film, but because it's the role of a glamorous princess and I suit it to a T. Whatever films I have signed so far, the only consideration has been my suitability and their faith in my ability to deliver the goods. Amitabh has nothing to do with it. He certainly isn't playing my godfather; nor is anybody else. I receive offers on my own steam.'

A television interview with Tabassum on the sets of *Namak Halaal*, where Parveen had praised her male co-star, was also seen as the sign of a blossoming romance. 'Tabassum asked me who my favourite actor is among the present generation of artists. So I told her that it was Amitabh, because he is a very good actor,' she declared quite matter-of-factly during the interview to the *Free Press Journal*. 'Now, you tell me, isn't he a very good actor? And, moreover, she wanted to know my personal favourite; so what was wrong if I mentioned his name? By [describing him as being] very good, I was not trying to undermine others. In fact, I did mention that there are other very good actors like Dilip Kumar, Sanjeev Kumar, Naseeruddin [Shah], etc., but my favourite is Amitabh. What was there to hide?'

Anyone in showbiz would attest to the fact that there's never smoke without fire. In this case, though, it was more like kindling ready to ignite. That Parveen had been obsessed with Amitabh Bachchan since they first worked together was clear to everyone around her. If the rumours were to be believed, what had changed now was that he had begun to show some interest in her.

Five films into his career as a director, the self-critical Mahesh Bhatt continued to be dissatisfied with his work. Despite the fact that *Lahu Ke Do Rang* had been declared a hit and had won two Filmfare Awards, he still sought self-validation.

It was at this juncture that the director decided to make the first of his many 'confessional', semi-autobiographical films – *Arth*, a fictionalized version of his extramarital affair with Parveen Babi, starring Shabana Azmi, Smita Patil and Kulbhushan Kharbanda. Shabana was cast in the role of the orphaned Pooja, who is emotionally and financially dependent on her husband Inder (enacted by Kharbanda) and whose character was apparently modelled on Mahesh's first wife Kiran. Inder, like Mahesh, is an ambitious film-maker, while Kavita Sanyal (played by Smita Patil) is a famous actress, who also happens to suffer from schizophrenia. From the day the film was launched and until its release on 3 December 1982, *Arth* was constantly in the news. This meant that Parveen was repeatedly badgered with questions about her views on a film that brought some of her darkest days into the public domain. It didn't help that Mahesh often contradicted himself on whether the film was autobiographical or not. Parveen was tired of all the curiosity generated by the film that had trained the spotlight, yet again, on the most intimate area of her private life. When asked during an interview for the *Free Press Journal* whether the film was, indeed, based on her life, she snapped, 'Why don't you ask Mahesh Bhatt to make up his mind? Anyway, I have no idea about his film.'

This was a rare instance where Parveen would let her public mask drop and reveal her true feelings to an outsider.

There are conflicting opinions on whether she had seen the film at all and, if she had, the reaction it had elicited from her. Xerxes, privy to Parveen's responses, says, 'She was proud of *Arth*. She really loved Mahesh and talked about him very fondly. She had made me listen to a tape where Mahesh had recited poetry to her and it was raining in the background. It was all very romantic. She respected him. I think Mahesh really loved her too.'

On the other hand, there were those who believed that the release of *Arth* pushed Parveen towards the breakdown that would result in her finally quitting Bollywood. The publicity generated by the film and the unhealthy curiosity about her illness must have been particularly traumatic for a person who had always been obsessed about keeping up appearances. Whether it was in college, where she had been eager to project herself as an 'It Girl', or throughout her career in films when she had devoted her every effort to earning respect as a professional actress, Parveen had worked really hard at creating the image of her choice. Since her breakdown in 1979, she had been struggling to come to terms with the realization that people other than her family and close friends were aware of the chink in her armour. Now, with the release of a film that was being screened for thousands of strangers across the country, it could not have been easy for her to handle the reality of some of the most intimate moments in her relationship with Mahesh – which also included, perhaps, episodes from her personal battle for sanity – being exposed to harsh public scrutiny.

Mahesh himself has never shied away from acknowledging how much of his real life he's chronicled on reel; *Arth* is no different. The film is peppered with moments and mannerisms that were lifted straight from the years he and Parveen spent together. Kavita, Smita Patil's character in the film, is shown to be clingy and insecure. She suspects that Inder is still in touch with his wife and sniffs his clothes when he returns home to find out if he's been with her. Parveen had, in fact, done the very same thing during the months leading up to her breakdown. The scene in the film where Kavita is sitting near a lamp, the only source of light in an otherwise dark room, and peering at the lines on her palm, is a moment inspired by Parveen's behaviour in real life.

Ved Sharma's wife Saavi remembers yet another moment that eventually found its way into *Arth*.

'This was around the time when Parveen wasn't feeling well in 1979,' she recalls. 'One day, I got home after running some errands. I saw Hanuman [Parveen's driver] sitting downstairs. Both Parveen and Mummy [the actress's mother Jamal] would come often to our house, so I didn't think much about it.'

Saavi recalls noticing that all the curtains in her home were drawn and the lights switched off. Before she could enquire about it, Parveen's mother explained to her that she had brought her daughter there, because she 'was acting strange'. Parveen, for her part, slept through most of the day.

'At some point in the evening,' Saavi remembers, 'Mahesh came to see her. He sat with Parveen for some time in the bedroom. When he was leaving, she followed him to the main door. She held his arm, like she was begging him not to leave. She was saying something like, "Do you want to leave me? You want to kill me?"'

With Ved being hounded by film-makers in the chaotic days that followed Parveen's breakdown, Saavi had completely forgotten about this moment – until she saw it being depicted on the big screen in *Arth*.

Mahesh insists, however, that Parveen didn't get to see the film. Those were the days before Hindi films had found their way into homes on VHS tapes and it is quite likely that Parveen didn't actually watch it. Either way, Mahesh has no regrets about making it.

'Making *Arth* was very important to me; it was my survival,' he explains. 'This was the most important, urgent experience of [my] life, which was compelling me to share my story. Everyone knew the story was based on my life. I've never been secretive about it. Smita [Patil] knew she was playing Parveen and she was absolutely okay with it. Autobiographical cinema, which has now found respectability, is something I stumbled upon because of that mishap in my life. Now bloodletting has become the mode of communication.'

This unflinching look at marriage and love didn't just push the boundaries because of its source material, which was strongly autobiographical. For decades, our films had glorified the potential of Indian women for sacrifice and forgiveness. Mahesh told his story, not from Inder's perspective, but from that of the two women who love him. 'I didn't want this to be a story of some guy wallowing [in self-pity] and playing the victim card. In fact, he's the perpetrator of the crisis. I remember Kulbhushan [Kharbanda] would say, "What kind of spineless man is he? I can't live with him in a lot of scenes." I've lived with him in the skin,' Mahesh says with his trademark bluntness.

He believes that *Arth* shows Parveen in 'a sympathetic light'. 'The movie roots for her as a helpless woman who's in love with a man, not someone else's husband; she also wanted her home,' he says.

But the film is, in essence, Inder's wife Pooja's journey from the shackles of patriarchy to discovering her own strength and a strong sense of self. In contrast, the image that remains of Kavita is one of a broken, unstable woman, whose life and relationships are haunted by fear. Her breakdown in the big, confrontational scene that precedes the film's climax is one of the most remembered scenes from *Arth*. She sits on a sofa, humming to herself as she peers into the mirror in her hand. This behavioural trait, Mahesh acknowledges, is also borrowed from Parveen's mannerisms. When Kavita notices Pooja entering the room, she politely asks her to sit down. But all semblance of that courtesy vanishes when Pooja asks her how she is feeling.

Kavita walks up to her and asks, 'Do I look mad?' Her impassive expression, unblinking eyes belie the thoughts and emotions churning within her. This is the image of Parveen that Mahesh has given the world.

It's hard to overstate the impact of *Arth* on its audience, especially in the way it would influence public perception of the actress. Fans would have read the normal celebrity stories about her – the affairs, the films, the rivalries and even her breakdown – but none of these had painted a picture quite as stark as the one Mahesh did with *Arth*. He had cherry-picked one aspect from the life of India's sex symbol, stripping off all the customary trappings and protections of celebrity to reveal the damaged psyche of a fragmented woman.

While Mahesh eventually acknowledged that Kavita's character was based on Parveen, he also admitted that he had her in mind while making *Phir Teri Kahani Yaad Aayi* and *Woh Lamhe*. Till now, people had only read and heard rumours of Parveen's mental illness – its on-screen portrayal was what irreversibly changed how the actress would be perceived by the media and audiences alike. An actress much admired for her beauty, poise and glamour would henceforth always be mentioned in the same breath as her debilitating illness.

Whether Parveen had watched *Arth* or not is irrelevant today. Just knowing that the details of her illness were now in the public domain left her already fragile self-esteem in tatters.

24

Parveen had never been single for this long. With an unfeeling mother like Jamal who had been content to do no more than her duty by her daughter, the actress had suffered from a sense of emotional deprivation all through her childhood and teenage years. More than ever, she wanted to believe what the books she read and the movies she watched promised her – that there was someone waiting to lavish love on her. She had spent most of her life oscillating between being hopeful and heartsick. After longing for a partner for years and looking for the perfect one, she was finally learning to live on her own, but she simply couldn't come to terms with it. It was a state of being she hated.

Every time she experienced that glorious, heart-stopping moment when she imagined she had found the love of her life, she loved the person with all her being. She loved everything he said and did; and she asked in return that he love her to the exclusion of all else and shower her with undivided attention. During these phases, she existed only because of his love and his acknowledgement of that love made her feel her existence was worthwhile. Perhaps because of the overwhelming intensity of her focus and feelings and the unhealthy possessiveness that accompanied them, none of the romantic relationships she had been involved in so far – and there had been quite a few – had lasted.

When she began working with Amitabh Bachchan as a co-star, what had started off as a desire and then an obsession to match his 'perfection' as an actor had, at some point, evolved into something far beyond that. The few who knew Parveen well at this juncture of her life believe that the nature of her obsession began changing only when she assumed her co-actor was reciprocating her feelings and she wasn't merely imagining his overtures. There was another thought playing at the back of her mind: being seen as 'Amitabh's woman' would, she felt, empower her in the eyes of the industry, in addition to helping her in her pursuit of perfection as an actor. The bonus, of course, would be to bask in his love and occupy the centre of his world.

Increasingly, however, Parveen's neurosis began affecting her professional decisions. She had been part of the original cast of director Saawan Kumar Tak's *Souten*, where her co-stars were Smita Patil and Rajesh Khanna. Parveen had already acted in three films with Khanna, including the most recent, *Ashanti*. She could not have been unaware of the decade-long rivalry between this male co-star of hers and Amitabh Bachchan that had begun on the set of *Namak Haraam* and had become a part of Bollywood lore. But now that she imagined she was getting 'close' to Bachchan, she felt impelled to establish her 'loyalty' to him and pick sides.

Unfortunately, she decided to do so and walk out of *Souten* after she had accepted a fee as advance payment for her role in the Rajesh Khanna starrer, all her costumes were ready and the crew was preparing to fly to Mauritius in a matter of days to start filming.

'Vedji went into panic mode,' Xerxes remembers. 'He tried to explain to Parveen that the director would be very angry and that he'd lose a lot of money. She didn't care. She told me that Amitji (she always called him "Amitji" or "Lambuji", never Amitabh) wouldn't like it if she did a film with Rajesh.'

Saawan Kumar remembers Ved returning the signing amount. 'He didn't really give a reason, but it seemed like Parveen wanted to work with one "camp",' he says. 'It was very gracious of her that she, at least, returned my money.'

It was obvious to those around her that her obsession with Amitabh Bachchan was boundless and on the verge of becoming

A still from Mahaan

all-consuming. Ved had begun to notice that Parveen was inclined to try and skip shooting for films where she wasn't paired with the superstar. She'd come up with excuses for her reluctance to shoot, and Ved would have to plead, cajole and somehow get her to the set.

Such was her fixation with him, that for the climax of *Mahaan*, she told Xerxes that Bachchan wanted her to wear yellow.

'I wondered why he would tell Parveen what colour to wear, but I didn't really want to argue,' says the designer. 'So I gave her swatches of yellow to pick the shade she wanted.'

Parveen picked a simple all-yellow salwar kameez.

In the years since 1980, when Xerxes had first started working with the actress, the duo spent entire days together and rarely had disagreements, let alone bitter arguments. Except for one evening in early 1983, a few months before Parveen's breakdown.

'I was tired of listening to her talk about Amitabh all the time,' Xerxes confesses. 'I finally told her this. While she talked about him all the time, he didn't even bother about her. It was a bad [bitter] fight and I left Parveen's house very angry.'

The next morning, the actress had a hundred roses delivered to his home by way of an apology, with a note addressed to 'my only love'. They were both able to forgive and forget this episode as if it had never happened, but Xerxes did learn a lesson from it: henceforth, he would never argue with Parveen about Amitabh Bachchan.

As much as she loved the idea of being in love with her 'Lambuji', there were those extremely rare moments when she felt trapped, perhaps, by what she recognized as a delusion. On 2 August 1982, Bachchan met with a near-fatal accident while filming a fight sequence on the sets of his film *Coolie*. In the weeks that followed, this injury was further complicated with a Hepatitis B infection that led to cirrhosis of the liver. While the actor was battling for his life in the intensive care unit (ICU) of Bombay's Breach Candy Hospital, millions of stunned fans across the country, along with the entire film industry, held their collective breath.

Far from everything that was going on at the hospital, Parveen was gripped with an overwhelming sense of fear and grief. This toxic combination would push her mind further into darkness. She seesawed between being worried sick about Bachchan's health and actually praying for his death.

'I hope he dies. I would be free of him,' she was heard muttering. The few people around her who overheard her words were horrified. This was an evil thing to wish on someone she loved, they felt – and the Parveen they knew wasn't evil.

***

By the end of 1982, the actress's mind was unravelling and she was slowly, but steadily losing touch with reality. She had begun to experience bouts of paranoia, to see things that weren't there and hear voices that didn't exist. Yet, she was able to continue living a functional life and maintain a flourishing career.

One of the films she was shooting for at this time was Hrishikesh Mukherjee's breezy comedy *Rang Birangi*, with Amol Palekar and Deepti Naval. Utpal Dutt played the hilarious Inspector Dhurandhar Bhatawdekar, a role that would win him the Filmfare Best Comedian Award. In what can only be described as counter-intuitive casting, the director had given Parveen, one of the most glamorous faces of Bollywood, the role of Nimmi, the exhausted housewife, neglected by her workaholic husband. Deepti Naval, on the other hand, best known for playing plain Jane characters, was cast as the feisty and desirable secretary.

When Hrishida, as the director was fondly called, told Deepti that Parveen was to play Nimmi, her first reaction was: 'Oh my god! If such a gorgeous girl plays the wife, why would her husband look at anyone else? The logic wouldn't work.' But the director had his own reasons for insisting on this unusual casting. 'Hrishida said that's the whole point with men – "looking elsewhere is always so much more interesting for them",' Deepti recalls.

Before shooting began, the director explained to Palekar, Dutt and Deepti, his regular collaborators, that Parveen wasn't too well and that they should keep that in mind when she was present. Once they started filming, however, Palekar found her no different from his other co-stars, who were all committed and disciplined.

'She would listen to the director with complete attention, which is the first thing that's required. She would also discuss scenes with me, which is normal,' the actor recollects, adding, 'she was able to deglamorize herself for that film so easily.'

Deepti, who worked with Parveen on *Rang Birangi* and the Ramsay production *Telephone*, also has fond memories of shooting with her co-star. *Telephone* would eventually release almost two years after Parveen had left the industry, following another breakdown.

'She was so beautiful and really affectionate towards me. We bonded on some level,' she observes. 'Whatever few scenes we shot together, I really enjoyed working with her. She was competent as an actor, but perhaps she wasn't realistic enough – her performance was a little studied. It wasn't something that surprised me, because I didn't expect her to suddenly play this down-to-earth character,' she says, remembering Parveen in the role of Nimmi.

Hrishida preferred shooting in authentic locations and there were times when Palekar could sense that Parveen was struggling.

'Particularly, during outdoor shoots, I could see she would suddenly not be her usual self and she'd clam up,' the actor remembers. 'She'd sit in a corner all by herself and it looked like she didn't want to be disturbed. I would give her that space, but I could see that she was struggling with herself and trying to snap out of it. After a while, she'd come back and be that lovely, warm, chatty person again.'

In the month preceding her next breakdown in the summer of 1983, Parveen's schedule was more packed than usual. Among the dozen new films she had signed and begun shooting for were Amjad Khan's *Ameer Aadmi Ghareeb Aadmi* opposite Shatrughan Sinha; *Karm Yudh*, *Deewana Tere Naam Ka* and *Avinash* opposite Mithun Chakraborty; Raj Sippy's *Sitamgar*, with Dharmendra and Rishi Kapoor; and *Yeh Desh* that had Shakti Kapoor playing Parveen's husband. At the beginning of the year, she had also joined Amitabh Bachchan and other actors on a series of international stage shows.

Her schedule was an extremely busy one and Parveen coped with it to the best of her ability. On good days, she enjoyed being on set, performing and hanging out with friends. Xerxes has fond memories of his visit to the US with her for the stage shows.

'We had such a blast on that trip,' he recalls. 'She had multiple costume changes during her act. She started with *'Jawaani jaaneman'*, for which I had given her a shimmery outfit. She carried roses that she threw out into the crowd. And then she had to quickly change into a saree. She changed in all sorts of crazy places. I remember, at times, holding the door shut with my body, because there was no latch, even as I helped her change outfits. It was mad and so much fun.'

The good days, he felt, however, were becoming few and far between.

Though she was feeling increasingly trapped by the delusions that seized her and the voices clamouring in her head, Parveen made a valiant effort to work through them.

Former journalist Nalini Uchil recalls spotting the actress in a corridor at Mehboob Studio during this period.

'I had gone to interview someone else and when I stepped out of their make-up room, I saw Parveen at the end of the corridor.' The two women were approaching each other from opposite ends of the same corridor and since Uchil had interviewed the actress earlier and known her for some time, she was mentally preparing herself for a quick chat. But as they got closer, the journalist was taken aback by Parveen's expression.

'There was no sign of recognition in Parveen's eyes, but what shocked me was that she looked terrified,' she says. 'Though there was no one else in that corridor, except for the two of us, she looked visibly scared. She was holding the wall and walking, almost as if she wanted to hide in the wall.'

Months later, when the news of Parveen's breakdown spread through the industry, Uchil's thoughts would go back to this odd encounter.

Ameer Aadmi Ghareeb Aadmi was Amjad Khan's second film as a director. He had made his directorial debut the previous year with *Chor Police*, which also featured Parveen. Vinay Sinha had produced both films. Both men had enjoyed working with Parveen so much that they didn't think twice before signing her on again.

'We had shot about sixty per cent of the film when Parveen started behaving erratically,' the late producer recalled in a conversation in 2018. 'Vedji would tell us that she'd reach by 10 a.m., but she'd turn up only post lunch. Once we even put up a set and waited for her to come, but she didn't turn up. Towards the end, she just stopped coming.'

A scene originally shot for Mr Aashiq *and eventually used in* Akarshan

The film was eventually reshot with Zeenat Aman and released in 1985. Amjad Khan didn't direct another movie again. Director Tanvir Ahmed's *Mr Aashiq*, with Akbar Khan and Smita Patil, was one of the last films that Parveen shot for before her breakdown. When she left the shoot midway, Ahmed scrapped the film and used the footage he'd shot for it as a special appearance in another film – *Akarshan*. He describes Parveen as 'being completely focused in between takes... But when she wasn't in front of the camera,' he adds, 'she would visibly tremble'.

Deepti Naval, who was a friend of Ahmed's, once landed up on his set to say a quick hello.

'I saw Parveen there and it was obvious that she wasn't well,' she says. 'She seemed jittery; like she was on the edge and very distracted. Her eyes seemed really focused and yet distant. She was a completely different Parveen from the one I had worked with just a few months before.'

After returning from Gstaad in the summer of 1980, Parveen had begun severing her ties with the man who had helped her recover after her breakdown – U.G. Krishnamurti. By 1982, she had completely dissociated herself from him; it was almost as if he had never been a part of her life. Forget meeting him when he visited Bombay, she didn't even mention him any more in her conversations with others. Pretending as if he didn't exist meant that she didn't have to remember his warnings of another possible mental breakdown. And if she didn't have to dwell on it, she reasoned, she could also stop taking her medication. She had never trusted the medicines or the doctors who had prescribed them. The only reason she had taken her medication regularly was that UG, whom she trusted then, had advised her to do so. As soon as he was out of her life, however, so were the medicines and the doctors.

In a 1981 interview to *Star & Style* for its 9–22 January 1981 issue, Parveen had equated UG's presence in her life to 'aspirin'. 'You can't depend on them totally, but definitely, if they have that something which you need, then just like an aspirin relieves our headache, they are able to guide you or stand by as a tower of strength when you face problems,' she had said. 'But eventually, as your problems slowly ease and fade into oblivion, you have to stand on your own feet.'

As the voices in her head became louder, Parveen realized that she needed help. And there was only one man she could trust.

'A month before she left for London, Parveen came over to my place to find out UG's current address,' director Vijay Anand revealed to *Star & Style* in an interview that was published in its 16–29 September 1983 issue. He added, 'The main problem with this girl is that she is so lonely. All around her, she has people who only want to get something out of her. Her mother is her only close relative. But it is said that Parveen gets antagonistic towards her own mother when she is ill. Kabir, Mahesh...all of them wanted something from Parveen. The only person who she feels is not making use of her in any way is UG and so she chose him to cure her.'

UG was one of the first people Parveen called when she landed in London for the stage show with Amitabh Bachchan and others. She promised that she'd visit him and Valentine in Gstaad, but eventually gave up on the idea.

※

In the cover piece Parveen wrote for the 29 January–4 February 1984 issue of the *Illustrated Weekly of India*, she described in her own words the days leading up to her departure from Bombay and her final farewell to a career in films:

> A few days later, I returned to India from London with a feeling in the pit of my stomach that all was not well. I kept up a bold, cheery front, which lasted precisely one night, most of which I spent sleeping. Next day, the familiar distrust returned and started to encompass all the areas of my life. I couldn't take it. At night, I broke down in front of my family and friends. In a desperate attempt to feel better, to feel serene, I tried a change of place — went to a friend's place, only to feel worse. A doctor was called in, medicine prescribed, which was no help at all. As I lay there on the bed, the truth dawned on me — this was the relapse. I was slowly but surely being consumed by it, and there was nothing I or anybody around me could do about it. This was the situation UG had so desperately and frantically tried to warn me about. One more thing became clear to me: last time, it was not the medicines that had helped me, and they would not help me this time. It was not within the power of medical science to restore a human being. It was UG's energy that had restored my health. All that time, he had been genuinely concerned about me, about my life, about my future.
>
> Now that I had realized the truth about a lot of things, there was just one thing I wanted to do. I wanted to talk to UG, not to thank him or to ask for his help again. I just wanted to speak with him.
>
> Next morning, I left the friend's house to return to my mother. I was concerned about her. She is old. How will she be able to take what is happening to me? Better than I had thought. Everybody

around me seemed OK—almost resigned to my inevitable ill fate. They couldn't help me, they all seemed so helpless themselves.

I called Gstaad. UG's familiar voice came on the line. The words that came out of my mouth were, 'UG, be with me in spirit.'

He laughed. 'When are you going to America?' he said. When I had called him up a week before from London, I had mentioned to him the possibility of my taking a trip to America. 'I will be in America in September for some shows. I want to see you, UG.'

'I will see you in America in September,' he said.

I put the receiver down and I knew I would see him in America in September — he had said so on the phone, and by now I knew enough to know that anything that came into UG's consciousness will certainly happen, anyhow.

At home, I tried to isolate myself from everything and everybody in the hope of feeling better — it didn't help. My condition was worsening. Suddenly, I heard my own voice dictate to me from within: 'Get out of Bombay. Get out of India.' I felt I had to get out and get to UG. He was the only hope, the only redeeming factor. I also knew that nobody, friends and family alike, would let me travel or let me move out of their reach in the condition I was in. There was no way I could share with them the faith, the confidence, the bond that I felt with UG. My mother had always viewed UG as an opportunist, an enemy of her daughter in the disguise of a friend, trying to take her beloved daughter away from her.

That night, I told my distraught secretary and mother that I wanted to go out of the country for a rest. In the midst of violent protestations, my secretary misplaced my address book, in which were the addresses of every single person I knew outside the country. My mother pleaded with me not to leave home.

I left. I had to. It was my entire life in question, in consideration.

It was the final curtain on Parveen's decade-long career in the movies.

25

During the layover in Dubai, Parveen called UG from the airport. She didn't know how he'd react to the fact that she was on her way to Gstaad to see him. Even in the middle of her psychotic episode, she recognized that UG had no obligation to see or help her. 'He had every right to refuse to even talk to me. I had hardly been a worthy friend to him,' she wrote in her essay for the *Illustrated Weekly of India*. Her fears, fortunately, were unfounded. Not only did UG arrange for Parveen to stay with a friend in London, while she obtained a Swiss visa and booked a flight to Zurich, he was at the airport to receive her as well.

Her faith in him was immense and so unshakeable that the actress truly believed that his very presence made her feel better. 'Within a few days, I started to look and feel better. The change in my physical condition was so apparent that everybody commented on it. A friend said I looked like a corpse when I arrived at Zurich airport. Everyone agreed that being with UG in Switzerland had done me a world of good. I myself couldn't have agreed more,' she wrote.

While Parveen admitted to feeling better, UG had reservations about her recovery. He had been down this path with her once and he didn't want to get involved again. 'He told me he would not be able to give me any advice,' she continued in her essay, 'that I was well enough to make my own decisions, and that he didn't want to get involved with the Indian film industry, directly or indirectly.'

It was no surprise, then, that when journalists from Bombay started calling UG, he was quite non-committal. He didn't want to get involved in the media circus that was Parveen's life. He told them that the actress had called her producers and informed them that she'd return to Bombay in the middle of September and that he himself would be travelling to the US. When Prochi Badshah, a journalist with *Stardust*, reached Parveen, the actress, as reported in the October 1983 issue of the magazine, pleaded, 'Please don't involve UG. He is a friend. He didn't invite me, nor did he call me here. I was tired and needed a break and he welcomed me. I am here only for a few days. I am coming back.'

Parveen did, in fact, call the many producers whose projects had been stalled by her unannounced departure from India and promised them that she would be returning to Bombay soon to finish shooting for their films. As the weeks passed, however, she realized that she couldn't go back to her old life. After her last breakdown, UG had warned her of a possible relapse if she returned to showbiz. She had doubted his words at the time, but now realized that he had been right.

'For better or for worse, truly there is no business like show business!' she wrote in the same essay. 'Either you stay in it and pay the price or you are out of it for good. You can't have it both ways. For me, it has come to this: if I stay in it, I lose my head. So I am staying out. Sorry, but I just can't take it any more. For the first time in my life, I am finished — done with it all; my fame, my success, my identity as an actress and my old life.'

Now that she had made the momentous decision, Parveen couldn't figure out what she wanted to do with her life next. Since UG and Valentine were scheduled to travel to the US, she decided to accompany them.

Parveen may have taken steps to escape her demons, but she left Ved Sharma in a world of trouble. At the time of her departure from Bombay, she was a part of nineteen films in different stages of completion. Some of them were more than half complete. Apart from *Kanoon Meri Mutthi Mein*, she was also a part of several 1985 releases like Amjad Khan's *Ameer Aadmi Ghareeb Aadmi*; Raj Sippy's *Sitamgar*, where she co-starred with Dharmendra, Rishi Kapoor and Poonam Dhillon; Ravi Tandon's *Bond 303*, where Jeetendra played the male lead; and the Ramsays' *Telephone*, where her co-stars were Marc Zuber and Shatrughan Sinha. At the time, Parveen was also a part of Chhotu Bihari's *Ricky* and Ravi Anand's *Sultaan*.

This was the second time in his decade-long association with her that Ved had had to face the wrath of producers and directors because of Parveen having left films midway. Unfortunately, this time too he was no better prepared to handle the situation. He simply didn't know what explanations to offer. 'Where has Parveen disappeared to?', 'Is she coming back; and when?' were questions he had no answers for.

'All I know is that Madam told me she was going away for a few days,' he would say to *Star & Style* that quoted him in its 25 November–8 December 1983 issue. 'She told me the atmosphere here was disturbing her and that she'd like to go away for a few days till things settle down.'

Like all good secretaries, Ved's immediate focus was on making sure that his artist didn't lose any work. In the weeks following Parveen's departure, he tried to keep a tight lid on the news or, rather, the utter lack of it. Despite his best efforts, it didn't take long for the uncertainty over the actress's whereabouts and future intentions to percolate from the Babi household to the film sets, where co-stars and technicians waited for her. Directors were told that the actress was unwell or had had to suddenly travel out of town. Ved Sharma was doing everything he could to buy her time.

Jeetendra, who was shooting Ravi Tandon's *Bond 303* with Parveen, was, understandably, furious.

'I have been reporting for shooting and waiting,' he was quoted as saying in *Star & Style*'s 16–29 September 1983 issue. 'Hours after my arrival, my clothes come and as I get dressed, I

With her co-star of seven films, Jeetendra

am told not to change, because Parveen hasn't arrived. It's the same story every time and has been happening far too often. I think it's high time something is done about it.'

Producer Vinay Sinha, who was bankrolling Amjad Khan's directorial venture *Ameer Aadmi Ghareeb Aadmi*, waited almost six months for Parveen to return.

'We had shot over sixty per cent of the film,' he recollected. 'Vedji kept telling us that she'd come back, so we waited.'

Amjad Khan's directorial debut *Chor Police*, with Shatrughan Sinha and Parveen, hadn't performed well at the box office and there was tremendous pressure on him to deliver with the new film. Even as *Ameer Aadmi Ghareeb Aadmi* continued to haemorrhage cash, the actor-director, who was best known for his role as the much-feared dacoit Gabbar Singh in the Amitabh Bachchan–Dharmendra blockbuster *Sholay*, was more concerned about Parveen's well-being.

'If, God forbid, anything has really happened to her and she needs my help, I'll do everything under the sun to help her,' he told *Star & Style*. 'If she has decided to settle down in London, I wish her all the best.' As for the fate of his film, he said, 'All I can do, if this is true, is to shoot my film with another heroine and change the script to suit the new girl.'

When they couldn't wait any longer, Zeenat Aman was cast as the female lead and the film was reshot, though Khan did decide to retain the song 'Har ek raasta saja ke chal' that he had shot with Parveen.

'We lost a lot of money because of the delay, but none of us complained about her, because she was such a nice lady. If she had a mental problem, what could anyone really do?' said the late Vinay Sinha.

Another film left in the lurch was Umesh Mehra's *Avinash*, co-starring Mithun Chakraborty. This was, in fact, the third time the director was working with the two actors. While they had already featured in his *Charlie's Angels*-inspired film *Ashanti*, he had also roped them in for a 'special appearance' song in *Teri Baahon Mein*, his version of Hollywood's Brooke Shields starrer *Blue Lagoon*, which marked the debut of yesteryear star Nutan's son Mohnish Behl and Ayesha Shroff (née Dutt).

Avinash was meant to be a Jason Bourne-esque thriller, with Chakraborty playing the eponymous spy. More than half the film had already been shot during an extensive schedule in Kathmandu. Just as the crew was prepping to film the rest of the movie in Bombay, the director heard about Parveen's disappearance through the grapevine. Umesh Mehra kept hoping against hope that the film's leading lady would return. But she didn't.

Unlike Amjad Khan, Mehra decided to retain the portion he had shot with Parveen as the female lead. As a result, the story needed to be rewritten so that the character she had been playing could be killed off and a new lead female character introduced into the plot. Therefore, in the second half of the film, Mehra used a body double to shoot a fire sequence where Parveen's character Nisha dies. As she takes her dying breath in Avinash's arms, Nisha spills out a few secrets. These disclosures facilitated the entry into the story of a character called Dr Sapna. The entry of Poonam Dhillon as Sapna, enabled Mehra to complete the film. *Avinash* released more than three years after Parveen's departure from Bombay. The delay in the film's release and its convoluted new storyline had their inevitable effect: the film failed at the box office.

It took years for the chaos Parveen had left behind to settle.

Of the nineteen films she had on hand at the time she left in 1983, ten released over the next seven years. The last Parveen Babi starrer to hit theatres was director Inderjeet Singh's *Iraada*, with Shatrughan Sinha and Suresh Oberoi. Though the writer-director retained her scenes in the film, he chose not to mention her in the film's credits. It was almost as if she had ceased to exist.

༺❀༻

When Parveen fled Bombay in the dead of night, she had set off the usual rumours about her. But once the dust had settled, the blame game began and gained momentum.

What had triggered the actress's breakdown? Who was responsible for pushing her over the edge? Both the industry and the media were looking for a scapegoat. Depending on whom one interacted with at the time, it was either Amitabh Bachchan's fault or Mahesh Bhatt's.

A few weeks after Parveen's departure from India, Prochi Badshah of *Stardust* spoke to UG. Reluctant to get involved, all he said was, 'She called me up in Gstaad and said she was tired and needed a break. She also said that she had seen *Arth* and was mentally disturbed by it.'

During the same phone call, Badshah also managed to speak to Parveen who said, 'It's true that I saw *Arth* and was upset. First,

I didn't think Mahesh would make a film like this. And second, it wasn't in the right perspective.'

When the journalist called the film's director Mahesh Bhatt with this information, however, he snapped, 'The last time I spoke to UG, that is, after you spoke to him, he told me that I shouldn't feel guilty, because Parveen hasn't seen *Arth*.' Defiantly, he continued, 'Everybody says that I have exploited my wife and Parveen, but I have exploited myself too. I have no false hang-ups. I am the first to admit that I am like a roadside leper selling his wounds. I make money from my humiliations.'

Mahesh maintained that he had warned Parveen about his film when it was released and advised her not to see it. 'My wife and I were having an argument one day, when she turned around and asked me where would I have been without Parveen and her? She was generous enough to include Parveen and I admired her for it,' he stated. 'Well, I was slightly high and I felt a genuine fondness for Parveen.' On an impulse, Mahesh had apparently called the actress at the Sea Rock Hotel, where she was shooting at the time, to thank her. 'She wished me luck for *Arth* and I told her, "Don't see the film. It's not good for you."'

It was obvious that the film-maker thought he was being blamed unfairly for Parveen's breakdown and her subsequent departure from the city.

In the same interview to *Stardust*, Mahesh started off by saying, 'No one can be blamed for Parveen's breakdowns,' before shifting the blame on to Amitabh Bachchan — and he didn't mince his words. The October 1983 issue of *Stardust* reported the film-maker stating, 'You cannot find simplistic solutions to this complex problem, but the fact remains that a lot of industrywallas took advantage of Parveen and the No. 1 Hero was one of them.' The reference was to Amitabh Bachchan at a time when most publications used a moniker ('middle-aged hero' and 'Lambuji' among others) instead of his name, following the imposition of a fifteen-year blanket media ban on the then superstar. 'In his white churidar kurta and shawl, he thinks he is some goddamn Messiah when, in actuality, he loves having an obsessed woman hovering around him. It makes him feel like God by dragging her for his show. He was taking advantage of a sick woman and her obsessions.'

He didn't spare Bachchan's wife Jaya either. 'She is also playing the Goddess, the sufferer,' he claimed. 'The only thing she is worried about is her position. She is not bothered [by] what she does to anyone to keep her own status intact.'

When the magazine asked Mahesh how the couple could know of Parveen's obsession, he dropped a bombshell. 'Of course, they know about it!' he cried out. 'And I know this for sure. I am not a fool. I knew all along that Parveen was having an affair with him, even when she was supposed to be in love with me. The only way I can figure out this obsession is that he spelt power and Parveen was obsessed with power. I was a nobody [in] those days. However demeaning it may sound to my own ears, it is a fact that I was kept by her. And I am honest enough to admit that I was a part of her entourage. She had a secretary, a hairdresser, a make-up man and a boyfriend.'

In the same interview, Mahesh recounted an instance when he visited Bachchan on the sets of Yash Johar's *Dostana* at Mehboob Studio to talk about Parveen. This was in 1979, when the actress was in Bangalore, recovering from her first public breakdown. Mahesh told the magazine that 'Parveen had woken up in the middle of the night, crying for the middle-aged hero'. Having witnessed her obsession, the film-maker had swallowed his pride and visited the actor's set to have a man-to-man talk with him. 'I still remember the humiliation I went through when I tried to explain her problem to him and begged him to be nice to her,' he says. 'He was very much aware of her problem and her obsession.'

To emphasize what he saw as Bachchan's utter lack of sympathy for Parveen's ailment, Mahesh shared yet another instance of the actor's unfeeling behaviour. 'Once Parveen had called him up in front of my eyes and when he came on the line, she just couldn't go beyond his name,' the film-maker said in the interview. 'She trembled, cried and kept on muttering his name over and over again. I snatched the receiver from her hand and spoke to the man myself. I apologized for her hysterical behaviour and not being able to talk. And he said, "Take care of her. She has so many films to complete!" That was all he was bothered about.'

Now that the blame had been shifted on to Amitabh Bachchan and the actor wasn't talking to the press, making his point of view hard to obtain, Prochi Badshah reached out to director Prakash Mehra.

The director had worked with both Parveen and Bachchan and had witnessed her breakdown in 1979. More importantly, he knew a little something about being blamed for it. 'The last time Parveen had a breakdown, I was blamed,' he told the *Stardust* journalist. 'Everybody said that she was petrified of me. The mention of my name made her shiver. I don't know how far it is true, but I don't think it's fair to blame anybody for her mental disorder.'

Mehra not only vehemently refused to lend credence to the allegations levelled against Bachchan, but even defended Mahesh. 'I know people are trying to blame Mahesh's *Arth* for Parveen's madness, but it's not fair,' he said. 'The boy has made a brilliant film and I don't think it could have affected Parveen in such a way that she lost total control of herself.' As for those blaming Bachchan for triggering Parveen's mental instability, Mehra countered the rumours with a question of his own. 'There are many heroines in this industry who are obsessed with my hero,' he said flatly, 'but have you heard of anybody flipping their lids because their interest is not reciprocated?'

Namak Halaal, Mehra's film starring both Parveen and Bachchan, had released a little more than a year ago. The filmmaker shared an incident from the set that he thought proved that Parveen had been struggling with some form of mental illness for quite some time. According to him, while the shoot was on, the actress had asked him to her make-up room one day. When he got there, he found her in tears.

'You are not happy with my work,' she told him.

'I asked her who had been telling her this and she said that she herself felt it. I fired her and warned her to not repeat the

Jwalamukhi performance with me again,' said the director. This was a reference to the time Parveen had suffered a psychotic episode during the shooting of Mehra's film *Jwalamukhi*, leaving him with no option but to replace her. 'I didn't want her to stop working in my film because of some silly phobias or imaginary fears about me,' he explained.

Over three decades later, there are just as many theories about what or who set in motion Parveen's decline. What most people tend to overlook is her history of mental illness. Before her breakdown in 1983, there had, in fact, been signs that the actress was quite unwell. Signs that she herself had ignored and others around her didn't recognize as something a little out of the ordinary. Parveen would experience certain very visible nervous tics that intensified with anxiety.

'She had a habit of constantly moving her chin,' Xerxes remembers. 'The more nervous she got, the more she clicked her chin. She'd also constantly scribble with her finger on the back of her hand.'

It's only now, in hindsight, that he thinks these could have been more than mere signs of nervousness. Bharat Godambe, who had done Parveen's make-up for years, and her driver Hanuman Patre mention how quiet she had become in the months leading up to both her breakdowns.

As a star, Parveen felt she was expected to be 'special'. This meant that she couldn't afford to reveal any chinks in her armour. And if any happened to become visible, they were either to be ignored, as if they didn't exist, or quickly covered up, before outsiders became aware of them. Her illness, coupled with the lack of a strong support system of relatives and friends in her life, failed to ensure that she received the medical treatment her condition urgently needed and pushed her deeper into a shell.

26

While the industry and her friends wondered where Parveen had disappeared to and theorized about what went wrong, she was continents away — blissfully unaware and enjoying the simpler life she had been yearning for. She travelled in the company of UG and Valentine, visiting Mexico City and Los Angeles, and eventually set up base for about six months in Corte Madera, a quiet suburb south of San Francisco. She lived a life of complete anonymity, doing the simple things that gave her joy. She tended to the garden, cooked meals for friends and shopped for groceries, free of the earlier incessant anxiety of having to project herself as perfect. There were no longer any masks she needed to hide behind. For the first time in a very long while, Parveen was under no compulsion to be anyone other than the person she was.

Robert Carr, a UG devotee who owned a restaurant in Larkspur, close to Corte Madera, recalls his association with the actress.

'Terry Newman, who was also a friend of UG's, had found the house for them. UG used to have an open house; so I would go over often or everyone would come to my restaurant to eat,' he explains.

Carr had met Parveen way back in 1979, when she was with Mahesh.

'It was my first trip to India and Chandrasekhar [Babu], whose house Parveen was staying in, had invited me over to meet UG. That was the first time I had met UG,' he says.

Someone had mentioned to him in passing that Parveen and Mahesh made movies, but Carr hadn't paid much attention. When he first heard, however, that Parveen was travelling with UG and Valentine, he was surprised.

'I learnt through the grapevine that she was more or less staying with UG and they had formed a platonic relationship and it stabilized her,' he says.

Though he had met Parveen casually on a few occasions, it was only during the time she spent in California that he would actually get to know her.

'I saw Parveen a lot and she seemed quite normal and friendly,' he observes. 'Though she wasn't very talkative, it was easy to see that she was very intelligent and had a very good grasp of what UG was talking about.'

When she wasn't running errands with Valentine or in the daily *satsang* (spiritual gathering), Parveen accompanied UG to Carr's restaurant where his chefs would rustle up a simple vegetarian meal for him.

'Both Parveen and UG enjoyed watching films,' Carr remembers. 'I had a large screen projector at home, so they would both come over to watch movies.'

One night, the actress cooked a special meal for her new American friend.

'She told UG she wanted to make non-vegetarian food for my friend Paul and I. UG was okay with it, so we had egg biryani that night,' Carr remembers fondly.

If he was wondering what a Bollywood film star was doing halfway across the globe, he didn't ask.

'She often talked about going back to Bombay and finishing her films,' he says.

It was during this period of contentment in sunny Corte Madera that Parveen wrote the cover article for the *Illustrated Weekly of India*, chronicling the story of her psychotic episodes and describing UG's crucial role in helping her to come out of them and follow the path he believed was best suited to her recovery. 'I have never felt more secure,' she wrote in her essay.

'I am peaceful and happy. What would have happened if UG had turned me away when I came to him from India? It would have been total destruction for me. This man — this extraordinary man — has saved me not once, but twice from destruction.'

Since she first began working, Parveen had come to believe that she was the person everyone around her depended on – and not just financially. UG, on the other hand, was the first person she had come to know who wanted nothing from her. And that's what had made her relationship with him unique in her eyes. 'I have no means to repay the enormous debt I owe him,' she would write in her essay for the *Illustrated Weekly of India*. 'He is one person who has given me everything within his power, without expecting or actually receiving anything from me in return. I have merely shown him some common courtesies, no more than anybody would do for a friend; arranging a stay for him in Kashmir, hosting him in Bombay, taking him for a drive, and such. Beyond these normal expressions of friendship, I have done nothing. In fact, he housed and fed me for months in Bangalore, and, even after me denouncing and turning on him [as she had, indeed, done at one point], in Gstaad. Reciprocity played no part in our so-called "relationship". He gave and I took. I have only received — he helped me when friends, relatives, acquaintances, including my own mother, had either been unwilling or unable to. He has given me strength, support, friendship and affection whenever I have needed it.'

When Parveen left Corte Madera with UG in the summer of 1984, their tentative plan was to travel to New York, then on to London and finally return to India, with a quick stop in Switzerland.

At the beginning of April 1984, a week after they had left Corte Madera, Carr received a call from the actress.

'She was in London and said that she had left a few thousand dollars in a bank here. She asked if I could help her withdraw that money. I told her it shouldn't be a problem. She could walk into any Bank of America branch and withdraw the amount,' he recalls.

Carr didn't think much of this conversation at the time, but less than a week later, the pieces of the puzzle fell into place.

On 4 April 1984, Parveen set in motion a series of events that would result in her virtually disappearing from the public eye for the next five years.

It all started with the trademark plainspeak that UG sometimes felt called upon to use when trying to persuade Parveen to do what would be right for her. In a letter he sent Mahesh from London – subsequently reproduced in the June 1984 issue of *Stardust* – UG wrote: 'As I told you, Parveen's present condition has been a great drain on my time, patience and energy. Ever since we left California, I have been making it crystal clear to her for some days that her idea of digging in her heels here and wanting to be with me forever is very unrealistic and that it is time that she started living her own life. She is such a sweet girl. We loved having her with us all these eight months. She has looked after Valentine so well that she is already missing her. Isn't it an eternal shame that she can't make anything of her talent and life now?'

He went on to describe Parveen's reaction to his advice and her subsequent exit from the house they were living in 'as sudden and as theatrical like last time'. 'She just got up from her chair,' he wrote, 'and said, "I don't want to be a burden on you. I am going to India right now."'

Parveen apparently didn't even bother to pack her belongings. 'She left all her things here and walked out,' was how UG put it in his letter. 'I gave her some money to take care of her tickets etc.'

And just like that, Parveen disappeared. UG had no way of knowing if she was still somewhere in London, had flown to some other part of the world or had returned to Bombay.

On 5 April, Parveen called Carr again in California. It was another quick, but strange call.

'She said she was in New York. She was going to the nearest bank to withdraw her money, but she wasn't sure about what exactly the procedure was,' he recalls.

Something about Parveen's tone set off alarm bells in Carr's mind. Though he had never witnessed her breakdowns, he was aware of her mental health-related challenges.

'She sounded very erratic, very disturbed,' he remembers. 'I spoke to her in a very calm voice and assured her that everything would be okay. I told her that she could come to California if she wanted. But she said, "No, I'm going to go to Texas."'

Two days later, Carr received another call from New York. It was from a stranger – an Indian doctor.

'He told me he had admitted Parveen to a hospital, because she was severely disturbed and behaving paranoid and suspicious,' Carr says. 'The doctor had found out my number from Parveen and called.'

The same doctor also called UG in London. The actress had apparently been detained at the John F. Kennedy International Airport in New York. On being asked by the airport authorities to show her identification papers, she had started behaving suspiciously. As a result, she was first handcuffed and, when she resisted the officials, was also ankle-cuffed and carried off by policemen to a general hospital. The Indian doctor who had witnessed the developments had immediately recognized her and rushed to her aid.

UG was reluctant to get involved. Going to New York to help Parveen would cost money, something he could ill afford. His travel companion Valentine was also getting on in years and neither of them was up to what amounted to a chase across the Atlantic. Most importantly, Parveen wasn't his responsibility. He called Mahesh who, in turn, implored UG to help her. After all, not only was he better placed, at least, geographically, but she always seemed to calm down in his presence. Eventually, the older man gave in and agreed to fly to New York to bring Parveen back with him to London.

Before he took the flight out, however, he called Kim Lawrence, someone he knew well in New York. Lawrence had briefly met Parveen in Corte Madera and UG now asked him to visit her at the hospital.

'I went to the hospital, but she refused to meet me,' says Lawrence. 'That's when we got to know that Parveen had bought a ticket to Houston, Texas. That's where she was headed when she was detained.'

By the time UG reached New York, the Indian Consul General there had been informed about Parveen's condition and had dropped in to visit her at the hospital.

In a letter dated 12 April 1984 – reproduced, subsequently, in the June 1984 issue of *Stardust* – UG shared with one of his New York-based followers the details of Parveen's condition and treatment: 'Parveen has been discharged from the general hospital this morning, but she needs and must have medical attention for a few weeks. Would you believe it? Her article in the *Illustrated Weekly of India* – it has been studied carefully by the whole panel of psychiatrists who studied her case – helped the doctors very much. And they have concluded that her case is one of misdiagnosis. Sometimes, it is difficult to distinguish between schizo[phrenia] and manic depression. They are going to put her on a drug for manics. There is no need for her to be in a clinic. They have carried out all the necessary tests and she has already been put on this drug. The doctors say that my presence will facilitate them to handle her case easily.'

The doctors treating Parveen informed UG that it would take six weeks for her to stabilize. But it would, perhaps, be a few years before she could take care of herself. She and UG were now staying at the Shelburne Murray Hill Hotel located in the city's posh Upper East Side. Parveen had initially resisted taking her medication, but had complied, once again, on UG's persuasion. For the next week or so, they fell into an easy routine, almost as if her hospitalization and the dramatic events leading up to it hadn't happened. Lawrence and his mother would drop in often to spend time with the two of them.

Then, one day, when UG came back to their hotel suite, after meeting some people, there was no sign of Parveen. Most of her belongings were gone. She had left, yet again.

After waiting for the next few days in the hope that she would return, UG eventually gave up. His final letter to Mahesh about Parveen, written on 25 April 1984, was a long one. 'The situation here is basically and insanely comical,' he wrote. 'I don't like waiting here for the Babi girl to turn up, so we are quitting this deluxe apartment hotel tomorrow and heading towards Washington DC by car. Kim [Lawrence] will join us a week later – just in case Parveen shows up in New York. Sooner or later, some information as to her whereabouts will turn up definitely when she runs out of funds. If she is trying to avoid medication and if this is the way to stay away from India, she is making a pretty good try. [And] my fear is that she might run into awkward situations. I hope not. She may not be all right in her head, but she can't be described as a dumb, runaway girl. But in her present state of mind, there is always the danger of [her] getting into trouble again. Well, I am afraid my usefulness has come to an end. Every time she reached out for help, I found it hard to let her down. My determination to prevent her from ending up in [a] mental hospital worked. I couldn't let this happen to her. Now she is spiralling towards disaster. This seems to be the final breakdown. She is plunging herself into a final manic depression. She is doing things which I thought she never would do. I am afraid she will completely and totally fall apart, with no hope of ever putting herself together without medical care.'

~

As the weeks stretched into months and the months into years, the film industry back in Bombay began to move on. Nobody talked about Parveen any more; and if they did, it was in hushed tones.

The actress's mother Jamal and her nephew Javed had moved back to Junagadh in 1983, following Parveen's departure from Bombay. Before she had left, she had bought a beautiful sea-facing penthouse in Riviera, a new building on Juhu Beach a stone's throw from her existing apartment in Kalumal Estate.

Spread over about 2,500 square feet, the apartment plan originally accommodated four bedrooms. Parveen preferred to have only two and had the space converted according to her specifications. Her favourite feature in the new pad was the huge terrace overlooking the beach. She had been very excited about her new home and had asked her friend Parmeshwar Godrej for her help in designing the apartment. She had even dispatched Javed to Markana, Rajasthan, to buy white marble that she intended using for the interiors.

After her sudden departure, however, Jamal had entrusted Javed with the responsibility of packing up most of Parveen's possessions and shutting down both homes in Bombay.

'I would come down every two three months to get both the houses cleaned and make sure that all the bills were paid,' Javed says. 'The Riviera apartment didn't have any furniture, so that was easy.'

There was, of course, no news from Parveen herself. Whatever little Jamal and Javed got to know about her was through magazine reports available during the time. When she disappeared from her New York hotel room in 1984, however, they would have no news of her at all for the next three years.

'We didn't even know if she was alive or not. We didn't know who to ask for help or what to do,' Javed confides.

Then, in 1987, while Javed was living in Junagadh with Jamal, they got a call from the US.

'It was a lady, who said she was calling from Houston, Texas. I think her name was Kalpana. She said that she was a lawyer and had seen Parveen in a police lockup in Houston. Thankfully, this lawyer's father lived in Ahmedabad and she managed to find our phone number through some people.'

The lawyer informed Javed that Parveen had been arrested at her local post office, where she had gone to mail some letters. There had been an altercation and she was taken to the police station in an agitated state.

'The lawyer said that Parveen seemed mentally disturbed,' Javed reports. 'Thankfully, an Indian spotted her. Otherwise, who knows how long she would have had to languish in that jail.'

This was the first bit of news Jamal had received about Parveen in nearly three years. Her first reaction was one of relief, because she had almost begun to believe that her daughter was dead. Once she knew Parveen was alive, however, she persuaded Javed to figure out a way to help her.

The very next day, Jamal, accompanied by Javed, travelled to Bombay to apply for an American visa.

'We went to the consulate and told them that we needed to help someone who was sick and in legal trouble,' says Javed.

Eventually, he was unable to accompany Jamal to the US. They decided that she would have to travel on her own.

'Mummy didn't speak English and she had never travelled on her own,' says Javed, explaining his anxiety over Jamal having to travel solo. 'But again, there was no choice. She was the only one who could help Parveen. Thankfully, we found someone we knew on the same flight who could help her.'

Once she reached Houston, Jamal paid Parveen's bail amount and the lawyer's fees and stayed with her daughter for a month. To anyone who asked her on her return about those thirty days she'd spent in the US, Jamal described them as a mixed bag, but mostly hellish. On most days, Parveen would be the daughter she had known. But when she lost her temper, she'd become someone Jamal didn't recognize at all. She constantly begged Parveen to return to Bombay or Junagadh and seek the medical help she urgently needed. It was this very suggestion, however, that seemed to trigger most of the actress's violent episodes. She would adamantly shoot down any suggestions about returning to India. Both mother and daughter reached the tipping point around the same time. Jamal realized that she wasn't making any headway with Parveen who, in turn, was fed up with her mother's constant nagging. The day arrived when she ordered Jamal to pack her bags and leave. And that's exactly what Jamal did.

A year later, Xerxes, who was planning to be in the US for some work, asked Ved Sharma for Parveen's address. He managed to locate her home and dropped in for a surprise visit.

'It was an apartment in a tall building in a very poor part of the city,' he recalls. 'Very run down. When I knocked, she opened the door, but refused to take the safety lock off. She didn't even let me enter her home.'

He recounts her telling him, 'Xerxes, you have your own life and I have mine. Please go away.'

'It broke my heart, but as a friend, I had to give her space,' he says, his voice tinged with sadness. 'She was suffering. Even in the Houston flat, I could see heaps of papers everywhere. There was a sofa, a centre table and a dresser in the corner. I could feel a heat wave from within the house. I asked her, "Why do you have the heat on? It's the middle of summer." She just kept telling me to leave. I wept like a baby. I knew I had lost my friend forever.'

27

Parveen's eventual return to Bombay was far less dramatic than her exit. After almost five years of no contact, she called Ved and Javed in the first week of November 1989. It was a short call.

'I am coming home,' she told them.

Parveen had been living in the US since 1984 on a tourist visa. Every six months, she would fly out to Mexico or one of the Caribbean countries and get an entry permit to return to Houston. That visa had finally expired and she had no choice but to return.

On 17 November 1989, Parveen returned to India after a seven-year-long self-imposed exile.

She had insisted that only Ved and Javed should receive her at the airport. Both men did a double take when she walked out to meet them.

Quoted in the March 2012 issue of *Filmfare*, Ved's son Lalit recalled his father's memory of that moment. 'Papa saw a fat lady with a soda bottle and [wearing] thick glasses at the airport, her hair all messed up, holding a board with her name! Parveen Aunty had put on a lot of weight and had changed beyond recognition.'

Her return made headlines in all the local dailies. In the years that Parveen had been away, a lot had changed, especially how and where film and celebrity news was reported. The once shadowy underworld of film news and unsubstantiated gossip wasn't limited to monthly or fortnightly magazines any more. The line between what was considered real reporting about 'important' matters and gossip that entertained, long blurred in

British and American media, had finally been breached in India. Mainstream newspapers were more than interested in salacious details about the private lives of celebrities. Even before Parveen's almost surreptitious departure from Bombay in the middle of the night, her lifestyle was believed to have been an encyclopaedia of excesses. And now that she was back, her sudden reappearance and every move that followed was considered as material for good copy.

In the first month after her return, there was a journalist or two ringing the doorbell at her Kalumal flat every single day. Parveen loved every minute of this attention. Not only did it feed into her delusion that she was still a big star, but these interviews also gave her a captive audience that hung on to her every word, no matter how ridiculous she sounded.

She told *Movie* magazine for its January 1990 issue that she had returned to Bombay to do 'what she ought to have done six years back. [To complete] a mission which she had left unaccomplished, [and] settle scores with the all-powerful man who had ruined her life'. But it was in a long interview to *Stardust*'s Omar Qureshi, published in the magazine's January 1990 issue, that Parveen launched into what would turn out to be a much-talked-about tirade against Amitabh Bachchan. 'In '79, I gave it all up and left the country, because then I had believed that I had gone mad,' she declared. 'From then on till '83, I chose to believe I was insane. The reasons were the numerous attempts to kill me by Mr Bachchan. What I am going to tell you is also written in this thousand-page handwritten letter that I have written to an eminent American tele-journalist, Ms Diane Sawyer. I have written everything in explicit detail and I expect her to take up my cause.'

Even as Qureshi sat there in stunned silence, Parveen explained why her former co-star wanted to kill her.

'Anyway, I was saying that I went away because I wanted to prove to Mr Bachchan that even if I knew that he was transferring money out of the country, I wouldn't talk about it,' she continued. 'But Mr Bachchan is an extremely untrusting man. And this knowledge of mine, coupled with me spurning his romantic overtures, made him decide to kill me. Mr Bachchan has been controlling my life like he controls the lives of everyone in the world. For he is the President of Organized Crimes in the world. He controls everybody. Everything!'

Once the tirade had started, there was no stopping Parveen and everything she said subsequently sounded more ludicrous than ever.

'Mr Bachchan has at his disposal all the chemical and energy weapons made available by science,' she went on. 'Every day, a new weapon was used on me. These chemical and energy weapons consisted of beams, of radiation and of energy pellets which constantly bombarded me. My make-up was contaminated so that every morning when I got up, I had to scrape off a thick residue from my face with a knife. My clothes, my food, everything around me was contaminated. In fact, fat cells were introduced inside my body to make me fat and ugly to others. Even my hair suffered the effect of all the toxins introduced within me and has become so bad. I remember I used to have such lovely hair once!'

As the evening progressed and night fell, Parveen sat there, silhouetted in the dim light cast by the room's solitary lamp. When Qureshi suggested that she switch on more lights, she shook her head.

'Mr Bachchan has had my electricity cut,' she claimed. 'Even my phone is dead. Only this lamp works.'

Many years later, in an article where he gave an account of this interview, Qureshi described Parveen as 'normal, affable, friendly, witty and very, very intelligent'. It therefore took him by surprise when she brought him a bottle of cola, recommending he drink it instead of the tea, because 'they' had been contaminating the milk. As reported in indiatimes.com on 10 August 2002, she said with a laugh, 'At least I get to open this bottle.'

Parveen also recorded the two-hour-long interview on her own Dictaphone, another habit she had developed and would persist with until the end.

In fact, her obsession with Amitabh Bachchan had become so all-consuming that regardless of the topic she was asked about, he not only featured in her reply, but was an integral part of it. Given the situation, the obvious question from Qureshi was whether she had ever been in love with the actor.

To which she replied, 'To fall in love with a person, there should be an equal response of warmth and affection from both sides. But there never was, so how could I fall in love? Of course, I had an affair with him, but that is not the same thing as a relationship. Of course, he did tell me that he was going to break up with Rekha then. But I did not want to intrude on their relationship in any way.'

In the same *Stardust* interview, Parveen insisted, 'Kabir Bedi was pressurized by Mr Bachchan to break up with me!' And she had a long-winded explanation to support this wild theory that started with *Amar Akbar Anthony* becoming a superhit. 'He wanted to use me professionally,' she claimed. 'Only I had gone off to the UK with Kabir. Also, then Amitabh had had a slight tiff with Zeenat Aman who was doing quite well for herself and had turned down *Kaalia* with him. That is why Mr Bachchan wanted to build up a heroine who was in direct opposition to Zeenat. Now since Neetu was just about to get married, Shabana was doing only offbeat roles and Smita not yet on the scene, I was the only choice left and even I had gone away. Then Kabir and I were very much in love and he was very nice and considerate. But in 1983, he went out of his way to be inconsiderate. To create a situation and to act in a manner that I disliked. It was almost as if he was pushing me to break up with him. Of course, it wasn't an unusual situation and it could be because he wanted to break up. But I was convinced otherwise when Kabir told me to go back to Bombay and contact Manmohan Desai who would give me work. I did just that, because I thought Manmohan Desai was a friend. It was only later that I realized that it was all a plan. So, in a way, Mr Kabir Bedi was the first person to sell me. Or rather sell out on me!'

During the interview, she didn't speak very kindly about her other ex-boyfriend Mahesh either. She claimed that the film-maker, while a good friend, was also 'exposing me to energy and chemical weapons; he was contaminating me'.

The *Stardust* journalist had managed to steer the conversation away from her wild accusations for a while, but it didn't take long for Parveen to come right back to the topic and start listing all the delusions that betrayed her persecution mania.

'I had a surgery performed in 1979, because my ears used to protrude. But during that operation, a tiny surveillance device was implanted behind my ear,' Parveen declared. 'There have been several plots to kill me. I am constantly being exposed to radiation. And everyone is made to believe I am mad. Just tell all my fans that mentally, I have never been saner. Though my physical health is suspect. My vaginal cream is tampered with, that damages my sex organs. My intestines are rotting. My liver is damaged. Oh! Why doesn't he leave me alone?'

This wouldn't be the first time or the last that Parveen made these absurd allegations in the presence of others. They cropped up often in private conversations with friends like Xerxes and Zarine Khan, whom she had attempted to reconnect with after her return. And they would appear in almost every single interview she gave until her final years.

The one close confidant Parveen didn't attempt to reconnect with on her return was Danny. They had had a fallout in the early 1980s, because Parveen suspected he was an agent for Amitabh Bachchan.

'[Amitabh] had given an interview to some magazine where he referred to me as "Danny, my friend",' the actor recalls. '[Parveen] had happened to read that interview. The next time I went to her house, she refused to let her housekeeper Maggie let me in. I knew she was standing on the other side of the door, so [I] asked her what [had] happened.'

Parveen accused Danny of being Bachchan's agent and forbade him from not just visiting her place in the future, but even from setting foot on her floor.

'I didn't want to argue with her, so I left after telling her to call me or come over to my home whenever she felt like it,' the actor says.

This was the last time Danny would speak to Parveen. Even if they crossed paths in their building compound or on a film set, she would evade him by leaving the spot in a hurry. Yet, during the explosive interview she gave *Stardust*, about seven years after she had declared Danny to be a spy for Amitabh Bachchan, he was the only one among her former lovers whom she didn't accuse of harming her.

༄༅༄

While she was away, Ved Sharma had been looking after her investments and income tax returns. One of the first things Parveen did after her return in 1989 was to call him home and take stock of her financial situation. From the time he received her at the airport, he had been deeply concerned about her state of mind. Deep inside, he knew that he didn't really want to work for Parveen any more. He just wasn't mentally prepared to come out with it. After all, he had known and worked for her for nearly two decades and was genuinely fond of her. However, it was Parveen herself who would announce at the end of their meeting that his services were no longer required. For a split second, he was relieved that the decision had been taken out of his hands, but then her accusations started. 'Parveen accused him of plotting to kill her and told him to never return,' Ved's wife Saavi says. It hurt Ved deeply that Parveen had chosen to end in this manner their long relationship, which was more than just professional. He had always thought of her as a member of his family.

Having lived on her own for years and made all decisions for herself, Parveen was no longer prepared to brook any interference from others. She and Jamal had always shared a rocky relationship and after Parveen's return to India, it just got worse.

'Mummy wanted Parveen to see a doctor again and get proper treatment. She couldn't understand why Parveen was publicly accusing people. She didn't want her to become a laughing stock,' Javed recalls.

Jamal stayed by her daughter's side for the first three months, but the fights became just too ugly. Every time they fought, Parveen's mother would return to Junagadh, but she could never stay away for long.

'After all, they had only each other,' Javed explains.

An important decision Parveen made after her return was to sell her Kalumal home and move into the sprawling sea-facing penthouse in Riviera, a few streets away. This move also eased the financial crunch she had faced after her return to Bombay. While Parveen was in the US, Jamal, left with no source of income, had been forced to sell the orchard she had so lovingly created and tended. The sale of the Kalumal flat, along with some investments she had made earlier, would keep Parveen afloat financially until the end.

It was also around this time that she decided she wanted to dabble in interior design. She had always been an avid lover of all things related to design and her personal aesthetic was cohesive

On an evening out with Jamal and Xerxes

and strong. Also, she felt she could leverage her celebrity status to draw clients. It seemed like a great idea at the time. She kept it simple with the company name – Parveen Babi Interiors International – and, soon, visiting cards and letterheads had been printed.

Parveen would go out to meet old friends and acquaintances in the hope of kick-starting her new career, but these meetings never led to anything constructive.

'People would just get weirded out by her,' says a friend who doesn't want to be named. 'Parveen came to me, wanting to collaborate on designing people's homes, but then she started talking about the chip behind her ear that the CIA had inserted. When she first said that, I remember laughing nervously. But then she started insisting that I touch her ear and I kept refusing. It was a very odd meeting and I ran out as soon as I could.'

Another work meeting ended even before it began, because the venue was in the same lane as Amitabh Bachchan's home in Juhu.

Parveen was trying to build a new life for herself, but she refused to acknowledge that the demons in her head were real. It's not impossible for those suffering from schizophrenia to live a regular life with appropriate medical treatment. Parveen, however, simply refused to see doctors. The situation was no different at this point in her life than it had been a decade ago — if anything, it had escalated.

Parveen had lost most of her friends, had no work to keep her busy and the absence of a spiritual guide like UG had left a hole in her life. While she had never equated spirituality with religion until now, it would be where she would seek solace in the years to come.

28

In 1997, two years after Bombay had been renamed Mumbai, Parveen was baptized by Father Arun Thomas at All Saints Church in the leafy by-lanes of Malabar Hill and her name entered in the records. She wasn't a regular churchgoer but the congregation welcomed her all the same.

Though she had been born a Muslim, there was an influence of other faiths through Parveen's early years. While her family wasn't particularly orthodox, she was taught to recite the kalimas every night. 'That was to ward off the evil eye, though I hardly understood about it,' she had told the *Free Press Journal* during an interview published in its 25 December 1980 issue. 'In the mornings, I used to hear chanting of Sanskrit verses by the Hindu priests. Then came my school. I was educated in a Christian school where we said our prayers in a chapel. So it was a mixture of all the three great religions in the world.'

Parveen would be introduced to Buddhism too through her relationship with Kabir, whose mother, Freda Bedi, was a Buddhist nun.

It's unclear what triggered Parveen's decision to convert to Christianity, though she often joked with friends that it was her desire to eat pork that had prompted it. It's also puzzling why she chose to join a church on the other side of the city, when there were many closer home. Reverend Dyvasirvadum, who took over as the church's pastor in 1998, remembers meeting Parveen for the first time at the All Saints Home for the Aged in Mazgaon during their centenary celebrations in the early 1990s. Parveen was a regular visitor there and residents of the home considered her a generous person who brought them gifts that ranged from transistors to toiletries. She even gifted an old television set to the home after her mother's demise.

After Reverend Dyvasirvadum came to know that she was a part of his parish, he tried reaching out to her, because she never attended the services. Then suddenly, she turned up one day at the priest's home, next to the church.

'She was very cordial and chatted with my two daughters,' he recalls.

Even after the priest moved to another parish, Parveen kept in touch with him and his family. She organized joyous meals to celebrate Christmas and Easter, not every year, but whenever she was feeling well enough to entertain. Reverend Dyvasirvadum describes her as being charming and absolutely fine when they met, though her stray comments about 'enemies who were trying to harm her' baffled him.

'She wasn't completely "normal", but we never asked her about it. It wasn't any of our business. We were there for when she wanted a prayer and comfort,' he explains.

After the initial media blitz that lasted a few months following her return, interest in Parveen waned all over again just as it had seven years ago. She spent the rest of the 1990s secluded in her home in Juhu. She rarely travelled out of Bombay any more, and now if she did go on any trips, they were mostly by road. She was afraid that she'd be killed if she boarded a flight or took a train. The one thing she did religiously every day was write. There were stacks of loose sheets and notebooks filled with her beautiful handwriting, chronicling all the ways in which 'they' were trying to harm her. Javed remembers Parveen sending him to get copies made of the hundreds of pages of letters she had written, and on one occasion spending three consecutive days at the nearest photocopy shop in Juhu. She would then hand these out to journalists who visited to interview her.

By the end of the decade, most of her former friends had ceased interacting with her. It wasn't as if she was always ranting against hidden enemies or spewing conspiracy theories. She was still capable of being charming and funny, but there were little things she did or said that threw people off.

Deepti Naval, for example, had a chance meeting with Parveen on the streets of Bombay in the early 1990s, when she was still living in her Kalumal flat.

'I was driving and a taxi stopped next to me. I saw someone who looked familiar, if a little chubby,' Deepti says. 'The signal changed, so I drove a little ahead and stopped by the side. Parveen got off her taxi and that's when I recognized her. We hugged and I was very happy to see her looking well.'

The hurried conversation ended with Parveen inviting her former co-star home.

'She seemed to be all there. Nothing had changed, except for the weight she had put on,' Deepti adds.

Since they hadn't exchanged phone numbers, a few days later Deepti simply landed up at the Kalumal flat.

'I rang the bell for a very long time, but no one opened the door,' she says. 'When I asked the building watchman, he said she was home. Eventually, I gave up and left.'

Something impelled Deepti to make another attempt to see her former friend and colleague a few weeks later. This time, Parveen did open the door.

'She invited me inside and it was all dark. We made small talk for a little while, which wasn't out of the ordinary, but then she started whispering, "The phone is going to ring. You wait, the phone will ring."'

Deepti's last memory of Parveen was the haunted look in her eyes and the fear in her voice.

She had driven everyone away by this point, including Xerxes.

'I loved her tremendously, but she was forever talking rubbish,' he explains. 'She wanted me to make some new outfits for her. So she had come to the studio. While I was taking measurements, she started saying that she had put on weight, because "they" were pumping her with steroids. Obviously, I asked her, "Who is 'they'?" And she started about Amitabh Bachchan again. She would say things like she was going to "finish them". It was just too much.'

Even Javed, who had been a steady companion to both Jamal and Parveen for so many decades, became alienated after Parveen accused him of attempting to poison her. By the beginning of the 2000s, she and Jamal were all alone. At least, for much of the time.

It was in 2000 that Enam Pir, a young man from Kolkata, would arrive in Mumbai, looking to make a mark in Bollywood as a writer. In an offhand conversation with some acquaintances, he mentioned that Parveen was his favourite actress of all time. Even as some in that gathering discussed her mental illness and wondered if she'd be open to meeting someone new, one of them called her on the phone.

'It was my lucky day, because not only did she answer the call, but she also agreed to talk to me,' Pir recalls.

He was just as shell-shocked by the turn of events as everyone around him.

'This was May 2000 and this conversation happened on a Friday,' he remembers. 'Parveen told me to come to her house on Sunday at 7 p.m. sharp. She told me not to come alone, but to bring along the person who had called her.'

That Sunday evening, when Pir and his friend reached Parveen's home, she greeted them warmly and was the consummate hostess.

'She was very kind and welcoming,' he recollects. 'She served us some cookies.'

The only oddity was that she switched on her Dictaphone as soon as the two of them sat down.

'This is Parveen Babi, 7 p.m. on Sunday. A fan of mine has come from Calcutta. His name is Enam,' she recorded, before asking him to log in his name, address and telephone number.

Posing next to her painting of Mother Teresa

There was something about Pir that obviously appealed to Parveen because after their first meeting, she called him home often for a meal or just a chat.

Eventually, she even trusted him enough to stop recording their conversations. Pir was so enamoured of Parveen that he didn't pay much attention to what he assumed to be a celebrity's harmless quirks.

'Once, she told me that now that I have become very friendly with her, there would be some people who might want to kill me. She asked me to call her every week or she'd worry if I was okay,' he adds.

Another time, Pir casually mentioned that he had met Zeenat Aman somewhere. Parveen asked him to leave immediately and wouldn't even hug him goodbye, because she insisted, 'Zeenat has transmitted something negative into you'.

With her career in interior design having failed to take off, Parveen started painting. Her home, which Pir described as 'a film set after shooting was over', was littered with canvases in different stages of execution. Among the completed pieces was a portrait of Mother Teresa and another of UG.

'Most of her paintings were very dark,' he says.

Javed recalls that Parveen had plans of reaching out to her friends, like Parmeshwar Godrej, to help her organize an exhibition of her works, but nothing came of it.

※

For a nonagenarian, Jamal was quite active. She continued to travel regularly between Junagadh and Mumbai. The amount of time she spent with Parveen in Mumbai, though, was dwindling progressively. Their relationship had steadily deteriorated. A time came when they were arguing about anything and everything. Parveen didn't want any advice from her mother, while Jamal strongly disapproved of her daughter's life choices. As age caught up with Jamal, she found she was losing the will to engage in endless arguments with her daughter, more so, because an angry

Parveen could be vicious and violent. Now, at the best of times, they were politely indifferent to each other. They had no choice; they had no one else in their lives.

Parveen was by her mother's side when Jamal passed away in early 2002.

The death of a parent is an insurmountable loss for anyone, but for someone already struggling with mental illness it can be devastating. Jamal's death triggered a maelstrom of grief, guilt, relief and loneliness, unlike anything Parveen had experienced before. She was now really and truly alone. Torn apart by her bereavement, she had no one to turn to for comfort. Eventually, she called Ved Sharma.

'As soon as Dad spoke with her, he understood that she needed help,' Ved's son Lalit says. 'He wasn't very well at the time, so I went along with him to her home.'

One day, Parveen called Lalit directly. She wanted a favour. 'She wanted me to file a case in the Bandra court on her behalf,' he explains.

In the handwritten complaints she would hand over to him, Parveen alleged that Bill Clinton, Al Gore, Robert Redford and Prince Charles, along with the US, British, French and Indian governments, the Roman Catholic Church and the Pope, the CIA, the CBI, the KGB and Mossad were plotting to kill her. Since she was afraid of stepping out of the house to get copies made of the complaint against each of these entities, Parveen had written a dozen identical letters by hand that ran into twenty-one pages each.

'She told me to go hire a lawyer who would file these complaints,' says Lalit. 'I was supposed to get a stamp on each. I went to the court, but no one there understood what the complaints were. The lawyers there just refused point-blank [to file her complaints], so I called her to ask for further instructions.'

Parveen's immediate reaction was: 'I knew they won't accept my complaint. It's a conspiracy.'

When he went back to her place to return her papers, Lalit, in a gesture of courtesy, decided to stay a little longer than he would have been expected to.

'The house was in [a] shambles,' he recalls. 'When she was still working and I was younger, we'd go to her Kalumal home often. It was beautiful and spotless. Her house in 2002 was filthy. There were dishes piled up in the kitchen, layers of dust on everything and piles of papers and newspapers everywhere.'

Even as Parveen raged about the court not accepting her complaint, she filled Lalit in on a previous 'attempt' to kill her.

The devastating earthquake, a little more than a year before, that had left large parts of Gujarat in disarray was a conspiracy by scientists and the government, because they knew there was a fault line under her building, was how Parveen interpreted the natural calamity, according to Lalit. 'Also, there was a water tank above her bedroom that she believed could have crushed her,' he adds, shedding light on the nature of her paranoia.

He remembers another man sitting quietly in the room at the time. He turned out to be the building's electrician, to whom Parveen had given a cheque for withdrawing money from her State Bank of India account.

'That's when she told me that she had stopped stepping out of the house,' says Lalit. 'Apparently, a BEST [Brihanmumbai Electric Supply & Transport Undertaking] bus driver had tried to run her over.'

The fear that she would be killed if she as much as stepped out of her house was so real that Parveen had stopped venturing out altogether. She had basic supplies delivered to her home. Once or twice a month, she would pay either the watchman or any handyman working in the building to withdraw money for her from her account. When Lalit left Parveen's home that evening, he felt sorry for her plight, but didn't know how he could help. The one thing he was sure about was that she wouldn't try to file another case in court.

A few weeks later, however, Lalit realized that even in the manic state that Parveen was living in, there was no stopping her. On 14 July 2002, she filed an affidavit, claiming to have in her possession highly incriminating documentary evidence against actor Sanjay Dutt for his alleged involvement in the 1993 Mumbai bomb blast cases. *Gulf News* reported on 20 August 2002, 'She has alleged that a conspiracy to acquit Dutt was hatched by the Central Bureau of Investigation (CBI) and that various international intelligence agencies were behind the bomb blasts, with Dutt being a pawn in their hands.'

The affidavit named a host of co-conspirators – the US, UK and Indian governments, intelligence agencies like the CBI, the ISI, the CIA and the British secret service, Amitabh Bachchan, Prince Charles and founder of the Shiv Sena, Bal Thackeray – who were also apparently trying to kill her.

In an interview published in the 26 August 2002 issue of *Outlook* magazine, Parveen defended her allegations against Sanjay Dutt. 'A majority in the industry has a nexus with the CIA,' she claimed. 'They function as [the] CIA's special contractors. It is within this framework that Sanjay Dutt executed the 1993 bombings conspiracy.'

Parveen insisted that the pieces of evidence she had with her 'are extremely cogent and irrefutable', but refused to explain how she had chanced upon them. She was summoned to depose in the Terrorism and Disruptive Activities (Prevention) Act (TADA) court, presided over by Judge P.D. Kode. On three separate occasions, she failed to turn up.

Outlook reported in the same issue that when asked about the reason for not showing up in court, she explained, 'I have evidence of a conspiracy to have me taken out of the court and get me killed on the way. They can come to my house and collect the evidence.'

According to the 20 August 2002 issue of *Gulf News*, Justice Kode eventually rejected Parveen's claims, by declaring, 'Her failure to specify evidence relevant to this trial leads to a logical inference that the said writer does not possess any evidence.' The judge also warned her 'that in future, she should not indulge in any such frivolous attempts' and directed the court registrar to send her a letter of warning, condemning her false claims.

Parveen had lived through the last decade in relative obscurity. But Sanjay Dutt's trial in the TADA court was one of the most high-profile cases anywhere in the country at the time and her allegations in relation to it were outrageous. They were bound to have repercussions, one way or the other. The relentless eye of the media had once again come to rest on her. What was different this time was that the focus was entirely on her mental state. And no one was pulling any punches. In articles that reported on the case, Parveen was described as a 'crack', a 'sex kitten' turned 'conspiracy theorist' and just plain '*pagal*' (insane).

By this time, people had forgotten about Parveen Babi the actress, and thought of her only as a crazy woman who caught the public eye every once in a while by making wild allegations. Just as Jamal had feared, her daughter had become a joke.

There were only a few interviews, like Rohit Khilnani's for the *Indian Express*, which truly captured Parveen's troubled mind with empathy. Every journalist worth his byline has to jump through hoops to get the interview he wants. In Parveen's case, these hoops always came across as extreme. For the *Indian Express* interview, published on 14 August 2002, Khilnani was first asked to read the eighteen-page affidavit, the twenty-two-page petition and the thirty-three-page complaint Parveen had drafted, all of which were attested by her, before they were handed over. She insisted that he record the interview on a tape recorder and that the accompanying photographer Mahendra Parekh carry 'two umbrella flashes and a digital camera – because digital cameras give you the best pictures'. After the photo session, Parveen used her own camera to click a photo of Khilnani and Parekh 'just for the record'.

Even as she was plagued by hallucinations and delusions, there was no denying that Parveen was still highly functional. For the petition she had filed in the TADA court, she didn't have a lawyer representing her. 'Filing an affidavit is a complicated process and certainly not a madman's job,' she said during the interview for the *Indian Express*. 'I conduct all my legal activism myself. I draft my legal documents myself and I take all legal decisions. This should be enough to prove my sanity.' Parveen pointed to the hundreds of notebooks, each filled, from start to finish, in her own handwriting, with all the 'evidence' she had collected.

Signs of the innate intelligence and photographic memory that had helped her learn a new language in college, do well in exams and learn her dialogues as an actress were still intact.

The *Indian Express* interview conducted by Khilnani turned out to be one of Parveen's last, where she talked about her bitterness towards her former colleagues and said it was justified. 'I never severed ties with the film industry. They broke their ties with me... They didn't respond to my phone calls or my party invitations. They didn't even invite me to their parties.' She confessed that she had become a recluse. 'I'm not in touch with anyone. Occasionally, I might bump into someone I have known, and I might say hello, but I have no friends at all.'

29

Her brief tryst with the spotlight, yet again, in connection with the Sanjay Dutt trial had consequences Parveen wasn't prepared for. The courts had dismissed her petition and the media had branded her insane. The bitter aftertaste pushed her deeper into the shadows.

The only time she stepped out of her home now was when her landline phone wasn't working. At these times, she'd go down to the building manager's office to make all her calls. She was suspicious of everyone except a handful of people like Enam Pir, the priests of All Saints Church, Ved Sharma and his son Lalit, her building's watchmen and, inexplicably, a handyman who painted homes in her neighbourhood. The joke in the building was that every time this painter had no work, he would land up at Parveen's home and offer his services. She was such a bleeding heart that she'd give in without hesitation, asking him to repaint a wall in her home that required no touching up at all.

It was these people who had become her community and her only links to the outside world. A few times a month, she'd ask either the handyman or the watchman to withdraw money for her. She never kept more than ₹3,000 in her home. There used to be a part-time maid who cleaned her place every few weeks, but towards the second half of 2004, even that service had been discontinued. What used to be a beautiful home that she had lovingly designed and maintained was now filthy and in a perpetual state of neglect.

If the building gossip between the maids and watchmen is to be believed, Parveen spent most of her days just writing, collecting clippings from newspapers and painting. Her diet consisted almost entirely of eggs and milk, with her consuming three dozen eggs a day. Every morning, she would prepare a concoction of milk and egg yolk and drink it through the day. She believed that these were the two things that couldn't be contaminated by anyone trying to harm her.

The one thing people who met her often had learnt was to never argue with her. If someone disagreed with her on any matter or attempted to correct her, Parveen would lose her temper and, as before, resort to physical violence, throwing whatever lay within reach.

Jyotsna, her roommate from college, who was in Mumbai on 4 April 2003 – Parveen's forty-ninth birthday – called to wish her and Parveen promptly invited her over.

'The first thing that struck me was how much make-up she was wearing,' Jyotsna recalls. 'She had never liked wearing make-up before. She'd only wear make-up when she was shooting, but almost never at home. We sat in the beautiful terrace that overlooked the sea.'

Parveen offered her tea, but quickly said, 'There's nothing in the house, because there are repairs going on.'

Jyotsna had noticed the scaffolding in the living room, and remembered Donald, her ex-husband, mentioning some painting job being carried out when he had visited Parveen two or three years ago.

'It felt odd that Parveen had had repairs going on for so long. So I asked her what she was getting done,' Jyotsna elaborates.

She remembers the sudden change in her friend's demeanour and the expression of sheer terror that came over her face.

'She looked around, almost as if to check that no one could overhear our conversation, and then whispered, "Supremo doesn't allow anyone to work in my house."'

'At normal volume, I asked, "Who is Supremo?", says Jyotsna. She became even more scared and whispered, "Amitabh."'

Not surprisingly, the visit didn't last long.

In her last years, the only time Parveen would socially interact with people was when she invited them over to celebrate a special occasion. A year after Jyotsna's visit, when she turned fifty, Parveen decided to celebrate her birthday by throwing a party. She drew up a menu, invited Ved's family and a few others, and even hired someone to serve her guests. This was a huge step for her. After a long time, she felt as if she was part of a community. She believed there were people who cared about her. She wore

Parveen at 50

her prettiest kaftan and applied the most flamboyant red lipstick she had in her possession. The table was laden with food she had cooked from scratch. Glasses were clinked and jokes were cracked. Under that bright veneer of fun, though, was anxiety. The laughs weren't as spontaneous as they would have been at one time. Her guests found it very hard to ignore the Dictaphone she had casually placed on the coffee table, in between glasses of mocktails and plates of food.

Nine months after her birthday party, she invited a much larger group over for Christmas. It included Reverend Father Avinash Rangayya, the new priest in charge of All Saints Church, along with former pastors Reverend Father Dyvasirvadum and Reverend Father Roy Varghese. Their wives were also invited. This was the first time that Father Rangayya would be meeting Parveen, though they had spoken over the phone a few times. The priest had almost turned down the invitation, because his two-month-old daughter's christening was scheduled for the very next day. On learning of this, Parveen had insisted that he bring along his baby and his in-laws. This was an important meal for her and she spent days planning the menu and getting all the supplies in order. She cooked a variety of meats, vegetarian sides and salads that were to be served with sweet wine.

That she had put together such an impressive spread and was an attentive and engaging hostess, despite the fact that she was clearly unwell, endeared Parveen to her guests. She had a broken tooth that she tried to camouflage with a lace handkerchief every time she opened her mouth to speak and was limping from what appeared to be a foot injury. Her guests asked if she had sought medical help, but Parveen shrugged aside their concerns with a smile and said that 'it's nothing major'. She had, in fact, sustained these injuries a few months ago. Her distrust of doctors, coupled with the paranoia that kept her homebound, meant that she hadn't sought any medical help at all. But the truth was not what she wanted to share with her guests. She wanted nothing to spoil her perfect Christmas party — which is it what it turned out to be.

It ended with Parveen receiving communion from Father Rangayya before he left.

'Everything, our meeting and the communion, happened at the right time. It's God's will,' the priest remembers her telling him, a fact that would be reported in the 25 January 2005 issue of the *Indian Express*.

30

During the first fortnight of 2005, Donald and Parveen spoke to each other often. He was planning a huge house-warming party in Ahmedabad and tried every trick in the book to persuade her to attend.

'I even offered to drive her down from Mumbai and back. She refused [the offer], but promised that she'd visit us soon,' he says.

Enam Pir had brought Parveen new outfits, because she had expressed a desire to check out a bar called Rain that had recently opened in her old friend Ranjeet's building.

'She said she hadn't been out shopping in a very long time, so she didn't have fun clothes to wear to a bar,' Pir says. 'I was travelling to Kolkata. So I offered help from my sisters [who agreed] to do some shopping for her.'

He dropped off the clothes at Riviera, but couldn't meet Parveen. He couldn't get her on the phone either.

'I tried calling a couple of times around the 15th or 16th of January and her part-time maid answered once, curtly saying that Parveen couldn't come to the phone.'

Pir didn't think much of it then.

Around 10 January, Parveen was running short of money. She asked the watchman, as usual, to withdraw money for her from her account, but he couldn't spare the time. So she borrowed some from the building's manager and gave him a cheque for the amount. A few days later, she called his office to ask him where she could get Gujarati food in the area.

'She said she was craving food like she used to eat in Junagadh and Ahmedabad,' the manager, who didn't want to be named, recalled. 'I recommended a restaurant in the area that would deliver.'

Inspector Sham Chavan had just entered Juhu Police Station around noon on 22 January 2005, when he was told that there had been a frantic call about Parveen Babi. At first, he didn't pay much attention to the news, because it was quite common for her to make panic-triggered calls to the station.

'She would call to complain about people who were trying to kill her,' says Chavan. 'Once, she had even said that the CIA was out to get her, but these calls had reduced over a period of time.' He realized it was serious when it dawned on him that it was the manager of Parveen's building who had made the call, not her. Apparently, Parveen hadn't collected the supplies left outside the main door of her seventh-floor flat for more than two days. Chavan immediately left for Riviera to investigate.

A keymaker was brought in to make a duplicate key so that the police could open the front door and enter Parveen's home. Time stood still while the keymaker did his job. Soon, there were more people inside the apartment than there had ever been in the past decade. Apartment 702, with its half-finished canvases, scattered clothes, medicines and stacks of newspapers had the melancholic air of a mute witness to the last chapter in the life of its occupant. Chavan and his team discovered Parveen, lying face up in her bedroom. There was no doubt in his mind or in anyone else's that she was no more.

'There was no sign of a struggle or any foul play,' Chavan adds.

It was a quiet end to a stormy life. The one constant was her loneliness. It defined her childhood, her desperate need for companionship in her prime and her last days in virtual isolation. Parveen was alone – in life and in death.

The girl who had set ramps on fire, the woman who had mesmerized millions on screen, now lay there dressed in a pair of discoloured white shorts and a tee shirt, a stained bandage on her left foot.

The forensic doctors at Cooper Hospital ruled that Parveen had died about twenty-four hours before her body was discovered and that her vital organs had ceased functioning. It was later revealed that the wound on Parveen's foot was gangrenous, triggered by diabetes. The building's manager remembers that a few months before her death, Parveen had developed an abscess on her foot. Sometimes, she'd call a doctor in the neighbourhood and describe the symptoms of whatever ailment she was suffering from. He, for his part, would prescribe medicines for it, which she then ordered from the neighbourhood pharmacy. This time, it seemed as if she had tried to treat the boil on her foot herself. The sore had developed gangrene, making it difficult for Parveen to walk and she requested the manager to buy a wheelchair for her.

A small police tag tied to her toe, with 'Token No. 62' written on it, was all that identified Parveen Babi in the hospital's morgue. With no immediate family around to claim her mortal remains, she had been registered as 'unclaimed body No. 16'. The other fifteen unclaimed bodies belonged to unidentified people who had died in road or train accidents. Parveen's was the only body laid out on a gurney on wheels, though; it was a favour extended to her in deference to her former stardom.

Epilogue

As soon as the news of Parveen Babi's death was reported by the media, a whole flock of her relatives descended on Mumbai. There was absolute confusion as cousins, aunts and uncles, some of whom confessed to never having even met Parveen, turned up to claim her body. Adding to the chaos was the counterclaim by the priests of All Saints Church that she had converted and had expressed her wish to be buried as a Christian. Eventually, the police handed her body over to an aunt – Farhad Sultan Babi, who had arrived from Balashinore, Gujarat. Almost a week after her body was found, Parveen was buried at the Juhu Muslim cemetery in Santacruz, Mumbai, next to her mother's remains.

At around 9.40 p.m. on 30 January 2005, Parveen was lowered into her grave. Danny, Kabir and Mahesh were among the few friends who attended her burial to say their last goodbyes. Stray tears were shed in between hushed conversations about who'd get her property and the circumstances surrounding her death. Along the boundary wall of the cemetery, a handful of curious onlookers stopped to peek in. The presence of camera-wielding journalists had attracted them. When it dawned on the onlookers that none of Parveen's famous colleagues was going to show up, the crowd shuffled away.

Parveen's life was like a mirror that had shattered into a million pieces. Each shard had its little story – of beauty, fame and fortune; of hard work, determination and humility. It was the shadow cast by her illness, however, that would never allow the mirror to be put back together and made whole again.

Parveen Babi's Films

Charitra (1973)
Directed and produced by B.R. Ishara

Dhuen Ki Lakeer (1974)
Directed and produced by Kishore Sahu

Trimurti (1974)
Directed and produced by Rajendra Bhatia

36 Ghante (1974)
Directed and produced by Raj Tilak

Majboor (1974)
Directed by Ravi Tandon; produced by Premji

Deewaar (1975)
Directed by Yash Chopra; produced by Gulshan Rai

Kaala Sona (1975)
Directed by Ravikant Nagaich; produced by Harish Shah and Vinod Shah

Bhanwar (1976)
Directed by Bhappi Sonie; produced by Shyam Keswani and Nand Mirani

Bullet (1976)
Directed and produced by Vijay Anand

Rangila Ratan (1976)
Directed by S. Ramanathan; produced by Ramchandra Bhikubhai

Mazdoor Zindabaad (1976)
Directed and produced by Naresh Kumar

Amar Akbar Anthony (1977)
Directed and produced by Manmohan Desai

Chalta Purza (1977)
Directed and produced by Bhappi Sonie

Darinda (1977)
Directed by Kaushal Bharati; produced by M.S. Gulati

Mastan Dada (1977)
Directed and produced by Satyen Bose

Mama Bhanja (1977)
Directed by Naresh Kumar; produced by Virendra Kumar

Chor Sipahee (1977)
Directed by Prayag Raj; produced by Shyam Sunder Shivdasani

Chandi Sona (1977)
Directed and produced by Sanjay Khan

Pati Patni aur Woh (1978)
Directed and produced by B.R. Chopra

Aahuti (1978)
Directed by Ashok Bhushan; produced by Ramchand Bashomal, Reeta D. Shah and R. Soni

Kaala Patthar (1979)
Directed and produced by Yash Chopra

Suhaag (1979)
Directed by Manmohan Desai; produced by Prakash Trehan, Shakti Subhash Sharma, Ramesh Sharma and Rajendra Sharma

Do aur Do Paanch (1980)
Directed by Rakesh Kumar; produced by C. Dhandayuthapani

The Burning Train (1980)
Directed by Ravi Chopra; produced by B.R. Chopra

Shaan (1980)
Directed by Ramesh Sippy; produced by G.P. Sippy

Gunehgaar (1980)
Directed and produced by Rahul Rawail

Ek Gunah aur Sahi (1980)
Directed and produced by Yogi Kathuria

Kranti (1981)
Directed and produced by Manoj Kumar

Khoon aur Paani (1981)
Directed by Chand; produced by A.A. Nadiadwala

Meri Aawaz Suno (1981)
Directed by S.V. Rajendra Singh; produced by G.A. Seshagiri Rao

Kaalia (1981)
Directed by Tinnu Anand; produced by Iqbal Singh

Raksha (1981)
Directed by Ravikant Nagaich; produced by P. Mallikharjuna Rao

Desh Premee (1982)
Directed by Manmohan Desai; produced by Subhash Desai

Namak Halaal (1982)
Directed by Prakash Mehra; produced by Satyendra Pal

Ashanti (1982)
Directed by Umesh Mehra; produced by Parvesh C. Mehra

Dil...Akhir Dil Hai (1982)
Directed by Esmayeel Shroff; produced by M.S. Gulati

Khud-Daar (1982)
Directed by Ravi Tandon; produced by Anwar Ali and F.K. Rattonsey

Yeh Nazdeekiyan (1982)
Directed and produced by Vinod Pande

Taaqat (1982)
Directed by Narendra Bedi; produced by Raj Grover and Shibranjan Majumdar

Mangal Pandey (1983)
Directed and produced by Harmesh Malhotra

Gehri Chot / Door-Desh (1983)
Directed by Ambrish Sangal; produced by Shamim Ahmed and Jagdish Bahroos

Arpan (1983)
Directed and produced by J. Om Prakash

Rang Birangi (1983)
Directed by Hrishikesh Mukherjee; produced by Rajiv Pandya

Mahaan (1983)
Directed by S. Ramanathan; produced by Satyanarayana and Suryanarayana

Jaani Dost (1983)
Directed by K. Raghavendra Rao; produced by Ashwini Dutt and M. Arjuna Raju

Razia Sultan (1983)
Directed by Kamal Amrohi; produced by A.K. Misra

Chor Police (1983)
Directed by Amjad Khan; produced by Shelha Khan and Vinay Kumar Sinha

Bad aur Badnaam (1984)
Directed by Feroz Chinoy; produced by K.D. Shorey

Teri Baahon Mein (1984) **(cameo)**
Directed by Umesh Mehra; produced by Pramod Pedder

Kanoon Meri Mutthi Mein (1984)
Directed by Chand and K. Prasad; produced by Venugopal Chettiyar and Dara Maruti

Ameer Aadmi Ghareeb Aadmi (1985) (cameo)
Directed by Amjad Khan; produced by Vinay Kumar Sinha

Sitamgar (1985)
Directed by Raj N. Sippy; produced by Bikram Singh Dehal

Telephone (1985)
Directed by Shyam Ramsay and Tulsi Ramsay; produced by Kumar Ramsay

Bond 303 (1985)
Directed by Ravi Tandon; produced by B.C. Devra

Karm Yudh (1985) (cameo)
Directed by Swaroop Kumar; produced by Dimppy

Avinash (1986)
Directed by Umesh Mehra; produced by Kavita Ramsay

Akarshan (1988) (cameo)
Directed and produced by Tanvir Ahmed

Iraada (1991)
Directed and produced by Inderjeet Singh

References
(in chronological order of publication)

'Six, not Sex', *Filmfare*, 15 June 1973.
'*Charitra* – What Flashes – and Flaws!', *Free Press Journal*, 11 November 1973.
'Rishi and Parveen: There's Nothing Fake Here', *Filmfare*, 11 January 1974.
'Parveen Babi/ Zahirra', *Stardust*, February 1974.
'Kabir–Protima to Split?', *Stardust*, March 1974.
'*Dhuen Ki Lakeer*: Smoke without Fire', *Free Press Journal*, 19 May 1974.
'I Won't Do Anything for Publicity: Parveen Babi', *Stardust*, September 1974.
'*Majboor* – Much, Much Majboori...', *Free Press Journal*, 8 December 1974.
Vohra, Bikram, 'Parveen Babi: My Work Is Very Elementary', *Filmfare*, 27 December 1974.
'I Don't Copy Anyone', *Stardust Annual*, 1974.
'What I Hate in My Mate', *Stardust*, January 1975.
Vohra, Bikram, 'Danny: Villain in Search of Sophistication', *Filmfare*, 21 March 1975.
'Studio Hopping: *Bhanwar*', *Stardust*, June 1975.
'Parveen Shifts Out!', *Stardust*, July 1975.
Rao, Uma, 'Beautiful Moments from a Beautiful Relationship', *Stardust*, February 1976.
'Small Talk', *Stardust*, September 1976.
Mirani, Indu, 'Danny Denzongpa Interview', *Filmfare*, 3–16 September 1976.
Bhatt, Shirin, 'Rajesh: "I've Known You for a Hundred Years, Parveen"', *Free Press Journal*, 19 September 1976.

Rao, Uma, 'Parveen–Protima: The Two Women Who Loved and Lost Kabir Bedi', *Stardust*, September 1977.
'From One Star to Another', *Stardust*, October 1977.
Gopalakrishnan, V.S., 'Parveen Babi: My "Affairs" Were Open', *Filmfare*, 23 December 1977–15 January 1978.
'Parveen Babi: The Men She Desires', *Stardust*, March 1978.
Rao, Uma, 'Parveen Babi Interview', *Stardust*, May 1978.
Rao, Uma, 'Court Martial: Parveen Babi', *Stardust*, July 1978.
Gopalakrishnan, V.S., 'Parveen Babi: Actually I Am a Loner', *Filmfare*, 16–31 December 1978.
Bakshi, Vanita, 'Parveen Babi: Fed Up of Being "the Poor Man's Zeenat Aman"?', *Stardust*, May 1979.
'Parveen Babi's Fight for Sanity', *Stardust*, December 1979.
Bharathi, N., 'Parveen Is Back!', *Star & Style*, 8–21 February 1980.
'Prakash Mehra Exposes Parveen', *Stardust*, June 1980.
Ragina, Prochi, 'Back to Normal!', *Stardust*, September 1980.
Venkatesh, Jyothi, 'What's Behind Jaya's Comeback?', *Free Press Journal*, 15 November 1980.
Sippy, Ramesh, '*Shaan* – The Biggest Challenge', *Free Press Journal*, 7 December 1980.
'What Religion Means to Them', *Free Press Journal*, 25 December 1980.
'Whoever Called Her Liberated?', *Star & Style*, 9–22 January 1981.
'Parveen's Strange New Foreign Lover', *Stardust*, May 1981.
Badshah, Prochi, 'The Babi Boom', *Stardust*, September 1981.
'Court Martial: Mahesh Bhatt', *Stardust*, September 1981.
Star & Style, 21 August–3 September 1981, pp. 28–29.
'Ved Sharma Interview', *Star & Style*, 16–29 October 1981.
'Smita–Parveen: Can the Two Actresses Overcome their Health Handicap?', *Stardust*, April 1982.
'Parveen's Second Breakdown', *Star & Style*, 28 May–10 June 1982.
'Parveen and Danny to Marry?', *Stardust*, June 1982.
Sushama, 'I Have No Godfather', *Free Press Journal*, 13 June 1982.
Sushama, 'Parveen Babi's Unpublicised Background', *Star & Style*, 10–23 December 1982.
Keni, Uma, 'Kabir Bedi Exposes the Lies Parveen Told', *Stardust*, April 1983.
'Parveen's Mysterious Disappearance', *Star & Style*, 16–29 September 1983.

Badshah, Prochi, 'A Common Factor in Babi's Three Breakdowns', *Stardust*, October 1983.

'Who's Diverting Parveen's Producer to Moon Moon?', *Star & Style*, 25 November–8 December 1983.

Babi, Parveen, 'The Confessions of Parveen Babi', *Illustrated Weekly Of India*, 29 January–4 February 1984.

Badshah, Prochi, 'Missing: Parveen Babi', *Stardust*, June 1984.

Qureshi, Omar, 'Sexual Perversions, Organised Crimes', *Stardust*, January 1990.

Ribeiro, Troy, 'Parveen Babi Interview', *Movie*, January 1990.

Bedi, Protima Bedi (with Pooja Bedi Ebrahim), *Timepass: The Memoirs of Protima Bedi*, Penguin Books India, 2000.

Bhatt, Mahesh, *U.G. Krishnamurti: A Life*, Penguin Books India, 2001.

Noorani, A.G., 'Jinnah and Junagadh', *Frontline*, 29 September–12 October 2001.

Qureshi, Omar, 'Parveen Babi: A Life Interrupted', indiatimes.com, 10 August 2002.

Raghunath, Pamela, 'Court Throws Out Plea of Film Actress', *Gulf News*, 20 August 2002.

Dwyer, Rachel, *Yash Chopra: Fifty Years in Indian Cinema*, Roli Books, 2002.

Bhatnagar, Manjari, 'Ruthless Revelations', *Society*, January 2007.

Christo, Bob, *Flashback: My Life and Times in Bollywood and Beyond*, Penguin Books India, 2011.

Farook, Farhana, 'The Myth & Madness of the Late Parveen Babi', *Filmfare*, 11 April 2012.

'Shah Rukh Khan in Conversation with Yash Chopra', YRF YouTube channel, 13 November 2012; https://www.youtube.com/watch?v=vq3eXwjAy2k

Banan, Aastha Atray, 'Revisiting Kabir Bedi's International TV Show *Sandokan*', *Mid-Day*, 29 December 2015.

Kumar, Anuj, 'Meet the Candid Kabir', *The Hindu*, 6 April 2017.

Mukherjee, Ram Kamal, *Hema Malini: Beyond the Dream Girl*, HarperCollins India, 2017.

Sanjay Khan, *The Best Mistakes of My Life*, Penguin Random House India, 2018.

Acknowledgements

It takes a lot of luck, patience and the wisdom of countless good friends to get a book out into the world.

I am deeply grateful for the help I received in researching this book. A huge thank you to everyone who shared their memories – some spanning years and others minutes – of Parveen Babi: Abdul Elah, Amol Palekar, Anju Mahendru, Anshul Balbir, Anwar Ali, Aruna Raje, Dr Ashit Sheth, Bharat Godambe, Bharathi Pradhan, Bindiya Goswami, Bindu, Deepti Naval, Dinesh Raheja, Reverend Dyvasirvadum, Enam Pir, Girish Shukla, Hanuman Patre, Hema Malini, Jeannie Nowroji, Johny Bakshi, Kavita Bhambani, Ketan Anand, Ketan Desai, Khurshid Ravji, Kim Lawrence, Lalit Sharma, Mala Shah, Mallika Sarabhai, Mamta Landerman, Manoj Kumar, Moon Moon Sen, Nalini Uchil, Parizad Damania, Pearl Goswami, Rahul Rawail, Rakesh Kumar, Ram Sethi, Randhir Kapoor, Ranjeet, Rauf Ahmed, Rashna and Bishu Basu, Ravi Tandon, Robert Carr, Rohit Khilnani, Saavi Sharma, Saawan Kumar Tak, Salim Durrani, Sanjay Khan, Sham Chavan, Shyam Ramsay, Suguna and K. Chandrasekhar Babu, Sushil Malik, Tanvir Ahmed, Vikas Desai, Vikram Sahu, Vinay Sinha, Vinod Pande and Zarine Khan.

Heartfelt thanks to Mahesh Bhatt, Kabir Bedi, Danny Denzongpa, Xerxes Bhathena, Javed Khan Babi, Donald Marks and Jyotsna Odedra for their generosity.

Thanks also to the dozens who didn't wish to be named but pointed me in the right direction with their insights, and agreed to verify or back up facts and anecdotes.

ACKNOWLEDGEMENTS

I have always loved libraries but researching this book has given me a whole new appreciation for librarians and archivists. Thanks also to Namrata Sanghani, who was a constant companion in dusty libraries across the city.

To my brilliant editors Poulomi Chatterjee and Mita Ghose, and the team at Hachette India, thank you for your patience and for pushing me every step of the way.

Everything I learnt from my former bosses and editors Suresh Nair, Ayaz Memon, Priya Tanna, Saira Menezes and Sonal Nerurkar helped me in researching and writing about someone as complex and fascinating as Parveen Babi.

To the Nosey Aunties and Secret Society of GSW, thank you for keeping me sane over the last three years. This book would not have existed without Sukanya Venkatraghavan. Thanks also to Mahua Kamat for lending me her 'eagle eye'.

For his encyclopaedic film knowledge, wisdom and answering my daily calls I thank my friend K.S. Sanjay.

I couldn't have written this book without the support and unconditional love of my family. Thank you for letting me whine and for celebrating the little wins with me.

And, finally, thank you Vishal, my husband, punching bag and personal cheerleader.

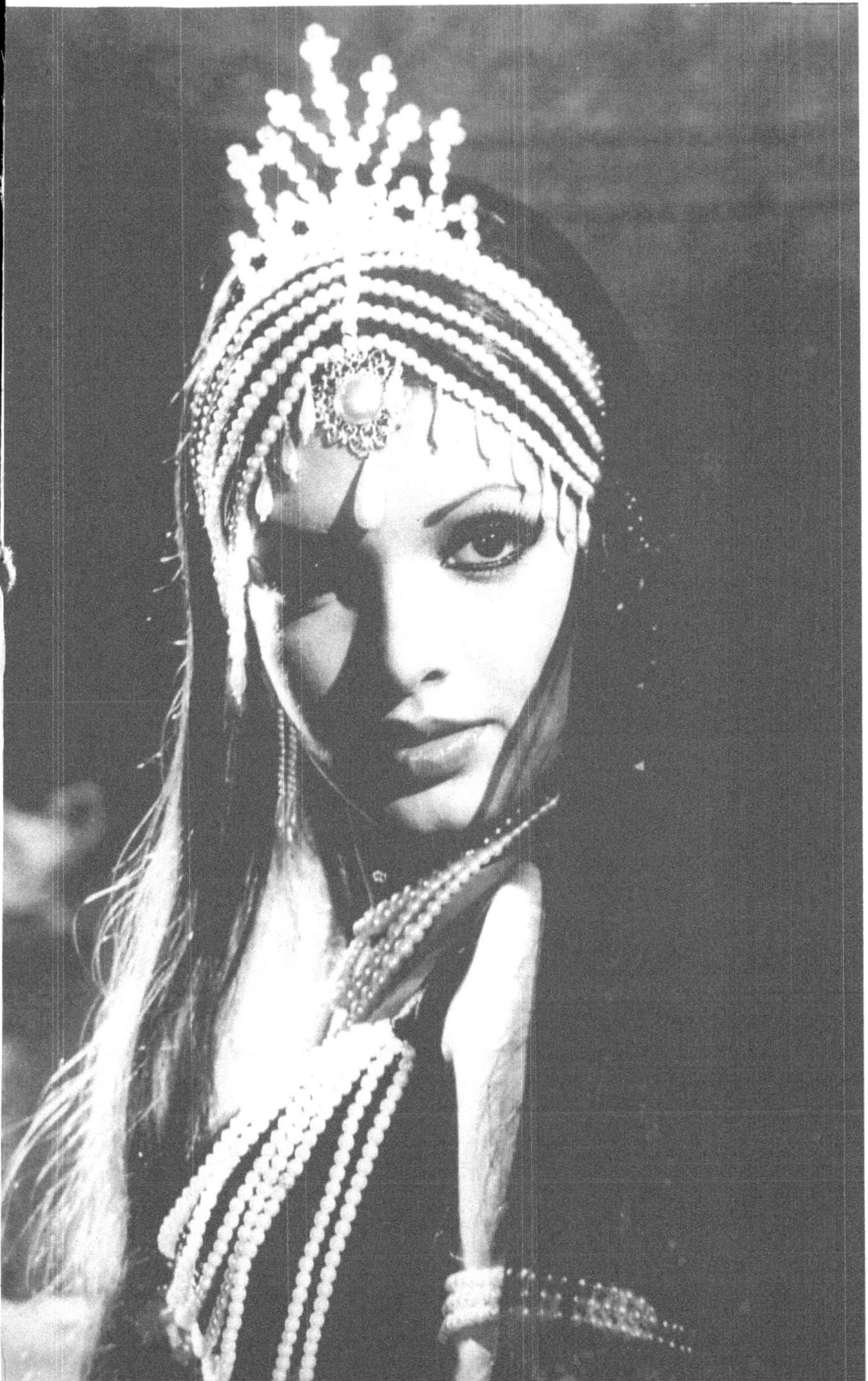